"Leydon's mission may be to enlighten us about movie history, but he also does a good job of entertaining us along the way. Damn fun!!!"

— Sable Jak, Author of *Writing the Fantasy Film*

"In bite-sized but insightful chapters, Leydon hits the highlights of film history, those movies that have become touchstones of their time, genre, or theme. Combining a scholar's insight and an enthusiast's passion, he discusses not only why these movies are great, but why they're important, further illustrating his points with comparisons to recent films and offering ideas for additional viewing. *Joe Leydon's Guide to Essential Movies* is a fun and thoughtful resource for all but the most casual movie fan."

— Melissa Prusi, Staff Writer, *AbsoluteWrite.com*

"Movies have become the social lingua franca in modern America. If you can't 'talk' movies, then you are considered culturally deficient. In this wonderful volume, veteran film critic Joe Leydon solves this problem by presenting in a brilliant series of concise, insightful, mini-essays everything you need to know about the movies that matter. The book will not only make you an overnight movie expert, it should be required reading for every student taking the basic course in film history."

— Garth Jowett, Author of *Film: The Democratic Art*

"Whether you want to fill in some gaps in your film knowledge, start from scratch with the basics, or simply be reminded of the movies that made a difference, this guide by one of America's most knowledgeable and fun-to-read critics is indeed essential."

— Jack Mathews, *New York Daily News*

"Joe Leydon's breezy prose takes the 'school' out of film school and makes looking at these classics fun — which is as it should be."

— Jeffrey M. Anderson, *San Francisco Examiner*

"As an aspiring screenwriter, and of course a bona fide movie lover, I was able to come at this massive movie guide from both angles, and found the book to be a stunning success all the way around. Not only did the actual choices of films inspire me (although many of them were shoo-ins!), but the many insights and little-known factoids surrounding these films delighted and entertained me into the wee hours of the morn. I just could not put this book down once I started reading through Leydon's top picks for the films that most influenced art, society, and culture."

— Ree Jones, Book Reviewer, *AbsoluteWrite.com*

"Along the gauntlet that leads from here to the future of American Cinema, safe passage will be afforded solely to those who can recognize the decisive turning points on the path and the pivotal creative milestones. Joe Leydon has laid out the map across the filmmakers' table, charting the course from Silent Films through Americana, from Song and Dance through CinemaFantastique, and from Suspense and Crime Drama to Funny Business and Foreign Influences. Pack your bags with Leydon's critical insights and must-read memoirs, because if you don't know where film has been, you can't appreciate where it's going, or how it will get there."

— Larry Sivitz, *Seattle Magazine*

"Joe Leydon combines good taste and thorough knowledge of the movies with a gift for colorful writing ... the result is a book that's informative, provocative, and great fun to read."

— Leonard Maltin

JOE LEYDON'S GUIDE TO ESSENTIAL

movies

YOU MUST SEE

if you read, write about, or make movies

Published by Michael Wiese Productions,
11288 Ventura Boulevard,
Suite #621
Studio City, CA 91604
(818) 379-8799, (818) 986-3408 (FAX).
mw@mwp.com
www.mwp.com

Cover design by John Hall
Interior design by William Morosi

Printed by McNaughton & Gunn, Saline, Michigan
Manufactured in the United States of America

Library of Congress Cataloging-in-Publication Data

Leydon, Joe, 1952-
  [Guide to essential movies you must see if you read, write about, or
make movies]
  Joe Leydon's guide to essential movies you must see if you read, write
about, or make movies / Joe Leydon.
      p. cm.
  ISBN 0-941188-92-2
  1. Motion pictures. I. Title: Guide to essential movies you must see
if you read, write about, or make movies. II. Title.
  PN1994.L456 2004
  791.43'75--dc22
                          2004004312

For Tom Bell and Joanne Harrison,

with eternal gratitude

for education and inspiration

TABLE OF
CONTENTS

INTRODUCTION

When it comes to reading and writing about film, some titles serve as useful shorthand. *The 400 Blows* is the yardstick for any drama about troubled adolescents. *Rashomon* describes any narrative that involves various, and often contradictory, points of view. (The term is so common, *TV Guide* editors think nothing of blurbing a *Seinfeld* episode as "a *Rashomon* situation.") If you're reading about a schlocky sci-fi melodrama best appreciated as a high-camp hoot, you can safely assume that, sooner or later, *Plan 9 from Outer Space* will figure into the commentary. And when dealing with a prime example of directorial hubris – well, let's just say that, had *Titanic* been a catastrophic flop, James Cameron would have been pelted with comparisons to Michael Cimino and *Heaven's Gate*.

Such allusions are by no means unique to film critics. Whether you're a screenwriter making a pitch to a producer, or simply a movie buff posting an online opinion, you're likely to use a single title to represent an entire genre: *48 HRS.* (slam-bang buddy-cop action-comedy), *Casablanca* (bittersweet wartime romance), *Shane* (lethal loner defends endangered innocents), *Sullivan's Travels* (picaresque road movie dotted with comical detours), *Alien* (bogeymen in outer space) and so on.

These and other key titles are basic elements in the common language used to write knowledgeably and authoritatively about film. It's a language you should master to fully comprehend what you *read* about film — especially while you're slogging through stuff written in the often arcane dialect of critic-speak — whether you're perusing some academic journal or paging through *Entertainment Weekly*.

And it's the language you *must* master if you want to become, and remain, a filmmaker. After all, how can you perform at pitch meetings — much less know where to seek inspiration, or how to avoid other people's mistakes — if you haven't taken time to learn the essentials?

Consider the advice given by Martin Scorsese in his 1997 book, *A Personal Journey Through American Movies*:

> "I am often asked by younger filmmakers: Why do I need to look at old movies? The only response I can give them is: I still consider myself a student. Yes, I have made a number of pictures... But the more pictures I make, the more I realize that I don't really know. I'm always looking for something or someone that I can learn from. This is what I tell young filmmakers and film students: Do what painters used to do, and probably still do. Study the old masters. Enrich your palette. Expand the canvas. There's always so much more to learn."

This book is intended as an introduction to movies you have to see if you want to talk, read, or write about movies, or pitch and make movies of your own.

It's a guide for casual fans and serious students — for stargazers and cineastes, megaplex attendees and art-house habitués. It's also a phrase book and ready reference for mastering the universal language of cinema.

Please understand: Unlike most other books of its kind, this is *not* a purely subjective guide to the greatest movies of all time. While some of the pictures discussed here are revered classics, others are noble failures — and many fall somewhere in between. A few are among the most influential films ever made. (Meaning, of course, other filmmakers are constantly "quoting" them — sometimes as loving homage, sometimes as shameless theft.) And a couple are so irredeemably awful, they've achieved near-legendary status.

What do they all have in common? For openers, these are films people mention most often when they talk or write about other films. They are the reference points, the defining terms, the standards of measure. Just as important, they are films that all current and future auteurs would do well to study — to gain a greater understanding of the medium, of course, but also to learn from good (and bad) examples.

Appropriately enough for our age of multitasking, this is a multipurpose book.

If you are an academic seeking a primary or supplemental text for an introductory film studies course, *Guide to Essential Movies* should fill your needs. If you prefer a home-schooling, do-it-yourself approach, you can use this book to teach yourself the rudiments of film literacy: View the films examined here at a comfortable pace — say, two a week over the course of a year — and you're guaranteed to wind up vastly more knowledgeable than most poseurs who call themselves film critics. (The late, great François Truffaut once warned fellow filmmakers that their work would be judged by reviewers who had never seen a film by F.W. Murnau; these days, filmmakers must endure half-baked assessments by "critics" who are unfamiliar with Truffaut's masterpieces.) If you seek consumer guidance for DVD and VHS purchases, you can parse these pages for advice while assembling a reference library of essential cinema.

And if you simply want a what-to-rent guide for those evenings when your friendly neighborhood Blockbuster has run out of the latest hot titles — consider this your handy-dandy tip sheet for uncovering hidden treasures on the back shelves.

Inevitably, a collection of any 60 or so titles will disappoint the most passionate advocates of those films and filmmakers not included in the final cut. But take heart: Just as every Hollywood box-office blockbuster is bound to inspire a sequel — unless, of course, that blockbuster happens to be *Titanic* — an enthusiastic response to this book likely will lead to *Essential Movies II*. Until such a follow-up appears, however, please remember what every savvy student eventually learns: Before you can attempt advanced studies, you need a firm grasp of the basics. There really is so much to learn.

— Joe Leydon

≈1≈
IN THE
BEGINNING

homas Edison, one of the founding fathers of cinema, was dubious about the long-range prospects for his mongrel offspring. Much as Bill Gates initially ignored the possibilities of the Internet, he failed to grasp the vast potential of the new medium, even as his own scientists were creating it. It took the singular achievement of Edwin S. Porter — ironically, one of the Edison Company's in-house directors — to help make Edison, and millions of others, fully appreciate the magic of the movies.

Edison originally envisioned "moving pictures" as a diversion roughly akin to music videos, to provide visual accompaniment for his marvel of late nineteenth-century high-tech entertainment, the phonograph. Sound and image, he theorized, would be synchronized on wax cylinders. ("Everything should come out of one hole," he memorably maintained.) But his associates, led by the resourceful William Kennedy Laurie Dickson, had different ideas.

As early as 1888, Team Dickson focused on celluloid roll film, newly developed by George Eastman, as the key to making movies. Edison gave his grudging approval, allowing Dickson and company to perfect the Kinetograph, a camera capable of imprinting images on up to 50 feet of film, at a speed of 40 frames per second.

Dickson struggled to find some way of projecting those images onto large screens for mass consumption. At first, however, Edison was content to exhibit his brief photoplays 30-second recordings of acrobatics, slapstick, hootchie-kootchie dancers and similar spectacles in a peep-show viewing device known as the Kinetoscope. As an inventor, he greatly appreciated the superior clarity of images viewed in a Kinetoscope. And as a businessman, he was certain he could make more money by showing movies to individual curiosity-seekers — who would pay a penny for each peek — instead of screening them in theaters filled with people who would quickly tire of a silly fad.

(Another consideration: Early projectors had an unfortunate tendency to overheat and explode. Unless you're selling explosives, fireworks, or Ford Pinto station wagons, it's never a good idea to sell something that might blow up while the buyer is using it.)

By 1894, Kinetoscope parlors were as plentiful and profitable throughout the United States as video game arcades in the late twentieth century. But Edison dismissed the phenomenon as a passing fancy that would soon fade from the pop-culture consciousness. Which is partly why, when he patented his newfangled devices, he refused to cough up the extra $150 that would have extended his U.S. rights to England and Europe.

Thanks to this tight-fisted and shortsighted decision, the brothers Louis Jean and Auguste Lumière were free to tinker with Edison's handiwork after attending a Kinetoscope exhibition in their native France. Within a year, they developed their own camera, dubbed the *Cinematographe*, which — *mirabile dictu!* — also printed and projected pictures. (Yes, you guessed it: This is where we get the word "cinema.")

On December 28, 1895, the date generally accepted as the birthday of motion pictures, the Lumière brothers presented their first program of short movies to a paying audience in a Paris bistro. The films were little more than fleeting glimpses of commonplace occurrences — the arrival of a passenger train, the departure of factory workers, the feeding of a baby by proud parents — but the viewers assembled in the basement of the Grand Café were astonished. A century before the advent of "reality television," the Lumières demonstrated the audience-grabbing appeal of what they called "actualities."

Not to be outdone by foreign competition, Edison belatedly recognized the commercial potential of big-screen exhibition. He obtained the rights to a projector perfected by another U.S. inventor, Thomas Armant, and marketed the device as an Edison Company innovation known as the Vitascope. Just as important, Edison continued to supervise production of short films for Vitascope *and* Kinetoscope presentation. While the Lumières and their European contemporaries tended to specialize in documentaries and travelogues, the Edison Company placed greater emphasis on vaudeville acts and snippets of legitimate theater. Both types of films actualities and entertainments — enjoyed tremendous popularity. For a while.

As the century turned, however, fickle audiences began to justify Edison's worst fears about the novelty value of moving pictures. Ticket-buyers tired of actions without context, sensations without story, while viewing clusters of 30- and 60-second shorts. The fad faded so drastically that, by the early 1900s, some vaudeville impresarios were programming "flickers" on their bills primarily as "chasers" — that is, off-putting attractions that would encourage steady audience turnover by discouraging patrons from staying in their seats too long.

It would be an overstatement, perhaps, to credit Edwin S. Porter with "saving" motion pictures by making *The Great Train Robbery* in 1903. And it definitely would be inaccurate to describe his 12-minute masterwork as the first narrative film. A year before Porter directed *Train Robbery*, French magician-turned-moviemaker George Melies premiered *A Trip to the Moon*, his exuberant account of a lunar misadventure. But whereas Melies' *Moon* remained, for all its trend-setting trick photography, hopelessly stagebound, Porter's film arguably is the first, and definitely the most influential, to fully exploit storytelling devices exclusive to cinema.

The story itself is childishly simple: Wild West outlaws subdue a telegraph operator, board and halt a train, rob the passengers, and gallop away to divide their ill-gotten gain only to be killed by a pursuing posse. (Censors and self-righteous politicians, take note: Right from the start, violence has been an intrinsic element of movies.) But Porter told the story with such then-innovative techniques as panning shots, parallel editing, elliptical jumps in time and non-sequential juxtaposition of scenes. Relying heavily on his experiences as a touring projectionist — a job that required him to assemble 15-minute and half-hour programs of unrelated shorts, thereby creating and varying moods like a modern-day dance-club d.j. — he sustained dramatic tension and narrative momentum for nearly an entire reel of film.

In doing so, Porter did more than establish many conventions of the Western genre. He also taught his contemporaries a lesson that, alas, is all too often ignored by twenty-first-century filmmakers: Spectacle is not enough; movies also have to tell compelling stories.

SUBJECTS FOR FURTHER RESEARCH:

Landmarks of Early Film — Worthy of inclusion in every home-video library, this remarkable Image Entertainment DVD contains late nineteenth-century Edison Company Kinetoscopes, the earliest movies of the Lumière Brothers — including *Exiting the Factory* and *Arrival of a Train at La Ciotat*, two of the very first motion pictures screened in 1895 — and two of the earliest narrative features: Georges Melies' *A Trip to the Moon* (1902) and Edwin S. Porter's *The Great Train Robbery* (1903).

Lumière and Company — To celebrate the 1995 centennial of motion pictures, 40 international filmmakers, each armed with a lovingly restored, hand-cranked *Cinematographe*, made their own one-minute films in the style of the Brothers Lumière (i.e., black and white, natural light, no synchronized sound). Assembled by documentarian Sarah Moon, and supplemented with remarks by the filmmakers, the shorts included on this Fox Lorber DVD range from Spike Lee's home movie–style view of his infant son to Claude Lelouch's elaborate ode to romance as a constant in cinema. Lasse Hallström, David Lynch, and Wim Wenders also offer contributions to this one-of-a-kind omnibus.

LESSON FOR FILMMAKERS:

"The cinema," Louis Lumière proclaimed in 1899, "is an invention without a future." Which just goes to show you: Even visionaries can be remarkably myopic.

≈2≈
SILENTS
PLEASE

THE BIRTH OF A NATION

If *The Birth of a Nation* were not the first great American movie, it would be inexcusable. Indeed, even for those who fully appreciate it as a groundbreaking and trendsetting masterwork, D. W. Griffith's notorious 1915 epic is almost impossible to watch without being electrified by alternating currents of outrage and embarrassment.

One moment, you're responding with hectoring giggles and slack-jawed amazement to some shameless flourish of Victorian-tinged melodramatic excess. The next moment, you're involuntarily cringing, or shouting rude things at the screen, as Griffith renders another bunch of African Americans (portrayed by white actors in blackface) as indolent buffoons, prideful dullards, sexual predators, bloodthirsty savages — or all of the above.

The most offensive scene? Take your pick. There's the infamous sequence inside a Reconstruction Era state legislature, where newly elected black representatives swill whiskey, feast on fried chicken, and prop their bare feet on desktops. Or the moment when a heroic white southerner, noting how easily black children are frightened by "ghosts" (i.e., playmates wearing sheets), is inspired to make a fashion statement as a Ku Klux Klansman.

To say nothing of the lasciviously detailed near-ravishing of virginal southern belles by a hormonally inflamed black soldier and — much worse, given the movie's implicit condemnation of miscegenation — an upwardly mobile mulatto.

9

And yet, for all that, *Birth of a Nation* must be acknowledged as a land-mark achievement. The sophistication of its technique and the epic sweep of its narrative were unprecedented. Its battle scenes, by turns intensely inti-mate and lavishly panoramic, were nothing short of stunning. Even more impressive — and, in terms of the film's effect on other filmmakers, more influential — was its innovative use of montage to enhance suspense, par-ticularly during two last-minute rescues in the final reel. After viewing the 1915 world premiere, an uncredited critic for the *New York Times* began a review by disapproving of the film's "melodramatic and inflammatory" content. "But of the film as a film," the critic added, "it may be reported simply that it is an impressive new illustration of the scope of the motion picture camera." For better or worse, the *Times* scribe made the right call.

The movie focuses primarily on two families — the Camerons of the South, the Stonemans of the North — backed by a supporting cast of carpetbaggers, Union scalawags, "crazed Negroes" (to quote one of the hyperbolic title cards), and President Abraham Lincoln (played in a handful of hagiographic tableaux by Joseph Henabury).

Before the war, the two families are on cordial terms, making it all the more bitterly ironic when, in the heat of battle, a young Cameron very nearly kills his Stoneman chum.

Unfortunately, both young men wind up dying at the hands of others. Even more unfortunately, during the Reconstruction period, "radical Republican" Austin Stoneman (Ralph Lewis) enables crafty mulatto Silas Lynch (George Siegmann) and the aforementioned crazed Negroes to gain dominance in the Camerons' home state of South Carolina.

Decent and God-fearing white folks are repeatedly humiliated by uppity Negroes (but protected by their faithful black servants). Sweet little Flora Cameron (Mae Marsh) jumps off a cliff to avoid being raped by a "renegade" black soldier. Elise Stoneman (Lillian Gish), the radical Republican's daughter, is sorely mistreated when she rejects the lusty Silas Lynch. It's up to young Ben Cameron (Henry B. Walthall) to save the day, with a little help from his army of hooded vigilantes.

David Wark Griffith, aptly described by a biographer as "fundamental-ly a nineteenth-century man who helped to invent the twentieth-century art," came to motion pictures only after failing in nearly every other field of endeavor. Unreadable as a poet, unremarkable as a playwright and chronically unemployed as a stage actor, he was thirty-two when, in 1907, he pitched a spec screenplay to Edwin S. Porter at the Bronx-based Edison Studio. Like many of his fellow thespians, Griffith viewed acting in "flickers" as the most demeaning sort of slumming. But after Porter rejected the script, Griffith swallowed his pride — temporarily, at least — when he was offered the lead role in an Edison one-reeler titled *Rescued from an Eagle's Nest.*

Within a few months, Griffith was working regularly, writing as well as acting, at the Biograph Studio in Manhattan. More important, he was a sharp observer and a quick study as he watched movies being made. By 1908, he was ready to direct his first film. By 1909, he had well over 100 one-reelers to his credit.

A great many film historians who should know better have credited Griffith with "inventing" such devices as establishing shots, expressionistic lighting, and crosscutting between simultaneous actions. In truth, each of these innovations appeared in other films long before Griffith embraced them. Griffith's indisputable genius was his ability to synthesize these and other tools in the creation of a uniquely cinematic storytelling syntax. To paraphrase a recent television commercial: Griffith didn't invent the close-up, he simply used it better than anyone ever had before.

During the final six months of 1914, Griffith used every trick in his book, and improvised quite a few new ones, while creating his magnum opus, *The Birth of a Nation.* He somehow managed to beg or borrow the enormous sum of $100,000 — up to that point, the biggest budget in motion picture history — to adapt Thomas F. Dixon Jr.'s *The Clansman,* an epic story set against the backdrop of the Civil War, which Dixon himself had previously adapted for the stage. Griffith, the son of an impoverished Confederate veteran, was especially impressed by Dixon's romanticized account of ordeal and triumph in a South Carolina town during the Reconstruction period.

Trouble is, even though Griffith made at least a token effort to excise or ameliorate the more savagely racist portions of Dixon's novel, his adaptation often comes across as impassioned justification, if not recruitment propaganda, for the Ku Klux Klan.

No doubt about it: *The Birth of a Nation* is a virtual textbook of innovative techniques that, in its time, greatly advanced cinema as art. As a historical artifact, it is invaluable. But, then again, so is Leni Riefenstahl's *The Triumph of the Will*. You can recognize the aesthetic significance of both films even as you despise their content.

SPECS:

The Birth of a Nation – Stars: Lillian Gish, Mae Marsh, Henry B. Walthall, Miriam Cooper, Mary Alden, Ralph Lewis, and George Siegmann. Directed by D. W. Griffith. Screenplay: D. W. Griffith and Frank Woods, based on the novel *The Clansman* by Thomas F. Dixon Jr. Running time: 187 minutes. Year of release: 1915. DVD distributor: Image Entertainment.

SUBJECTS FOR FURTHER RESEARCH:

Intolerance (1916) — Defiantly responding to pressure groups that sought to censor *The Birth of a Nation*, D. W. Griffith defended his concept of "free speech" with an even more spectacular epic, which interweaves stories of unjust persecution from four separate historical periods. Audiences stayed away in droves — then as now, "message pictures" are dicey box-office draws — but *Intolerance* has gradually gained acceptance as a major work of cinematic art (which many critics deem superior to *Nation.*)

Way Down East (1920) — One of D. W. Griffith's greatest critical and financial successes, this sentimental melodrama about a country lass who's betrayed in the big city features an exquisite lead performance by the immortal Lillian Gish, and a much-imitated cliffhanger climax that finds Gish trapped on an ice floe drifting toward a waterfall.

The Triumph of the Will (1935) — Leni Riefenstahl's infamously Hitler-worshipping documentary, shot during the 1934 Nazi rallies in Nuremberg, remains one of the most influential films ever made. Indeed, it's hard to watch TV coverage of sporting events or political conventions without noting similarities to Riefenstahl's record of the '34 extravaganza (which, not unlike modern entertainments, was meticulously stage-managed for the cameras). Along with *The Birth of the Nation*, however, it must be ranked among the most morally contemptible masterpieces ever produced.

LESSON FOR FILMMAKERS:

Rave reviews are nice, but a celebrity endorsement sometimes can be more easily exploited in advertisements. President Woodrow Wilson merits a footnote in film history as the very first Blurbster in Chief: Upon seeing *The Birth of a Nation*, he provided an eminently quotable comment: "It is like writing history with Lightning. And my only regret is that it is all so terribly true."

NOSFERATU:
A SYMPHONY OF
HORROR

Decades before web surfers began to swap music files without bothering about the niceties of copyright law, F.W. Murnau felt entitled to attempt a different type of unauthorized downloading. Although he couldn't or wouldn't obtain movie rights to the late Bram Stoker's *Dracula*, he went ahead and filmed the novel as *Nosferatu: A Symphony of Horror* in 1922.

Critics were enchanted, audiences were enthralled — but that meant little to the executors of Stoker's literary estate. Even though Murnau changed names and places to protect the guilty — Count Dracula was christened Count Orlock, scenes were shifted from London to Bremen — he retained nearly the entire original plot, and many identifying details of the novel's characters. Stoker's widow was so incensed, she filed suit to have all copies of the film destroyed.

That *Nosferatu* survives in any form whatsoever can be credited to fortuitous happenstance. (A few prints here and there somehow managed to avoid the Stoker-sanctioned roundup.) But the enduring power of the movie to enthrall and unsettle is a result of Murnau's coldly calculated artistry. This isn't merely the first (and in many ways most influential) *Dracula* movie. It's also, quite literally, the most monstrous.

Count Orlock, the Ur-vampire portrayed by Max Schreck, is unlike any of the dozens of Draculas who have followed in his wake. In sharp contrast to the suave and silken bloodsuckers later played by Bela Lugosi and Christopher Lee, or the tragically brooding outcast essayed by Gary Oldman in Francis Coppola's 1992 extravaganza, Schreck's Orlock comes off a pure evil on the hoof, complete with the pointed ears, extended fangs, and the skittish movements of a steroid-enhanced rodent. When Orlock first emerges from the shadows of his decaying Transylvanian castle, you can't help wondering why visiting real estate agent Thomas Hutter (Gustav Von Wagenheim) doesn't run screaming into the nearby woods. (Maybe the count has offered to pay an irresistibly huge commission for new living quarters in Bremen?)

Later, Orlock methodically feasts on the sailors aboard the ship carrying him to Germany, then unleashes in Bremen a plague represented by the mangy rats transported within his coffins. Talk about your enemy alien: The misshapen vampire stands — or skulks — as the very personification of a "foreign presence" who visits death and destruction upon an unwary populace.

Chief among his potential victims: Ellen (Greta Schroeder), Hutter's ethereally beautiful wife, whose feelings toward her callow husband appear more maternal than connubial. Orlock longs for a necking session with the dreamy-eyed damsel, a fatal weakness that Ellen selflessly exploits to save her beloved Thomas. Truth to tell, however, she does appear just the *teensiest* bit drawn to an admirer who, although hideous, may be appreciably more vigorous than her fey and flighty spouse.

Thanks to a unique confluence of artistic trends and sociopolitical upheavals, Murnau found an exceptionally receptive audience for *Nosferatu*. Much like the folks in Depression-ravaged America, Germans during the heyday of the Weimar Republic (1919-33) distracted themselves from harsh realities of postwar deprivation by seeking escapism at the movies. Historical romances, costume dramas, and lavish epics based on ancient legends were prime box-office attractions. Equally popular, however, were dramas of the macabre and fantastical — tales of horror, phantasms, and science fiction, ranging from *The Golem* (1920) to *Metropolis* (1926) — that allowed audiences a safe way to savor catharsis through the playing out of worst-case scenarios.

Nosferatu is very much of its time in its Expressionistic intermingling of light and shadow, style and substance, modern psychology and ancient myth. And yet it stands apart from most other similarly stylized films of its era by grounding its fantasy in a recognizable reality. E. Elias Merhige's *Shadow of the Vampire* (2000) mischievously exaggerated Murnau's penchant for verisimilitude. (The demanding director didn't hire a *real* vampire for the lead role — honest! — and he didn't allow his cast to be killed off during production.) But Murnau did indeed spurn the stylized studio sets that were common in fantasy films of his age. Instead, he preferred to shoot on actual locations, often venturing outside to ground his extraordinary story in ordinary surroundings.

To be sure, he occasionally used the '20s equivalent of high-tech trickery: fast-motion, stop-action, photographic negatives depicting white trees against a midnight-black sky. But by emphasizing the natural as much as possible while rendering the supernatural, Murnau rightly figured he could enhance the horror of *Nosferatu*. Many years later, critic Roger Ebert would write: "This movie seems to really believe in vampires." No kidding.

SPECS:

Nosferatu: A Symphony of Horror – Stars: Max Schreck, Greta Schröder, Gustav von Wangenheim, Alexander Granach, and John Gottowt. Directed by F. W. Murnau. Screenplay: Henrik Galeen (based on *Dracula* by Bram Stoker). Running time: 81 minutes. Year of release: 1922. DVD distributor: Image Entertainment.

SUBJECTS FOR FURTHER RESEARCH:

The Cabinet of Dr. Caligari (1919) — Another masterwork of German Expressionism, justly famous for its purposefully bizarre set, costume, and make-up designs, Robert Weine's fever dream of a melodrama (about a sideshow charlatan who controls a murderous sleepwalker) has been a thematic and/or visual influence on countless subsequent scary movies.

Dracula (1931) — It's stodgy and stagy by contemporary standards, but Tod Browning's genuinely spooky version of Bram Stoker's novel is irresistible as a showcase for Bela Lugosi's definitive performance as the suavely sinister count.

Horror of Dracula (1958) — Among the first and best of the revisionist horror shows from England's Hammer Studios, director Terence Fisher's take on Bram Stoker's tale is frankly sensuous and graphically violent (by '50s standards, at least) even while eschewing many aspects of the vampire mythos. (In this version, bloodsuckers can't turn into wolves or bats.) Christopher Lee establishes his bogeyman cred with his authoritatively evil Count Dracula, a character he would reprise in several sequels.

LESSON FOR FILMMAKERS:

Fidelity to source material is optional. It was F. W. Murnau, not Bram Stoker, who came up with the notion that vampires disintegrate in sunlight. (Dracula actually tours London by day at one point in Stoker's novel.) Murnau used the plot device to cap off a grand romantic gesture at the end of *Nosferatu*, when Ellen sacrifices her life while delaying Orlock's departure until daybreak. Almost every vampire movie produced since *Nosferatu* has followed Murnau's lead.

T̲H̲E̲ G̲ENERAL

An internationally acclaimed auteur follows the biggest hit of his career with a budget-busting action-comedy epic. The production values are prodigious — a single sight gag requires one of the most expensive single shots in movie history — and the death-defying stunt work is spectacular.

But the critical response is scathing. *Variety* bluntly blasts the production as "a flop." *Life* magazine condemns the cringe-inducing mix of comedy and carnage. *The New York Times* huffily complains that the director "appears to have bitten off more than he can chew." Negative buzz abounds, unfavorable word of mouth spreads. Despite the marquee allure of the above-the-title star, audiences stay away in droves.

Sound familiar? It could be the story of *1941*, or *Last Action Hero*. But the embarrassing under-achievements of those box-office duds are fairly inconsequential when viewed in the big picture of Hollywood history. Buster Keaton's *The General*, arguably the first action-comedy epic, merits special consideration as a far more significant "failure."

Today, Keaton's dauntingly ambitious and remarkably accomplished 1927 comedy is universally recognized as one of the enduring classics of the silent era. Indeed, many critics and academics insist *The General* is one of the greatest movies ever made in any period. Back in the 1920s, however, it was such a resounding flop that Keaton's career was forever blighted by its long shadow.

To be sure, Keaton remained active — most often as an actor, sometimes as a director or uncredited writer — in features and shorts until his death in 1966. He appeared as a befuddled time-traveler in a memorable *Twilight Zone* segment, displayed remarkable dignity (and undiminished comic verve) in such teen-skewing trifles as *Pajama Party* (1964) and *How to Stuff a Wild Bikini* (1965), and gave a poignantly funny final performance in Richard Lester's *A Funny Thing Happened on the Way to the Forum* (1966). But he never again enjoyed the artistic freedom and financial wherewithal he was granted when he made *The General*.

Even in his heyday, Keaton often found himself on the wrong end of unflattering comparisons to a more celebrated contemporary, Charlie Chaplin. Viewed in retrospect, however, the *dissimilarities* between the two comic greats are more pronounced. As critic Andrew Sarris astutely noted in *The American Cinema*, "The difference between Keaton and Chaplin is the difference between poise and poetry, between the aristocrat and the tramp, between adaptability and dislocation, between the function of things and the meaning of things."

To put it another way: While Chaplin often risks everything, even his life, while soaring on flights of dream-stoked fancy, Keaton customarily remains more earthbound, doggedly ignoring the chaos around him while obsessively focused on purely practical matters. Chaplin romanticizes women as luminous mysteries to be worshipped; Keaton expects a woman to pull her weight even after he falls in love with her. (At one point in *The General*, his character is so exasperated by the clueless klutziness of his lady love that he very nearly strangles her before opting to kiss her instead.) Whereas Chaplin might be driven batty by his dehumanizing drudgery on a high-speed assembly line (*Modern Times*), Keaton is more determined to impose control over troublesome technology, likely through sheer force of will.

Consider one of the many unforgettable moments in *The General*, the Civil War saga of a Confederate engineer's misadventures while trying to retrieve a wood-burning locomotive hijacked by Union spies. (The title refers to the locomotive, not a military officer.) As Johnnie Gray, the improbably and imperturbably heroic southerner, Keaton is so busy chopping wood to keep his engine running while pursuing his stolen General, he remains totally oblivious as his train passes retreating Confederate forces, then an advancing Union army. His absurdly disproportionate attentiveness to detail is not unlike that of the bomber crewman in *Dr. Strangelove* who fastidiously corrects a log error moments before his big-bang vaporization.

Throughout *The General*, Keaton lives up to his nickname as The Great Stone Face, making only the most minute adjustments to his expression to signal shifts between amusement (rare) and befuddlement (frequent), despair (he volunteers for the Confederate army, but is rejected because of his value as an engineer) and exultation (he proves his heroism to the southern belle who once thought him a coward). Just as important, Keaton also illustrates the contradiction — the hilarious dichotomy between stillness of form and fluidity of movement — that is his hallmark as a comic artist.

After the enormous success of his *Battling Butler* (1926), a relatively slight farce about a faux boxer, Keaton co-wrote and co-directed *The General* (with Clyde Bruckman) as another star vehicle. Even so, the latter movie's notoriously expensive sight gag (estimated cost: $42,000) is keyed to the flabbergasted response of a minor supporting character, a Union commander who watches helplessly while a train falls through a burning bridge and into a river far below. Keaton used a real bridge, a real river — and, yes, a real locomotive. Back in 1927, such excessive spectacle in a *comedy* struck many critics and audiences as bewildering, if not downright unseemly.

Viewers of the era were even more upset by the outrageously dark comedy of a scene in which Keaton fails to notice while his Confederate comrades are felled by a Union sniper. Just in the nick of time, our hero saves himself simply by waving his sword. The loosened blade flies off the handle, and plunges into the enemy marksman.

Mind you, we don't see the moment of impalement, just a brief glimpse of the dead sniper. But that was too much for most folks in the 1920s. Critic Robert E. Sherwood complained in *Life* magazine: "Someone should have told Buster that it is difficult to derive laughter from the sight of men being killed in battle. Many of his gags at the end of (*The General*) are in such gruesomely bad taste that the sympathetic spectator is inclined to look the other way." Time passes, tastes change: In 2000, when the American Film Institute released its list of the 100 funniest movies ever made, *The General* ranked higher – number eighteen – than any other silent comedy on the list.

Buster Keaton was far ahead of his time, which is why he remains immortal.

SPECS:

The General – Stars: Buster Keaton and Marion Mack. Written and directed by Buster Keaton, Clyde Bruckman. Screenplay: Running time: 75 minutes. Year of release: 1927. DVD distributor: Image Entertainment.

SUBJECTS FOR FURTHER RESEARCH:

Sherlock Jr. (1924) — Sixty years before Jeff Daniels played a '30s movie star who wandered off the screen and into the audience in Woody Allen's *The Purple Rose of Cairo* (1985), and more than seven decades before Tobey Maguire was transported from his '90s living room to a '50s TV sitcom in *Pleasantville* (1998), Keaton was smudging the line between reality and fantasy by playing a projectionist (and would-be detective) who daydreams his way into a movie he's presenting.

How I Won the War (1967) — Director Richard Lester (*A Hard Day's Night*) offered a bold mix of comedy and carnage in his darkly humorous satire of war (and war films). Much like *The General*, Lester's film angered critics who were outraged by the unsettling juxtaposition of style and content. (Lester previously directed Keaton in the latter's final movie, 1966's *A Funny Thing Happened on the Way to the Forum*.)

The Blues Brothers (1980) — John Landis's demolition derby of a comedy features John Belushi and Dan Aykroyd as deadpan blues musicians who matter-of-factly forge an interlocking chain of spectacular car crashes and steadily escalating cataclysms. It's easy to spot the influence of several Buster Keaton films (especially 1922's *Cops*).

LESSON FOR FILMMAKERS:

"If I could be compared to one filmmaker," Jackie Chan has said,

"I would want it to be Buster Keaton." Ever wonder why Chan is so frequently compared to Keaton? Take a close look at the no-sweat gracefulness of the latter's astonishing physicality in *The General*. See how Keaton lunges into frames, dives under tables, spins into pratfalls, and skips across the tops of moving trains – all the while maintaining his unsmiling aplomb and, like Chan, risking life and limb while never using a stunt double. "I just want that one day, when I retire," Chan once told an interviewer, "that people will still remember me like they remember Buster."

CITY LIGHTS

There may be folks who can remain dry-eyed and hard-hearted during the final moments of Charlie Chaplin's *City Lights*, but take care: Anyone that cynical shouldn't be entirely trusted.

Chaplin's silent masterworks, one-reelers and features alike, are continually rediscovered by new generations, and recognized as timeless classics by adoring audiences and fellow filmmakers. ("For me," François Truffaut famously enthused, "they are the most beautiful films in the world. Chaplin means more to me than the idea of God.") To be sure, Chaplin's relatively few talking pictures — especially *Limelight* (1952) and *The Great Dictator* (1940) — also inspire admiration and affection. But his pre-talkie efforts are the wonderments that guarantee his immortality, that ensure his very name will forever serve as an adjective for any attempt, successful or otherwise, to mix pratfalling and heart-tugging in a crowd-pleasing comedy.

The Kid (1921) may be more aggressively sentimental, and *The Gold Rush* (1925) perhaps is more commonly acclaimed as his magnum opus, but *City Lights* (1931) is by far the most *Chaplinesque* of all Chaplin movies, being an absolutely magical commingling of graceful pantomime, knockabout tomfoolery, inspired silliness and — perhaps most important — profoundly affecting poignancy. It's also, not incidentally, a project Chaplin insisted on shooting as a silent movie long after talking pictures had become the accepted norm.

City Lights begins, of course, with Chaplin cleverly introduced in his familiar role as The Little Tramp, the elegantly mustached gentleman whose shabby attire (derby hat, frock coat, baggy trousers, outsized shoes) is offset by his courtly manner and cane-twirling, hat-tipping panache. And it proceeds with the sort of seemingly improvised but intricately choreographed funny business that many comic actors still emulate. (Check out his classic bits in a raucous nightclub and a high-society party.) In the closing scenes, however, *City Lights* gradually builds to an epiphany of sweetly painful pathos, leading to a final, indelible image of a man smiling with hopeless longing at a woman whose love he fears he could never — not now, not in a million lifetimes — deserve.

Throughout much of *City Lights*, Chaplin maintains a lighter mood, even as The Little Tramp — a.k.a. Charlie — is repeatedly abused or embarrassed. (Chaplin customarily billed himself as *Charles* Chaplin for his writing and directorial credits, but always stuck with *Charlie* to identify himself as star of the show.) When a blind flower girl (Virginia Merrill) naively assumes he is a free-spending dandy, Charlie is so smitten that he resorts to drastic measures — including, most hilariously, his participation in a boxing match — to earn enough money to sustain the mistaken identity.

Periodically, Charlie enjoys an evening's revelry with an alcoholic millionaire (Harry Myers) who drinks to steadily increasing excess in the wake of his wife's departure. Whenever the millionaire sobers up, however, he never recognizes Charlie as his boon companion from the night before. His selective memory proves to be awfully inconvenient for Charlie: After giving the Little Tramp enough money for the flower girl to have an operation that will restore her eyesight, the millionaire forgets all about his generosity. Which, unfortunately, leads to Charlie's arrest and imprisonment.

After his release, Charlie looks even more bedraggled and destitute than he does in the opening scenes. The good news is, the flower girl, who has opened a flower shop, can now see. The bad news is — well, she can now see *him*.

"She recognizes who he must be by his shy, confident, shining joy as he comes silently toward her," critic James Agee wrote in 1949. "And he recognizes himself, for the first time, through the terrible changes in her face. The camera just exchanges a few quiet close-ups of the emotions which shift and intensify in each face. It is enough to shrivel the heart to see, and it is the greatest piece of acting and the highest moment in movies."

SPECS:

City Lights – Stars: Charlie Chaplin, Virginia Sherrill, Florence Lee, Harry Myers, Allan Garcia, and Hank Mann. Written and directed by Charles Chaplin. Running time: 87 minutes. Year of release: 1931. DVD distributor: Image Entertainment.

SUBJECTS FOR FURTHER RESEARCH:

Modern Times (1936) — Chaplin's final silent classic (which includes, almost grudgingly, some music, sound effects, and gibberish dialogue) is a brilliant parody of mind-numbing mechanization and assembly-line innovation. But wait, there's more: The Little Tramp actually gets the girl (Paulette Goddard, then Chaplin's off-screen significant other) in a beautifully upbeat finale.

Nights of Cabiria (1957) — Federico Fellini borrows liberally from *City Lights* while detailing the seriocomic misadventures of a lonely, love-starved prostitute (luminously played by Giulietta Masina, Fellini's wife) who comes off as a female version of Chaplin's pummeled-yet-plucky Little Tramp.

50 First Dates (2004) — While repeatedly wooing and winning a beautiful woman (Drew Barrymore) with short-term memory loss, Adam Sandler borrows a page or two from Chaplin's relationship with the forgetful millionaire in *City Lights*. It's worth noting, by the way, that Sandler also manages fleeting moments of Chaplinesque pathos in *Big Daddy* (1999), a broad comedy clearly influenced by Chaplin's *The Kid*.

LESSON FOR FILMMAKERS:

The final image of *Manhattan* (1979), Woody Allen's melancholy romantic comedy, is a loving homage to the heart-wrenching finale of

City Lights. It's to Allen's considerable credit that his version is almost as affecting as Chaplin's original, which Allen admits he carefully studied. "*City Lights* was funny and also tragic," Allen told the *New York Times* in 2000. "Some think it's sentimental, but to me, it's an honest film about love." For all his careful appraisal of Chaplin's works, Allen says he still can't fully deconstruct the magic of the master: "I don't believe Chaplin was aware of creating a new vocabulary for film comedy. He just happened to be that gifted, that superb. Very few have taken that extreme leap into a realm that is indefinable and unexplainable."

≈3≈
AMERICANA

MR. SMITH GOES TO WASHINGTON

In an age when radio talk shows, all-news cable networks, and seemingly infinite arrays of internet websites offer round-the-clock reports of thievery, adultery, and brazen stupidity on the part of politicians, it may be well-nigh impossible to believe there ever was a time when Americans were less cynical, and more respectful, in their views of elected officials.

Indeed, as far back as 1939, when filmmaker Frank Capra unveiled *Mr. Smith Goes to Washington*, American voters already were accustomed to logrolling and pork-barreling as instinctive behavior of political animals. But the transition from healthy skepticism to deep-rooted distrust — or profound disgust — on the part of the electorate is a relatively recent phenomenon. Capra's classic comedy about virtue triumphant (though just barely) over Washington corruption is a throwback to the days when most people still wanted to believe that public servants really served the republic.

Jefferson Smith, the soft-spoken but steel-spined hero stirringly played by James Stewart, is a small-town do-gooder. He heads the local branch of a Boy Scouts-type organization, quotes Thomas Jefferson and Abraham Lincoln at exhaustive length and, evidently, thinks his best gal pal is his dear old mom.

(A random thought: Can you imagine the contortions that contemporary screenwriters would go through to immediately indicate that this bachelor scoutmaster isn't really — well, you know, gay?)

In short, Jeff is such a starry-eyed naïf that he seems a perfect choice to serve as "honorary stooge" when one of his state's U.S. Senators dies. Political boss Jim Taylor (Edward Arnold), a robustly venal string-puller, voices a few doubts about appointing this "big-eyed patriot" to serve the remaining two months of the late legislator's term. But the state's other senator, Joseph Paine (Claude Rains), a silver-haired paragon of faux virtue, insists that he'll be able to keep the "simpleton" in line. Yeah, right.

Initially, Jeff appears every bit as green and gawky as his handlers hoped. As soon as he reaches Washington, D.C., he slips away on his own to take a bus tour of the nation's capital. (Cynics often point to this sequence — a shamelessly sentimental and spirit-pumping montage of the Washington Monument, the Lincoln Memorial, and similarly impressive icons — as representing the worst excesses of what detractors label as "Capra-corn." In his defense, Capra claimed that when *he* first took the Washington tour, he felt the same rush of excitement — "I got a bad case of goose pimples!" — that inflames Jeff Smith.) Later, while Jeff is being tutored by his cynical secretary, Clarissa Saunders (Jean Arthur), the dewy-eyed newcomer decides he should pay a visit to Mount Vernon, for inspiration, before his first day of duties in the Senate.

It doesn't take long, however, before Jeff gets wise to the ways of Washington. Our hero is horrified to discover that Senator Paine — a long-time family friend who knew Jeff's late father, a crusading newspaper editor — is part of a plot to procure federal funding for a dam on property purchased by Taylor and other scalawags. Worse, when he tries to expose the dirty dealing, Jeff is framed as a corrupt hypocrite by Senator Paine himself. But don't worry: Jeff may have a few dark moments of doubt, but he ultimately rises to the occasion. In the movie's most famous sequence, he defends himself — along with truth, justice, and the American way — in a passionate filibuster that he sustains at great cost to his health and reputation. Gravely conscience-stricken, Senator Paine eventually admits his chicanery on the Senator floor, instantly vindicating Jeff. As Woody Allen once said in an entirely different context: "If only life were like this!"

Viewed today by jaded audiences, *Mr. Smith Goes to Washington* might seem quaintly timid in its treatment of money-grubbing politicos, hard-drinking reporters and well-heeled power brokers. In 1939, however, many members of the political establishment loudly decried the movie as scurrilous libel. Washington reporters were enraged by Capra's depiction of the Washington press corps as boozy and irresponsible. (Thomas Mitchell plays the booziest of the lot, and very nearly steals the picture.) The hostile response to a preview screening in Washington, D.C. remains the stuff of Hollywood legend. Joseph P. Kennedy, then U.S. ambassador to London, reportedly went so far as to press Columbia not to release *Mr. Smith* in Europe, lest American prestige be undermined just as Adolf Hitler was making such a nuisance of himself.

The delicious irony is, Capra didn't realize what a subversive piece of work he had concocted until long after the cameras stopped rolling. As he explained in his 1971 autobiography, *The Name Above the Title*, Capra intended *Mr. Smith* as a valentine to American democracy, a heartfelt tribute to a form of government that guaranteed a single, right-thinking individual had the opportunity to stand up and be counted. Propelled by the kind of foursquare, flag-waving patriotism that perhaps only an appreciative immigrant wouldn't deem extreme, Capra — a Sicilian native who reached U.S. shores at the age of six — wanted his small-town hero to represent all that was noble, honest and idealistic about America and Americans.

Decades later, many Americans continue to view Jefferson Smith as the kind of elected official they'd like to have. (Politicians as diverse as Bill Clinton and the late Sonny Bono have cited *Mr. Smith* as a major influence on their decision to run for office.) Trouble is, most Americans also recognize Senator Paine as the kind of elected official they usually have to settle for.

SPECS:

Mr. Smith Goes to Washington — Stars: James Stewart, Jean Arthur, Claude Rains, Edward Arnold, Guy Kibbee, and Thomas Mitchell. Directed by Frank Capra. Screenplay: Sidney Buchman. Running time: 129 minutes. Year of release: 1939. DVD distributor: Columbia/TriStar Home Video.

SUBJECTS FOR FURTHER RESEARCH:

It's a Wonderful Life (1946) — Frank Capra's evergreen comedy-fantasy features James Stewart as George Bailey, a small-town Mr. Nice Guy who's driven to the brink of suicidal despair. A guardian angel convinces George to stay alive by showing him what his small town would be like if he'd never been born. The shock therapy works, which explains why the movie is widely embraced as uplifting and inspirational. Pay close attention, however, and you can detect a heart of darkness beating just beneath the sentimental surface of so-called "Capra-corn."

The Seduction of Joe Tynan (1979) — Alan Alda does double duty as star and screenwriter in Jerry Schatzberg's understated drama about a liberal U.S. senator (Alda) whose idealism curdles into opportunism as he faces more alluring temptations (including a sexy associate played by Meryl Streep) than Jefferson Smith ever encountered.

Dave (1993) — When a corrupt U.S. President (Kevin Kline) is felled by a stroke, his equally corrupt advisers replace him with an innocent look-alike (also Kline). Unsurprisingly, but very amusingly, the imitation chief executive turns the tables on the string-pullers by appealing directly to the American public.

LESSON FOR FILMMAKERS:

Unlike many other indie filmmakers — including some who profess to be deeply influenced by the late, great John Cassavetes — Cassavetes himself refused to sneer at the idealist who made *Mr. Smith Goes to Washington.* "Frank Capra," Cassavetes proclaimed, "is the greatest filmmaker that ever lived. Capra created a feeling of belief in a free country and in goodness in bad people ... Idealism is not sentimental. It validates a hope for the future. Capra gave me hope, and in turn I wish to extend a sense of hope to my audiences."

GONE WITH THE WIND

Movie buffs and film academics tend to agree that 1939 was one of the greatest years — if not *the* greatest year, period — in the history of cinema. And with good reason: Even as clouds of war loomed darkly over Europe, the Hollywood studio system was operating at peak efficiency and capacity. With the creative engines of the Dream Factory firing on all cylinders, audiences were treated to such instant classics as *Stagecoach*, *The Wizard of Oz* and *Mr. Smith Goes to Washington*, to name just a few.

Amid this bounty, however, one title continues to overshadow all others: *Gone With the Wind* remains, now and forever, a thrilling romantic melodrama on the grandest imaginable scale, a textbook example of the epic sweep and scope that only movies — even movies made in the pre-Cinemascope era — can provide.

And yet, at the same time, *GWTW* is a beguilingly intimate epic — "basically a film of interiors and medium shots," as author William Bayer (*The Great Movies*) has noted. It may be set before, during, and after the Civil War, but it most certainly isn't a "war movie." In fact, we see nothing but the *aftermath* of bloody clashes, or the collateral damage (i.e., the burning of Atlanta, altercations among retreating civilians). Only one of the main characters ever fires a gun — and even then, only once. For the most part, the War Between the States exists only as a frightful imposition, exploited by the filmmakers to shape destinies and impede romances among the lead characters.

During the opening scenes, the coquettish Scarlett O'Hara (Vivien Leigh) dismisses talk of an impending war by a posse of obsequious suitors. She insists that her would-be boyfriends turn their complete attention to her, while she concentrates on the blandly handsome Ashley Wilkes (Leslie Howard). Unfortunately, Wilkes turns party-pooper by announcing his engagement to the more conventionally demure Melanie Hamilton (Olivia de Havilland). Scarlett is so shocked by the bad news, she pays only minimal attention to the actual outbreak of armed conflict between North and South.

Throughout the rest of *GWTW*, Scarlett survives through sheer force of will, enduring both wartime hardship and postwar deprivation with indomitable spirit and resourcefulness. All the while, she carries a blazing torch for Ashley, even during her occasional marriages of convenience and, more important, despite an aggressive courtship by the charmingly roguish — but not, alas, infinitely patient — Rhett Butler (Clark Gable).

The unsynchronized passions of Scarlett and Rhett are played out against such striking tableaux as the Atlanta conflagration, the burnt-orange sunsets at the Tara plantation and, most famously, the gracefully fluid and awesomely eloquent crane shot of the sprawling train yard filled with scores of wounded Confederate soldiers. But even when the screen is filled with such dramatically and emotionally potent imagery, the spectacle never overwhelms the individual characters or their interpersonal conflicts. In sharp contrast to most other cinematic epics, *GWTW* has a perfect sense of balance.

As an exemplary Old Hollywood confection, *GWTW* is irresistibly entertaining and only occasionally campy. Unmistakably a product of the 1930s, a period when American movies raced at full gallop from one melodramatic scrape to the next, it may be the speediest four-hour movie ever made. Indeed, during one especially busy ten-minute stretch near the end, there are two deaths, a miscarriage, and a near-nervous breakdown.

The performances are thoroughly attuned to this bold, breakneck style of storytelling: Even relatively minor roles — such as Jonas Wilkerson, a slimy slave overseer portrayed by Victor Jory, or the blustering Yankee captain briefly essayed by Ward Bond — are cast and played with an eye toward propelling the narrative with incandescent bursts of vivid character acting.

Consider the compelling work of Thomas Mitchell, character actor extraordinaire, who conveys rooted-to-the soil sincerity with blast-to-the rafters grandiloquence as Gerald O'Hara, Scarlett's Irish-born father and master of Tara. All Mitchell needs is a minute or so of screen time to get across O'Hara's misty-eyed romanticism and steel-willed practicality. All the audience needs is the image of Scarlett as she listens, raptly and receptively, while her father waxes eloquent about the need to hold on to your land — or, in his case, your plantation — by any means necessary. After that, we know everything we need to understand Scarlett's subsequent actions in regard to maintaining Tara.

Contemporary viewers may be discomforted, or worse, by the slave/servant stereotypes rendered by Hattie McDaniel (who earned an Oscar as the cantankerous Mammy) and Butterfly McQueen (who grates on the nerves — even as she earns laughs — as the whiny Prissy). It's worth noting, however, that their characters have appreciably more sass and substance than many similar but nobler characters in more politically correct recent films (such as the ghastly *Gods and Generals*).

(It's also worth noting that O'Hara's ode to landowning, along with Scarlett's vow to "never be hungry again," doubtless had profound resonance among 1939 moviegoers who had been displaced, unemployed, or otherwise scarred by the Great Depression.)

Leslie Howard, as the namby-pamby Ashley, and Olivia de Havilland, as the compulsively self-effacing Melanie, are competent yet colorless. But the leads are everything they should be, and much, much more. Clark Gable's Rhett Butler remains the most charismatic rascal in the annals of cinema — insolently brazen when it comes to mocking hypocrisy, yet profoundly moving in his moments of grief. And Vivien Leigh is a radiant vixen as Scarlet O'Hara, an alluring mix of shameless flirt, implacable obsessive, and unlucky-in-love intriguer, forging the archetype for later generations of radio and TV soap-opera *femmes fatales*.

Which brings to mind a sobering thought: If Margaret Mitchell's Pulitzer Prize-winning novel were published today, *Gone With the Wind* likely would be filmed as a TV miniseries. And it just as likely would be spun off as a weekly series.

SPECS:

Gone With the Wind — Stars: Clark Gable, Vivien Leigh, Olivia de Havilland, Leslie Howard, Hattie McDaniel, Butterfly McQueen, and Thomas Mitchell. Directed by Victor Fleming. Screenplay: Sidney Howard, based on the novel by Margaret Mitchell. Running time: 233 minutes. Year of release: 1939. DVD distributor: Warner Home Video.

SUBJECTS FOR FURTHER RESEARCH:

Jezebel (1938) — Bette Davis, one of many candidates for the role of Scarlett O'Hara, earned an Oscar for playing an equally vixenish Southern belle in William Wyler's delectable romantic melodrama set in pre-Civil War New Orleans.

Dr. Zhivago (1965) — The Russian Revolution is awfully inconvenient for the title character, an idealistic poet-physician (Omar Sharif) who's torn between his beautiful well-born wife (Geraldine Chaplin) and a gorgeous political firebrand (Julie Christie), in David Lean's lush historical epic. Maurice Jarre's haunting musical score is every bit as unforgettable (for better or worse) as Max Steiner's thunderous theme for *GWTW*.

Titanic (1997) — The untimely appearance of an iceberg interrupts a budding romance (and, not incidentally, causes hundreds of deaths) in the internationally adored Oscar-winner directed by James "King of the World" Cameron. Arguably the most popular romantic epic since *GWTW*, *Titanic* — not unlike its predecessor — proves that audiences don't always need, or want, a tidily happy ending.

LESSON FOR FILMMAKERS:

Be careful what you wish for. Victor Fleming may be credited as its sole director — even though many scenes were overseen by George Cukor (who was fired, reportedly at Clark Gable's insistence, weeks into film-ing) and Sam Wood — but producer David O. Selznick is indisputably the true *auteur* of *GWTW*. The control-freakish mogul intended the epic romance to be his magnum opus, and spared no expense in his obsessive quest to make a masterpiece. Unfortunately, he spent the rest of his life in the shadow of his grandest achievement, despite several determined efforts — most notably and notoriously, *Duel in the Sun* (1946) — to duplicate its success.

CITIZEN KANE

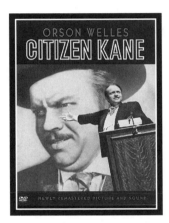

It's the greatest movie ever made, but don't let that scare you away. Critic Pauline Kael once described *Citizen Kane* as "the one American talking picture that seems as fresh now as the day it opened." She's right — great heavens, how she is right! — and that, more than anything else, is what separates it from the usual run of certified classics.

Unlike certain other staples of film-school syllabi — did I hear someone say *Potemkin*? — Orson Welles' 1941 debut feature has nothing stale or stately about it, nothing that smacks of required reading or museum artifact. It's a bold American masterwork with a rude vigor in its vernacular, and a sassy zest in its storytelling. It's a whoopee cushion slipped under the seats of those grim-faced academics who would insist that art is serious stuff.

It is, quite simply, a blast.

Blame it on the arrogance of youth. Legend has it that the first time he visited a Hollywood movie set, Welles — already a living legend at the tender age of 25 — described the amalgamation of magic-making machinery as the greatest toy train set ever designed for a kid to play with. And then, with all the rash, breakneck enthusiasm of a child enchanted by a new plaything, he set the machinery a-spinning.

Very much like some indulgent father who continually signs the checks and brings home newer, more lavish toys, RKO Pictures gave Welles carte blanche to pull the levers, blow the whistles, and chug-chug down the tracks as recklessly and rapidly as he desired. All they asked in return was the speedy delivery of the final product he boldly promised: A new and exciting motion picture melodrama about the rise and fall of a fabulously wealthy publishing tycoon, Charles Foster Kane, whose resemblance to real-life media mogul William Randolph Hearst would be not at all coincidental.

Employing the best technicians Hollywood had to offer, the finest actors he could import from New York, and the most dazzling vocal and visual effects from his celebrated stage and radio productions, Welles broke most of the moviemaking rules, including a few that had not yet been recorded in the rulebook. And he blithely disregarded the advice of his elders whenever they told him that something he wanted to do was ill-advised, unprecedented, or simply impossible.

What's that? You say you never show ceilings in a room, because it's easier to light a scene with nothing overhead? Balderdash! Put the camera down, way down — hell, bolt it to the floor! — and tilt upward. Then you'll have to have a ceiling! You'll have to have lots of them!

Say what? You have to break a sequence into individual shots, so you can propel the narrative and direct the audience's attention? Hah! Meet Gregg Toland, ace cinematographer and maverick risk-taker. Welles knew Toland could shoot entire scenes in deep focus, enabling the audience to see foreground objects, middle-ground drama and background activity all at once, all with equal clarity. That way, Welles knew, he wouldn't have to cut — entire sequences could be played out before a fluidly graceful camera, and viewers could decide on their own what they wanted to watch.

(Check out the scene where young Charlie Kane's mother and her lawyer are in the foreground, deciding the boy's future, while Kane's father huddles off in a corner — and outside, on the other side of a rear-wall window, Charlie is playing in the snow with his very special sled, blissfully unaware that his childhood is about to end.)

Citizen Kane appears to have been made in one single, spontaneous burst of creative energy, by collaborators — Welles, Toland, co-scriptwriter Herman J. Mankiewicz — clearly intoxicated by the sheer power of their medium. Intoxicated, yes, and impatient with their era's customary niceties of film narrative.

Right at the start, *Kane* shoots to thrill, shocking the audience by cutting from a somber, stylized death scene to a shrill *March of Time*–style newsreel. The transition is audacious, but no more so than the clever use of the newsreel itself, which provides, highly compressed, all the exposition the audience needs to understand the flashbacks that follow.

Then the newsreel ends, the journalists banter in a shadow-streaked screening room, someone mentions "Rosebud" — the dying Kane's final word — and the chase is on.

Throughout the rest of the movie, a dogged reporter assembles bits and pieces of the late tycoon's life by interviewing the people who knew him — or, more precisely, *thought* they knew him — at key points in his tumultuous life. Their interlocking flashbacks serve as pieces of a panoramic jigsaw puzzle, fragments that gradually coalesce into a multi-faceted portrait of an elusive enigma. Of course, the portrait remains teasingly incomplete, even after the "Rosebud" mystery is solved (for the audience if not for the folks on screen). *Citizen Kane* ends by indicating that, ultimately, some people are simply *unknowable*. But never mind: The search for answers to unanswerable questions is so exhilaratingly rendered, with such brilliantly kinetic flair, that you can't help feeling grateful for the wild ride toward a dead end.

SPECS:

Citizen Kane — Stars: Orson Welles, Joseph Cotten, Dorothy Comingore, Everett Sloane, Ray Collins, George Coulouris, Agnes Moorehead, Paul Stewart, and Ruth Warwick. Directed by Orson Welles. Screenplay: Orson Welles, Herman J. Mankiewicz. Running time: 119 minutes. Year of release: 1941. DVD distributor: Warner Home Video.

SUBJECTS FOR FURTHER RESEARCH:

The Power and the Glory (1933) — Often cited as an inspiration for the flashback structure of *Citizen Kane*, William K. Howard's sentimental drama (based on an early screenplay by Preston Sturges) focuses on a self-made millionaire (Spencer Tracy) whose life is re-examined by his intimates after his suicide.

Keeper of the Flame (1943) — Spencer Tracy again, this time as an inquisitive reporter in a drama (directed by George Cukor) with echoes of *Citizen Kane*. The reporter wants to write a biography of a "great American," but he's troubled by conflicting testimonies, and impeded by his subject's not-so-grieving widow (Katharine Hepburn).

The Bad and the Beautiful (1952) — A notorious producer (Kirk Douglas at his anti-heroic hunkiest) is exposed through the flashbacks of estranged associates (Lana Turner, Dick Powell, Gloria Graham) in Vincente Minnelli's deliciously pulpy inside-Hollywood melodrama.

LESSON FOR FILMMAKERS:

Early in Orson Welles' must-see masterpiece, an impudent young Charlie Kane explains why he wants to take over the moribund *New York Inquirer*: "I think it would be fun to run a newspaper." Watching *Citizen Kane*, it's easy to assume it would be even more fun to make a movie. Little wonder that French New Wave auteur François Truffaut once praised *Kane* as "probably the film that has started the largest number of filmmakers on their careers." Echoing those sentiments, fellow New Wave icon Jean-Luc Godard has said of Welles: "Everyone will always owe him everything."

ROCKY

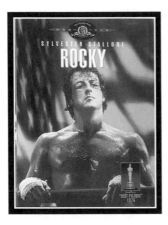

Even after inspiring countless rip-offs and put-ons, not to mention a string of sequels that illustrated the law of diminishing returns, *Rocky* remains in a class by itself as a true-blue, two-fisted American original.

Never mind that its underdog-against-the-odds plot seemed secondhand even when the movie first appeared in 1976. And pay no attention to the grandiose spectacle that Sylvester Stallone made of himself in several subsequent pictures. *Rocky* represents an almost miraculous confluence of actor and role, emotion and manipulation, entertainment and zeitgeist. In a post-Watergate era of cynicism and disillusionment, Stallone and director John G. Avildsen (*Save the Tiger*) found a way to uplift and exhilarate audiences by offering a feel-good fantasy in the credible guise of a street-smart, kitchen-sink drama. And yet, even though *Rocky* is very much a product of its time, it remains timeless in its appeal.

Indeed, this must-see movie has been accepted as a classic for so long that most folks have forgotten its humble origins. In many respects, this small-budget labor of love — which wound up wining an Oscar as Best Picture — was as much of an "indie" production as anything picked up by Miramax or Fox Searchlight at a typical Sundance Film Festival. At the time he wrote the screenplay, Stallone was eking out a career as a character actor in TV guest spots (*Kojak*, *Police Story*) and movie bit parts (*Capone*, *The Lords of Flatbush*). And while he evidenced promise, few people took notice. He wrote *Rocky* almost as an act of desperation, intending the drama as a showcase for himself. And he refused all offers from anyone who wanted to retrofit the script as a vehicle for someone else.

If you haven't viewed *Rocky* since its initial theatrical run — or if you're familiar with it only through its reputation — you may be shocked by how grubby and gritty much of it seems. After an unfortunately pretentious display of the title, accompanied by the cascading trumpets of Bill Conti's now-familiar score, the movie immediately rights itself by leaping into the unromanticized brutality of a small-stakes prizefight. Rocky Balboa is introduced as a self-described "ham-and-egger," an unremarkable club fighter who earns chump change in neighborhood matches throughout Philadelphia. When we first see him, Rocky manages to recover from a vicious head-butt, and knocks out his younger opponent. But the rowdy audience remains unimpressed. "You're a bum!" a blowsy woman shrieks. "You heard that? You're a bum!" Rocky, it should be noted, doesn't bother to argue the point with her.

Out of the ring, Rocky struggles to maintain his proud swagger and his tattered dignity, even while he works as a collection agent for a slimy loan shark. Unfortunately, he doesn't have it in him to be as violent with delinquent debtors as his boss demands. (A nice touch: Rocky has to don reading glasses before scribbling the name of the next guy he's supposed to lean on.) And despite his best efforts to rehearse snappy patter in front of his bedroom mirror, he can't quite break the ice with Adrian (Talia Shire), the painfully shy young woman who works at the neighborhood pet store. Worst of all, Rocky can't even keep his locker at a dingy gym, because he's been branded as an undesirable — a "cheap leg-breaker" — by Mickey (Burgess Meredith), the grizzled trainer who runs the joint.

Rocky devotes the better part of an hour to credibly establishing its title character as sorely needing — and, yes, entirely deserving — a shot at redemption. It takes a fair amount of contrivance, but fortune eventually smiles on our hero: Apollo Creed (Carl Weathers), the flamboyant heavyweight champ, chooses to fight Rocky as a well-hyped publicity stunt when a more worthy contender is sidelined. The twist of fate is frankly fantastic — almost as incredible as Stallone's off-screen struggle to get *Rocky* made in the first place — but you have no trouble accepting it. Why? Because, by that point in the movie, you *want* to. Just as you want Rocky to accept the gruff but achingly vulnerable Mickey as his trainer, and to wear that silly and oversized robe in the ring as a favor to his buddy Paulie (Burt Young).

But even a fairy tale must be true to its own logic. One of the great things about *Rocky* is its refusal to pander to its audience by having Rocky score a knockout and grab the heavyweight title. (Compared to most other sports-themed dramas that have followed in its wake, this one comes across as almost cruelly realistic.) Winning, *Rocky* dares to say, really *isn't* everything. Torn by self-doubt, and yet driven by a desire to prove he's not "another bum from the neighborhood," Rocky Balboa figures he will do enough if he simply "goes the distance" and remains standing when the final bell sounds. That, the movie implies, is the best any man can hope for.

SPECS:

Rocky – Stars: Sylvester Stallone, Talia Shire, Burt Young, Carl Weathers, and Burgess Meredith. Directed by John G. Avildsen. Screenplay: Sylvester Stallone. Running time: 119 minutes. Year of release: 1976. DVD distributor: MGM Home Entertainment.

SUBJECTS FOR FURTHER RESEARCH:

The Bad News Bears (1976) — Walter Matthau stars to perfection as a boozy ne'er-do-well who coaches a motley crew of Little Leaguers. Much like *Rocky*, this box-office smash (which inspired two sequels and a short-lived TV series) didn't feel compelled to provide a climactic triumph for its long-shot heroes.

Chariots of Fire (1981) — Another sports-themed Oscar-winner, this uplifting drama focuses on two temperamentally dissimilar but equally prodigious runners at the 1924 Olympics. The mood-enhancing, emotion-rousing score by Vangelis is central to the movie's impact, not unlike Bill Conti's much-imitated score for *Rocky*.

Girlfight (2001) — Karyn Kusama's gritty indie drama about a determined Latina boxer (a star-making performance by then-unknown Michelle Rodriguez) often plays like a gender-switched *Rocky*. The big difference is, *Girlfight* really did make its initial splash at the Sundance Film Festival.

LESSON FOR FILMMAKERS:

"It really was an indie film," Sylvester Stallone said in 2003 of the movie that launched him as a cinematic multi-hyphenate. "Except indie films really weren't so prevalent back then. So when (United Artists) agreed to do the film, they approached it more like it was, maybe, second-bill fare for drive-ins. I was told that: 'This is not "A" material, per se.' It was done with unknowns, under a budget of $1 million. And we had twenty-eight days to make it. I never, ever thought it was going to be shown in a first-run theater... The funny thing is, I've been told by reigning studio executives that *Rocky* would today be considered high-concept. And I think, 'OK. The guy is wearing Converse sneakers, and he lives in a cold-water flat. And this guy is high concept.' Sure."

ALL THE PRESIDENT'S MEN

The Most Devastating
Detective Story Of This Century.

REDFORD/HOFFMAN
"ALL THE PRESIDENT'S MEN"

For the sake of full disclosure, I must admit at the outset that I was a journalism major in college during the tragicomic sideshow of Watergate. So my view of *Washington Post* reporters Bob Woodward and Carl Benstein as true-blue American heroes — as fearless and relentless seekers of truth who helped to bring down the most corrupt President in U.S. history — is, perhaps, a bit skewed. But that isn't the only reason why I consider Alan J. Pakula's *All the President's Men* to be, incontrovertibly, a must-see movie.

The simple fact is, just as Woodward and Bernstein (collectively nicknamed Woodstein) set new standards for American journalism, and inspired thousands of idealists — along with more than a few amoral glory-hounds — to follow in their paths, *All the President's Men* established a new paradigm for big-screen docudramas in general, and true-life tales of uncovered malfeasance in particular. (Think about it: Was there a single review of 1999's *The Insider* that *didn't* cite Pakula's classic as a prime influence?)

Just as important, it also provided an invaluable counterbalance to the stereotypical movie image of newspaper reporters as boozy buccaneers who talk fast, crack wise, and raise hell — a la the ink-stained rogues of *The Front Page* — while they comfort the afflicted and afflict the comfortable. In this movie, reporters spend most of their time getting doors slammed in their faces, digging through voluminous records, and walking or driving endless miles to follow leads that go nowhere. Glamorous, it ain't.

Robert Redford (who also produced the picture) plays Woodward, Dustin Hoffman plays Bernstein, and they're both terrific. (Hoffman is slightly more terrific, if only because he gets some meatier, showier scenes, but never mind.) And Jason Robards is a hoot in his Oscar-winning portrayal of *Post* editor Ben Bradlee, who pops up periodically to remind Woodstein — and the audience — just how high the stakes are. ("We are about to accuse Bob Halderman — who only happens to be the second most important man in this country — of conducting a criminal conspiracy from inside the White House. It would be nice if we were right.") But the leads give full-blooded performances, not one-dimensional star turns, and the movie's enduring stature has relatively little to do with the names above and below the title.

Given the task of fashioning a compelling narrative from events at once overly familiar and off-puttingly confusing to a 1976 moviegoing public, screenwriter William Goldman earned an Academy Award by rising brilliantly to the challenge of imposing structure and generating suspense. Director Pakula — whose thrillers *Klute* (1971) and *The Parallax View* (1974) can be viewed in retrospect as warm-up exercises — does his utmost to ensure that every scene of *All the President's Men* percolates with paranoia. Even so, he strives for a realistic, even semi-documentary look, and rarely invokes his dramatic license to hype the truth with stylistic hyperbole.

On a couple of occasions, Pakula and ace cinematographer Gordon Willis (*The Godfather*) artfully underscore the against-all-odds nature of the Woodstein investigation by viewing the reporters at a distance, from far, far overhead. (Note the casually brilliant sequence in the Library of Congress, as the camera pulls further and further back to show the dutifully plodding duo seeking the truth in the very center of a labyrinth.) More often, though, Pakula goes for unvarnished verisimilitude, occasionally allowing scenes to unfold in what feels like real time.

About midway through the movie, there's a mesmerizing cat-and-mouse game played by Bernstein and a Committee to Re-Elect the President bookkeeper (Oscar-nominated Jane Alexander) who's too scared to be forthcoming, but too honest to be deceptive. Bernstein finagles his way into the woman's living room, and plants himself on her couch while her sister — obviously no fan of the bookkeeper's bosses — brings him coffee. The CREEP bookkeeper refuses to talk. Bernstein insists he will listen. And then, gradually, the ice starts to melt.

Against her better judgment, and despite her worst fears, the bookkeeper speaks volumes with tremulous nods and half-whispered monosyllables. Bernstein listens attentively, sympathetically. All you have to do is look at his eyes to tell what the guy is thinking — "Jeez, I can't believe what I'm hearing! God, don't let me screw this up!" — and note his tense body posture to appreciate what an effort he's making to appear relaxed. But his smile remains pleasant and deferential; his voice, noncommittal but gently prodding. He's not merely coaxing information from her — he's seducing her into doing what she really wants to do. Ever wonder how reporters get ordinary people to make extraordinary revelations? Pay close attention to this scene, which should be mandatory viewing at every journalism school.

Other scenes — including some of the movie's funniest — resound with a similar ring of truth. At one point, Woodward makes a cold call to a GOP official, and so is amazed when the official himself answers the phone that he's momentarily lost for words. (He vamps, none too effectively, by twice introducing himself as "Bob Woodward of the *Washington Post*.") Later, as the Woodstein team questions Hugh Sloan (Stephen Collins), a former White House insider, Sloan insists that he's a good Republican. "So am I," Woodward interjects, obviously trying to ingratiate himself. Bernstein says nothing, but shoots his partner an ambiguous glance that can be read as hectoring skepticism ("What a crock!") or stunned disbelief ("You're a *what*?")

Pakula and Goldman wisely chose to conclude *All the President's Men* shortly after Woodward and Bernstein make a major goof that briefly stalls their investigation. It's a daring move, ending a movie when it appears the protagonists have been defeated. (It's also a quintessentially '70s touch that few contemporary filmmakers would risk.) But the final image of Woodward and Bernstein at work in the newsroom, pounding away at their typewriters as a televised Richard M. Nixon looms triumphantly, is a masterstroke. We don't need to read the newswire bulletins that chart Nixon's eventual downfall. All we need to see are the two reporters doggedly pursuing the truth, illustrating how doing the right thing entails so much hard, thankless, and seemingly unexciting work.

SPECS:

All the President's Men — Stars: Robert Redford, Dustin Hoffman, Jack Warden, Martin Balsam, Hal Holbrook, and Jason Robards. Directed by Alan J. Pakula. Screenplay: William Goldman, based on the book by Carl Bernstein and Bob Woodward. Running time: 139 minutes. Year of release: 1976. DVD distributor: Warner Home Video.

SUBJECTS FOR FURTHER RESEARCH:

The China Syndrome (1979) — James Bridges' paranoid thriller none-too-subtly argues that advocacy journalism is morally superior to objective reporting. A TV features reporter (Jane Fonda) graduates to hard news when a whistleblower (Jack Lemmon) alerts to her potential catastrophe at a nuclear power plant.

Absence of Malice (1982) — Sydney Pollack's morally ambiguous drama is a kinda-sorta counterpoint to *All the President's Men*. The chronically underrated Sally Field plays an investigative journalist who causes tragedy while rushing to judgment in her coverage of a murder suspect (Paul Newman).

The Insider (1999) — Investigative journalism gets, if not a blackened eye, then a rap across the knuckles in Michael Mann's docudrama about a tobacco-industry whistle-blower (Russell Crowe) who feels betrayed and exploited after he provides info to a *60 Minutes* producer (Al Pacino).

LESSON FOR FILMMAKERS:

Chris Carter, creator-producer of *The X-Files*, admits his cult TV series and its movie spin-off were strongly influenced by *All the President's Men*. "It was a great film that just broke so many rules," Carter told

Variety in a 1999 interview. "To use the non-dramatic image of someone sitting on a telephone trying to glean information took some guts. And as a former journalist interested in investigative journalism as a young man, that kind of storytelling and investigative approach fascinated me... It's a kind of entertainment that largely doesn't play any more. Tabloidization has had a great impact, unfortunately. We're not interested in journalists who adhere to a standard of their own. So you couldn't do an *All the President's Men* any more."

TAXI DRIVER

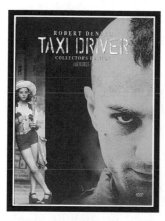

Just a few hours after John W. Hinckley Jr. tried to gatecrash his way into history in 1981 by shooting President Ronald Reagan, the Associated Press reported that the would-be assassin already was claiming extenuating circumstances: The movies made him do it.

According to an AP news bulletin, Hinckley was obsessed with unrequited love for actress Jodie Foster, who at the time was still best known for playing a twelve-year-old prostitute opposite Robert De Niro's troubled Travis Bickle in *Taxi Driver*. Five years after the Martin Scorsese film had shocked audiences and polarized critics worldwide, Hinckley supposedly decided to imitate De Niro's character and take aim at Reagan. Why? Because Hinckley figured this would impress Foster. After all, the AP reported, De Niro told Foster at one point in Scorsese's movie: "If you don't love me, I'm gonna shoot the president."

Quite a shocking story. Trouble is, it was no more accurate than Hinckley's aim.

Yes, Hinckley did indeed harbor lust in his heart for Foster. And yes, he did see *Taxi Driver*. But, no, De Niro never says anything remotely like the aforementioned line in Scorsese's classic. (A personal note: In 1981, I was interim entertainment editor at the *Dallas Morning News*. Minutes after the bulletin hit the wire, I called AP to report the error. I'm sure other journalists in other cities did the same. But if a correction ever ran, I never saw it.) In point of fact, De Niro's Travis Bickle isn't amorously inclined toward Foster's under-age hooker — even though he "rescues" her by killing her slimeball pimp (Harvey Keitel). The real object of Bickle's obsessive affection is a presidential primary campaign worker played by Cybill Shepherd — who, it should be noted, has never complained about going unmentioned in all the post-Hinckley stories about *Taxi Driver*.

Time and again since the dawn of cinema — most recently, in the wake of the 1999 high school massacre in Littleton, Colorado — critics and commentators have heatedly debated whether there's a direct link between on-screen violence and real-life mayhem. *Taxi Driver* might easily be cited as Exhibit A by anyone who wants to build a case against the insidiously antisocial influence of Hollywood. But free-speech absolutists can use the same film — and the notoriety attached to it by a lovesick would-be assassin — to illustrate how dangerous it can be to rush to judgement in matters of cause and effect. For these reasons alone, *Taxi Driver* deserves a place on your list of must-see movies.

Another compelling reason: More than a generation after *Taxi Driver* first made darkness visible on theater screens, the movie remains every bit as profoundly discomforting and bleakly fascinating.

For that, much credit should go to the inspired direction of Martin Scorsese, the edgy screenwriting of Paul Schrader — and the eloquent cinematography of Michael Chapman, which vividly conveys (particularly during Bickle's nighttime drives through the meanest streets of New York) a foreboding ambiance of neon-lit decay and rain-washed dread.

But even more credit is due Robert De Niro, whose Oscar-nominated triumph in the lead role is, for better or worse, his defining achievement as an actor.

By now, De Niro's performance as Bickle is so firmly established in our collective pop-culture consciousness that it's almost impossible to imagine another actor ever was considered for the role. But it's true: Screenwriter Paul Schrader has admitted there was a period during pre-production when it appeared Scorsese would have to hire Jeff Bridges to obtain financing. It's intriguing to consider how this alternative casting could have affected Bridges' career. (If he had played Travis Bickle in 1976, would audiences have accepted him as a boyishly attractive romantic lead during the next decade and a half?) But perhaps not playing Bickle would have had an even greater impact on De Niro.

Let's face it: For all his prodigious talent as a movie actor, and despite his unlikely emergence in the late 1990s as an action hero and comic lead, De Niro has never been a "movie star" in the traditional sense of the term. Audiences may respect him, and frequently are amazed by him, but they haven't been able, or willing, to warm up to the guy. And some of this is De Niro's own fault. With very few exceptions — his animated hustler in *Night and the City*, his tongue-tied romantic in *Mad Dog and Glory*, his self-satirical Mafioso in *Analyze This* — his performances rarely convey any discernible pleasure in performing on camera. De Niro can be very good — hell, he can be downright astonishing — but you rarely get the feeling that he's enjoying himself. As opposed to, say, Tom Hanks, who gives the impression of being someone who just can't wait to get to the set each morning. Like it or not, that's the sort of thing that invariably colors an audience's response to an actor.

And even if De Niro injected more jolliness into his on-screen appearances, he would still have to deal with the legacy of Travis Bickle, the isolated and inarticulate Vietnam vet who's driven to assert himself through savage violence. Nearly three decades after he stunned audiences with his mesmerizing portrayal of "God's lonely man" (as Bickle describes himself), De Niro continues to be so strongly identified with the role that I suspect most moviegoers simply don't trust him. That is, I think even people who have never actually seen *Taxi Driver*, or who have only glimpsed clips of Bickle's "You talkin' to me?" monologue, still have it in their heads whenever they see De Niro on screen that — uh-oh! — this guy could go postal at any second. This has less to do with the naïveté of moviegoers than the utterly fearless, drop-dead brilliance exemplified by one of our greatest film actors. Such is the power of an indelibly memorable performance in an equally unforgettable movie.

SPECS:

Taxi Driver — Stars: Robert De Niro, Jodie Foster, Albert Brooks, Harvey Keitel, Peter Boyle, and Cybill Shepherd. Directed by Martin Scorsese. Screenplay: Paul Schrader. Running time: 114 minutes. Year of release: 1976. DVD distributor: Columbia/TriStar Home Video.

SUBJECTS FOR FURTHER RESEARCH:

The King of Comedy (1983) — Think of it as *Taxi Driver II: The Comedy*. Martin Scorsese directs Robert De Niro in another story about a socially maladroit outsider who snaps after enduring repeated rejections, and becomes an obsessive stalker. This time, however, De Niro is a would-be stand-up comic who kidnaps his showbiz idol, talk-show host Jerry Langford (a perfectly cast Jerry Lewis).

Falling Down (1993) — In Joel Schumacher's contrived but compelling drama, Michael Douglas is superb as a laid-off defense worker who goes postal (or, perhaps more precisely, goes Travis Bickle) and violently responds to various indignities and injustices of everyday life in L.A.

Punch-Drunk Love (2002) — Could a simpatico sweetheart ever "cure" Travis Bickle? Paul Thomas Anderson indirectly raises that provocative question with this offbeat comedy-drama. Adam Sandler is excellent as a barely repressed rageaholic who seems as lonely and isolated as Travis until he connects with the nurturing Emily Watson.

LESSON FOR FILMMAKERS:

The cause-and-effect debate over movie violence has continued unabated since *Taxi Driver* was linked to a real-life would-be assassin. Mary Harron addressed the controversy — and admitted her ambivalent attitude — in a *New York Times* essay she wrote prior to the release of her *American Psycho* (2000): "Once you accept the idea that the representation of violence is in itself harmful to society, much of the finest world cinema could be banned, from Eisenstein to Kurosawa to Kubrick and Polanski to Coppola and Scorsese. Most genre films would have to go too: *film noir*, horror, gangster films, Westerns. This form of censorship, taken to its logical conclusion, clearly means the end of art. However, it does have a point, because no matter how moral or ironic or satirical a filmmaker might think a work is, he or she can have no control over how a member of the audience will receive it. No sane person could watch *Taxi Driver* and decide it was a good idea to shoot the president — but an insane person did. And who is to say that your audience will always consist of the sane?"

SMOKEY AND THE BANDIT

A textbook example of a hand-tooled star vehicle that forever labels the star in its driver's seat, *Smokey and the Bandit* also is noteworthy for being the movie most often credited — or, perhaps more precisely, blamed — for kicking off an action-comedy subgenre best described as Cross-Country Demolition Derby.

Two lesser sequels and at least one long-running TV series (*The Dukes of Hazzard*) can be traced directly to this broadly played hodgepodge of high-speed driving, lowbrow humor, and spectacular car crashes. But wait, there's more: *Smokey and the Bandit*, the debut feature of stuntman-turned-filmmaker Hal Needham, also inspired literally dozens of other pedal-to-the-metal extravaganzas — mostly redneck melodramas and cornpone comedies, along with Needham's own in-jokey *Cannonball Run* movies — throughout the '70s and '80s. Decades later, its very title still serves as shorthand for a particular type of undemanding crowd-pleaser with smart-alecky heroes, dim-bulb authority figures, and more high-octane action than a month of NASCAR events.

The thin plot is a serviceable excuse for stringing together scenes of cartoonish frivolity and vehicular misadventure. Bandit (Burt Reynolds), a swaggering prankster and maverick trucker, wagers that he can transport contraband beer from Texas to Georgia in record time. While a faithful friend (Jerry Reed) does much of the actual driving in the lager-stocked 18-wheeler, Bandit darts about in a souped-up Trans Am, on the lookout for any "smokey" (i.e., highway cop) who might impede their high-speed progress. Complications arise when Bandit arouses the ire of an especially grizzly smokey, Sheriff Buford T. Justice (Jackie Gleason), by picking up a perky hitchhiker (Sally Field) who just happens to be the runaway bride of the sheriff's cretinous son (Mike Henry).

Initially dismissed as a freakish regional hit at Deep South drive-ins, *Smokey and the Bandit* gradually proved equally popular in major metropolitan markets, and wound up in the record books as the second-highest grossing film (right behind *Star Wars*) of 1977. Some have credited its phenomenal popularity to its subversive allure as fantasy fulfillment: Bandit repeatedly outsmarts and humiliates Sheriff Justice and all other law-enforcement officials who dare to impinge on his God-given right to ignore any posted speed limit. (Some academic somewhere doubtless has earned a doctorate by explaining why so many pop tunes and popcorn flicks of the '70s equated driving over 55 with all-American rebelliousness.) Most other observers, however, credit the movie's appeal — for contemporary viewers as well as '70s ticketbuyers — to the once-in-a-lifetime matching of player and character.

Even moviegoers not yet born when *Smokey and the Bandit* first screeched into theaters reflexively think of the hard-driving, trash-talking trucker whenever they hear Reynolds' name. Part of that can be explained by the virtually nonstop exposure of Needham's movie on cable and home video. But it's instructive to consider Reynolds' own role in erasing the lines between actor and character, man and mythos.

In the wake of his becoming an "overnight success" after years of journeymen work in television and movies, Reynolds embraced typecasting — and tongue-in-cheek self-promotion — with unseemly fervor. For the better part of a decade, he chronically reprised his Bandit shtick — winking insouciance, naughty-boy sarcasm, zero-cool self-assurance — in motion pictures *and* TV talk shows. It was funny, for a while, and then it wasn't. Trouble is, by the time it stopped being funny, the image was firmly affixed in the public's collective pop-culture consciousness. So much so, in fact, that even after demonstrating his versatility in a wide range of character roles — most memorably, as the prideful porn-film director in Paul Thomas Anderson's *Boogie Nights* (1997) — Reynolds appears destined to always be remembered best for one indelibly defining character.

On the other hand, there are far less pleasant ways for an actor to ensure his immortality. When asked about his enduring linkage to Bandit in 2003, more than a generation after playing the cocky trucker, Reynolds addressed the mixed blessing with typically self-effacing humor.

"I'm very flattered," he said, "by how some people still respond to that character. I still have guys in Trans Ams pull up to me at stoplights and yell, 'Dammit! You're the reason I got this thing!'

"But I also remember a while back, when I was offering an acting seminar in Florida, that I was afraid they'd go over to the auto-racetrack looking for me, instead of the theater. And even when they did show up at the right place, I felt I should tell them: 'Those of you who are wearing your racing gloves — take them off, we're not going to need them, we're going to talk about other things.'"

SPECS:

Smokey and the Bandit — Stars: Burt Reynolds, Sally Field, Jerry Reed, Jackie Gleason, Mike Henry, Paul Williams, and Pat McCormick. Director: Hal Needham. Screenplay: James Lee Barrett, Charles Shyer, and Alan Mandel. Running time: 96 minutes. Year of release: 1977. DVD distributor: Universal.

SUBJECTS FOR FURTHER RESEARCH:

Vanishing Point (1971) — An appreciably more serious precursor of the Cross-Country Demolition Derby, Richard C. Sarafian's existential cult fave follows a risk-taking, pill-popping driver (Barry Newman) who races a Dodge Challenger from Denver to San Francisco while avoiding — but, miraculously, never injuring — hundreds of cops in hot pursuit.

Convoy (1978) — Sam Peckinpah often referred to himself as "a good whore" while working on lesser projects. He lived down to that reputation when he transformed a Top 40 hit about truckers, "smokies" and C.B. radios into a fitfully exciting melodrama with Kris Kristofferson, Ernest Borgnine and Ali MacGraw.

Black Dog (1998) — Patrick Swayze moves from dirty dancing to road rage in Kevin Hooks' stripped-for-speed B-movie as a trucker tricked into transporting illegal weapons. Few laughs — well, okay, few *intentional* laughs — but lots of Smokey-style chasing and crashing.

LESSON FOR FILMMAKERS:

If the audience loves a character (and, better still, the actor playing that character) the character can get away with practically anything, even coming off as a bona fide egomaniac. Midway through *Smokey and the Bandit*, Burt Reynolds recalls, "There's a moment when Sally asks me, 'What is it that you do best?' And I say, 'Show off.' And she says, 'Yeah, you do that well.' At the time we made the film, I thought to myself, 'If I can get that line out and they still like me — "they" being the audience — we're home free.' Because basically, that's who (Bandit) was, what he was all about." The line got big laughs, indicating just how much the audience really, *really* liked Bandit. And, of course, the actor who played him.

DO THE
RIGHT THING

Throbbing to the beat of a rap-music rant, percolating to the heat of long-simmering rage, Spike Lee's *Do the Right Thing* is an audacious and exhilarating film, at once joyous and foreboding, screamingly funny and terrifyingly tragic. It is as vast and full of teeming energy and emotional contradictions as life itself. Yet it also is intimate enough to offer a half-dozen or so full-bodied, warts-and-all character portraits of exceptional detail, texture, and dramatic truth.

Quite simply, this is a great film. But be forewarned: Very little else about *Do the Right Thing* is at all simple. In fact, for some audiences, this 1989 must-see masterwork may still be too complex for comfort.

That it sparked debate and stirred controversy during its initial theatrical run came as no surprise to Lee, an African-American filmmaker who has devoted most of his career to provoking thought and outrage in equal measure. He first attracted attention with *She's Gotta Have It* (1986), a no-budget, black-and-white erotic comedy that dared to suggest a woman might have a sexual appetite as hearty as any man's. His next picture, *School Daze* (1988), was a flawed but ambitiously energetic musical drama about bigotry among blacks at a Deep South college where light-skinned "Wannabes" (as in "wanna be white") feud with darker-skinned students.

But Lee didn't make waves of tsunami proportions until he unleashed *Do the Right Thing*, which gives us the vitality of urban street life and the viciousness of racism in a single, brightly bedecked, booby-trapped package. Throughout the movie, Lee weaves a tapestry of many colors, contrasting his basic black with whites, Asians and Hispanics during one very hot summer day in the life on a block in Brooklyn's lower-middle-class Bedford-Stuyvesant. It's worth noting that, because of the film's sustained emphasis on interracial tensions, many sincere people of all races genuinely feared *Do the Right Thing* might incite riots during the summer of 1989. It's also worth noting, however, that those fears proved unfounded.

Not the least of Lee's many achievements here is his ability to create a vital, compassionately drawn white character: Sal (Danny Aiello, giving the performance of his career), a burly Italian-American whose Famous Pizzeria has been a neighborhood institution for twenty-five years. Compare this character to the bland black clichés you still find in many movies by white filmmakers, and you will be even more impressed by Lee's underappreciated even-handedness.

Sal's Famous Pizzeria is the center of a small, richly detailed universe where colorful characters react and interact, often with explosively funny results. The Corner Men, three middle-aged black fellows who serve as a funky Greek chorus, sit and watch the world go by. They drink beer, trade insults, swap boasts, and remark on the intrusion of Korean immigrants who are taking over fruit and vegetable stores. In a rare self-aware moment, a Corner Man claims blacks should blame themselves, not only white racism, for their failings. But such serious talk is tiring, and requires another beer.

Among the other folks in the pizzeria's orbit: Da Mayor (Ossie Davis), a grandiloquent neighborhood drunk; Radio Raheem (Bill Nunn), a brutish-looking young black man who brandishes his blasting boom-box like an offensive weapon;

Mother Sister (Ruby Dee), the block's resident sage, philosopher, and all-purpose busybody; Pino (John Turturro), Sal's son and co-worker, a sneering racist who can't abide the live-and-let-live attitude of his more easygoing brother, Vito (Richard Edson); and Buggin Out (Giancarlo

Esposito), a would-be activist who wants to know why Sal won't include photos of blacks as well as Italian-Americans on the pizzeria's wall.

"You want brothers up on the Wall of Fame?" Sal responds. "You open your own business, then you can do what you wanna do. My pizzeria, Italian-Americans up on the wall."

Buggin Out counters: "Sal, that might be fine, you own this. But rarely do I see any Italian-Americans eating in here. All I've ever seen is black folks. So since we spend so much money here, we do have some say."

Both men are right, both men are wrong. As the movie progresses, their petty dispute escalates, igniting a slow-burning fuse that leads to a devastating climax.

Long before that terrible fury is unleashed, there is a sense of impending danger beneath the hugely entertaining panorama of music, movement, and moving performances. Lee allows his film to hip-hop gracefully, even defiantly, between heightened realism and Bertolt Brecht-style anti-realism. In one riveting sequence, characters of various hues directly address the camera, screaming every racist (and anti-Semitic) epithet in the book. A local disc jockey, Mister Senor Love Daddy (Samuel L. Jackson, then billed simply as Sam Jackson), tells his listeners they need to chill out — "And that's the truth, Ruth!" — but the resentments fester. Later, in a scene that recalls the conflict represented by Robert Mitchum's homicidal preacher in *The Night of the Hunter* (1955), Radio Raheem depicts the battle between light and darkness with his brightly bedecked hands: One has rings that spell out LOVE; the other, HATE. The image lingers in your mind, then returns with full-screen impact near the end.

So who does the right thing? Da Mayor tries, offering the wisdom of age to younger people not inclined to listen. Sal basically is a decent fellow, quick to admonish Pino for his racist blather, but quicker to pick up a baseball bat when he gets angry. And Mookie, Sal's cheerfully feckless deliveryman, tries to smother the brush fires when bitterness leads to heated arguments.

Lee himself plays Mookie, very well, and makes the young man likable, if not admirable. (He's unabashedly irresponsible in dealing with his girl-friend and their small child.) But then the cops show up at Sal's store, a young black man is killed, and Mookie — not some hair-trigger malcontent — throws a trashcan through Sal's front window. A riot ensues. A tragedy that could have been avoided, isn't.

"Up to that point," Lee told me in a 1989 interview, "I think for a lot of the white audience, Mookie is the one character in the film they can identify with. They're not gonna like Buggin Out, because he's a troublemaker. And they're not gonna like Radio Raheem. Because everybody has these preconceived notions of these black youths, these angry, insane, raping, mugging black youths that terrorize inner-city America, walking around with these giant radios, with their rap music blasting. It would have been too easy to have somebody like this throw a garbage can through the window.

"So it's a big surprise. And we get you. Because throughout the beginning of the movie, Mookie is this nice, young black character. The one you wouldn't mind having come over to your house, and not feel you have to lock up your silverware and your color TV. And then, at the last minute, he is the one who throws the garbage can through the window."

Do the Right Thing ends with two seemingly contradictory quotes: from Dr. Martin Luther King Jr., a condemnation of radical violence; and from Malcolm X, a claim that violence in "self-defense" against racism is justifiable. But what happens at Sal's isn't really self-defense: It's an impulsive, impassioned assault at the only available target that might represent the white power structure. The rage is impotent, misdirected — and, for a dreadfully exciting moment in time, intoxicating.

Some commentators have accused Lee of glorifying violence in *Do the Right Thing*. That's a bum rap. A more substantial charge is that Lee's film muddles its message with mixed signals. To a large degree, it does. But the ambiguity is intentional. Certainly, Lee doesn't make it easy for the audience. On the other hand, who says an artist is *supposed* to make it easy? Lee doesn't offer answers, doesn't make excuses. Instead, he slaps on your plate a raw, juicy slice of life. It's tough, troubling food for thought. And, sadly enough, it seems just as fresh today as it did in 1989.

SPECS:

Do the Right Thing — Stars: Danny Aiello, Ossie Davis, Ruby Dee, Richard Edson, Giancarlo Esposito, Spike Lee, Bill Nunn, John Turturro, Samuel L. Jackson, Rosie Perez, and John Savage. Written and directed by Spike Lee. Running time: 120 minutes. Year of release: 1989. DVD distributor: Universal Home Video.

SUBJECTS FOR FURTHER RESEARCH:

Boyz N the Hood (1991) — John Singleton's harrowing, heartfelt drama about black youths at risk in the South Central district of Los Angeles helped launch the movie careers of Cuba Gooding Jr., Ice Cube, and Angela Basset. Just as important, Singleton's film – along with Allen and Albert Hughes' even more brutal *Menace II Society* (1993) — set the tone for a subgenre of '90s movies about urban African-Americans.

Friday (1995) — A much lighter view of aimless African-American youths in L.A.'s South Central district, F. Gary Gray's essentially plotless yet amiably amusing comedy (co-written by star and co-producer Ice Cube) can be viewed as the link between the so-called "angry black cinema" of the post-*Do the Right Thing* era and the subsequent cycle of ensemble-in-the-hood comedies with predominantly black casts.

25th Hour (2002) — While charting the final 24 hours of freedom savored by a convicted drug dealer (Edward Norton), Spike Lee borrows several stylistic flourishes from his own *Do the Right Thing*. Overall, however, *25th Hour* — Lee's first movie with a predominantly *white* cast — is more subdued and pensive. A furiously melancholy drama about life and dread in post-9/11 New York City, it catches all of its characters at a moment when their selfish concerns are increasingly overshadowed — whether they want to admit it or not — by events beyond their control.

LESSON FOR FILMMAKERS:

Kevin Smith cites *Do the Right Thing* as a major influence on the narrative structure of his debut feature, the low-concept, mini-budget *Clerks* (1994). Spike Lee's must-see masterwork is "a film I was very inspired by, and cribbed from mercilessly for my first film. Just as *Do the Right Thing* takes place in a 24-hour period on one small block, so too did *Clerks*. However, I didn't have that much to say, whereas (Lee's film) explodes with so much social commentary that the celluloid can barely contain it all. Very seldom can a film artist craft a story in which everybody's right and everybody's wrong at the same time, and hang it on authentic and recognizable characters so wonderfully complex that their motivations are never as simple as black and white."

≈4≈
MEN AND WOMEN

HIS GIRL FRIDAY

It's the kind of grand Old Hollywood story that, if not true, should be. Filmmaker Howard Hawks claimed on several occasions, to a variety of sympathetic interviewers, that he was entertaining dinner guests in his home during the late 1930s when someone steered the conversation toward the fine art of movie dialogue. Hawks flatly announced that the best dialogue he'd ever heard came from Ben Hecht and Charles MacArthur, and that the very best Hecht-MacArthur dialogue came from *The Front Page*, their exuberantly cynical 1928 stage play about roguish reporters covering an execution in a colorfully corrupt Chicago.

To prove his point, Hawks produced two copies of the original *Front Page* script. (Pretty convenient, his just happening to have those scripts on hand, but never mind.) He gave one copy to a young lady in attendance, and asked her to read the part of Hildy Johnson, the veteran reporter who vows to quit the wordsmith racket so he can marry into wealth and respectability. Hawks himself read the part of Walter Burns, the robustly unscrupulous editor who will use any means, fair or foul, to keep Johnson on the staff of his newspaper.

"And in the middle of it," Hawks recalled, "I said, 'My Lord, it's better with a girl reading it than the way it was!'" Which led, according to Hawks, to his remaking *The Front Page* — previously filmed in 1931 by Lewis Milestone, with Adolph Menjou and Pat O'Brien in the leads — as *His Girl Friday*.

Fact or fiction? As author Todd McCarthy notes in his admiring biography, *Howard Hawks: The Grey Fox* of Hollywood, it's mighty strange that no dinner guest, including the unidentified woman who read Hildy, ever mentioned being present during this fateful evening in Hawks' home. And it's even stranger to imagine Hawks, aptly described by McCarthy as "the antithesis of the fast-talking, hard-driving verbal type," zipping through the rapid-fire repartee penned by Hecht and MacArthur.

But so what? To paraphrase a line from John Ford's *The Man Who Shot Liberty Valance* — spoken, appropriately enough, by a newspaper editor — when the legend becomes accepted as fact, why print anything but the legend? The story may be apocryphal, but it exemplifies an anything-goes, seat-of-the-pants creative process that we've come to accept, even romanticize, as typical of Hollywood's golden age.

In much the same way, *His Girl Friday* — arguably more than the Hecht-MacArthur original, and definitely more than any other film it inspired — indelibly established the stereotype of reporters as rudely sarcastic iconoclasts who talk fast, crack wise, and raise hell while they comfort the afflicted and afflict the comfortable. When Hawks' Hildy Johnson (a Hildegard rather than a Hildebrand) makes her grand entrance into the press office of the Chicago Criminal Courts Building, to join the deathwatch for a luckless bumbler who accidentally shot a cop, she rubs her fashionably padded shoulders with a vibrantly motley crew of ink-stained wretches. Despite her claims to the contrary, she looks and sounds like she's precisely where she's meant to be, because she can talk faster and crack wiser than anyone else in the room.

Rosalind Russell wasn't Hawks' first choice, or even his fifth, to play Hildy Johnson, but her image-defining performance as the sassy and brassy newspaperwoman is swell enough to suggest that no one could have done it better. (Whenever I screen *His Girl Friday* for college-level film courses, female students seem particularly impressed by Russell's portrayal of a woman liberated way before women's liberation was cool.) Her most attractive attribute: She is a spectacularly worthy opponent in verbal jousting with Cary Grant, perfectly cast as Walter Burns, her conniving ex-editor and, more important, ex-husband.

Months after divorcing Walter, Hildy returns to the *Morning Post* news-room, only to announce her engagement to Bruce Baldwin (Ralph Bellamy), an affably bland insurance salesman. Bruce has no connection to the madcap world that Hildy wants to leave behind, a fact Hawks subtly underscores by having Walter wait outside a newsroom gate marked "No Admittance" while Hildy bids Walter good-bye.

But, of course, Hildy doesn't fare well while trying to say farewell: Walter tricks her into doing what she really wants to do, which is remain a reporter who comes alive most fully when she's on the prowl for a big story. And while Walter and Hildy may be, like Elyot and Amanda of Noel Coward's *Private Lives*, unable to live happily either apart or together, there is no doubt that they are soul mates who speak the same language with the same warp-speed alacrity.

Such rhetorical virtuosity is a defining characteristic of screwball comedy, a genre that thrived throughout the 1930s and early '40s. Films of this sort were an escape from the harsh realities of Depression-era life, offering carefree and attractive characters behaving with abandon and freedom in a world filled with colorful but (usually) harmless eccentrics and blustering but (usually) impotent authority figures.

Like many other screwball classics, Hawks' must-see masterwork belongs to the subgenre known as "Comedy of Re-Marriage," being the story of divorced partners who simply must be reunited because they bring out the best in each other. Walter may be a sneak, and his motives are hardly selfless, but he genuinely admires — and values — Hildy's professional abilities. Hildy has every reason to distrust Walter — except, of course, when he's telling her that no one else would appreciate her, and encourage her, the way he does.

His Girl Friday ranks among the finest and funniest screwball comedies, largely because Hawks, with a little help from Hecht and MacArthur, gives his characters so much to say so quickly and memorably. Although chronically averse to theorizing or philosophizing about technique, he hinted at the key to his movie's appeal with this pithy quip: "They're moving pictures. Let's make them move."

SPECS:

His Girl Friday — Stars: Cary Grant, Rosalind Russell, Ralph Bellamy, Gene Lockhart, and Helen Mack. Directed by Howard Hawks. Screenplay: Charles Lederer, based on *The Front Page* by Ben Hecht and Charles MacArthur. Running time: 92 minutes. Year of release: 1940. DVD distributor: Columbia TriStar Home Video.

SUBJECTS FOR FURTHER RESEARCH:

Bringing Up Baby (1938) — Another exemplary screwball comedy by Howard Hawks, this fleet and funny farce memorably pairs Cary Grant as a bumbling paleontologist with a jones for dinosaur bones and Katharine Hepburn as a madcap socialite with a motherly fondness for her pet leopard. Unlikely romance proceeds apace while rapid-fire repartee abounds.

Switching Channels (1988) — Brutally dismissed by purist critics during its initial theatrical run, Ted Kotcheff's update of *His Girl Friday* can be appreciated on its own terms as a zippy satirical comedy. Burt Reynolds is slyly amusing as a cable-news network honcho, Kathleen Turner shines as his star reporter (and ex-wife) — and Christopher Reeve is impeccably silly as the boring businessman who foolishly assumes he can lure Turner into domestic bliss.

The Hudsucker Proxy (1994) — Joel and Ethan Coen try their hand at full-tilt screwball comedy in this farcical fable about a wide-eyed innocent (Tim Robbins) who's groomed for the role of fall guy by a corporate shark (cast-against-type Paul Newman). Jennifer Jason Leigh appears to be channeling Rosalind Russell *and* Katharine Hepburn as a fast-talking, wisecracking reporter.

LESSON FOR FILMMAKERS:

Many filmmakers have acknowledged their debt to Howard Hawks, but Quentin Tarantino specifically referenced a Hawks classic in directorial notes for a screenplay. In the published script for *Pulp Fiction*, Tarantino describes the opening scene: "Their dialogue is to be said in a rapid-pace *His Girl Friday* fashion." In the movie, it's clear Tim Roth and Amanda Plummer took this cue to heart.

DARK VICTORY

hroughout the final quarter-century of her life, in countless feature films, TV dramas, and talk-show appearances, Bette Davis (1908-89) went out of her way to sustain a self-satirizing image as a bug-eyed, raspy-voiced, age-ravaged eccentric. For movie buffs who came of age in the wake of *What Ever Happened to Baby Jane?* (1962), the career-reviving gothic-camp extravaganza that permanently recast her as a cantankerous harpy, it sometimes comes as a shock to be reminded of the unconventionally beautiful and uniquely charismatic superstar that Davis was in her prime.

Fortunately, film is a medium that ensures even the dearly departed are always in the present tense, at their very best. In *Dark Victory*, the must-see 1939 tearjerker directed by Edmond Goulding (*Grand Hotel*), Davis continues to delight and dazzle in a role that she ranked among her favorites. And despite the passing of years — not to mention the abundance of remakes, rip-offs, and spot-on parodies — the movie itself still packs a potent emotional wallop.

Davis earned her third Academy Award nomination for her cunningly dynamic portrayal of Judith Traherne, a fast-living, hard-drinking Long Island socialite who lives her life as one long New Year's Eve party until she realizes her occasional dizzy spells and blurred vision can't be blamed on hangovers. Dedicated surgeon Frederick Steele (George Brent) — who, not surprisingly, falls in love with Judith — identifies her malady as a brain tumor. But, of course, the audience knows better: Judith has Old Movie Disease, a humbling affliction that strikes only carefree and capricious leading ladies. Victims become progressively more beautiful, and increasingly less self-absorbed, as they stoically approach a peaceful quietus. (Sporadic spasms of kookiness are common symptoms.)

For no very good reason, her doctor and her best friend (Geraldine Fitzgerald) opt to keep Judith blissfully ignorant of her death sentence. When she inadvertently learns the truth, she turns against her confidants, and resumes her wastrel ways with bad influences. (Chief among the latter: a pre-presidential Ronald Reagan, who's unsettlingly convincing as a party-hearty libertine.) Ultimately, however, Judith decides to spend her final months as a supportive wife for Frederick. During the profoundly affecting final scenes, she refuses to tell him of her abruptly fading eyesight — the telltale sign, alas, of a rapidly approaching demise. Instead, she sends him off to an important medical conference, so she can die alone — to the accompaniment of Max Steiner's heart-wrenching musical score — in bed.

Dark Victory is a textbook example of the glossy Hollywood product that rolled off dream factory assembly lines during the heyday of the studio era. And like most similar product – especially the brand produced by Warner Bros. — it features a strong supporting cast of contract players. Brent, an actor best remembered for providing handsome window dressing in movies built around remarkable leading ladies, is impeccably noble as Frederick. Fitzgerald makes the most of a largely thankless part, while Reagan is amusingly lightweight as Alec, a feckless fellow who spends most of the movie in various stages of inebriation. And third-billed Humphrey Bogart struggles manfully with an on-again, off-again Irish accent as Michael O'Leary, a virile horse trainer who'd like to corral Judith.

The main attraction, though, is Bette Davis. Whether Judith is gliding coquettishly through a country-club gathering, or bravely comforting a weepy buddy before striding off to her solitary destiny, Davis demonstrates just what being a gloriously larger-than-life movie icon is all about. An underrated element of her timeless appeal: She's not afraid to appear infuriatingly selfish, if not aggressively unlikable, when a scene calls for potentially off-putting extremes. That alone is sufficient to set her far apart from most image-conscious stars of any era. If they don't make movies like *Dark Victory* anymore, maybe it's because there's no one like Davis — *this* Davis, the luminous immortal of 1939 — to star in them.

SPECS:

Dark Victory — Stars: Bette Davis, George Brent, Humphrey Bogart, Geraldine Fitzgerald, and Ronald Reagan. Directed by Edmond Goulding. Screenplay: Casey Robinson, based on the play by George Emerson Brewer Jr. and Bertram Bloch. Running time: 106 minutes. Year of release: 1939. DVD distributor: Warner Home Video.

SUBJECTS FOR FURTHER RESEARCH:

Jezebel (1938) — Davis does her selfish-turns-selfless thing to Oscar-worthy perfection in William Wyler's antebellum melodrama about a mercurial Southern belle who pays dearly for toying with a proud suitor (Henry Fonda).

All About Eve (1950) — Nightclub impressionists and fabulous camp followers are especially fond of this much-quoted classic starring Davis as an "aging" (that is, over 40) and self-dramatizing stage actress whose toadying acolyte (Anne Baxter) covets her boyfriend (Gary Merrill) *and* her stardom. Yes, this is the one in which Davis snaps: "Fasten your seatbelts, it's going to be a bumpy night!"

Love Story (1971) — Phenomenally popular in its time, this class-conscious *Dark Victory* variation features Ali McGraw as a blue-collar girl who makes a better man of rich-boy husband Ryan O'Neal by dying of Old Movie Disease.

LESSON FOR FILMMAKERS

Never argue with a star who has a sharp eye for spiffy vehicles. Bette Davis saw *Dark Victory* on the stage, and pressed mogul Jack L. Warner to buy screen rights for her. Warner reluctantly agreed, even though he famously groused: "Who wants to see a dame go blind?"

CASABLANCA

Breathes there the man with soul so dead who never to himself has said, "Here's looking at you, kid"?

Casablanca, sixty-plus years young and doubtless immortal, is more than a classic movie, more than a paradigm of Old Hollywood artistry — and much, much more than the sum of its Dream Factory machine-tooled parts. It is, to borrow a line from another popular Humphrey Bogart picture, the stuff that dreams are made of.

Conceived in haste, produced in chaos, and launched with more than a little last-minute trepidation, *Casablanca* has survived — no, make that *thrived* — for well over a half-century, defying changing tastes and remaining forever fresh. It is the type of grand romantic gesture that moviemakers rarely attempt in this irony-obsessed age. And yet it is the very sort of intoxicating hokum that drew most of us to movies in the first place.

At once cynical and sincere, hard-boiled and softhearted, worldly wise and dreamily romantic, it is great, glossy fun of the kind that no medium other than cinema can deliver in such bountifully generous measure.

Inspired by an unproduced play called *Everybody Comes to Rick's*, and freely adapted by screenwriters who continued to write and rewrite during actual production, the wartime romance pivots on a device not unlike one of Alfred Hitchcock's "McGuffins." In all likelihood, neither the Third Reich nor Vichy France ever authorized those all-important exit visas that propel so much of the action. But, hey, who cares? If Peter Lorre says he stole them, Humphrey Bogart accepts them, and

Ingrid Bergman and Paul Henreid are so desperate to obtain them, who are we to quibble?

As Rick Blaine, the sardonically evasive man of mystery who came to Casablanca "because of the waters," Bogart is very much a man ahead of his time — an existential hero long before existentialism was cool. Having survived the pain of lost love and lost causes, Rick insists he lives only for the moment as the apolitical operator of Rick's Café Americain, the swankiest night spot in French Morocco. Sometimes, a woman makes the mistake of thinking she can break through Rick's shell, only to be harshly disappointed. ("Where were you last night?" "That's so long ago, I don't remember." "Will I see you tonight?" "I never make plans that far ahead.") Sometimes, a man makes the even bigger mistake of thinking he can count on Rick's help, only to be brutally rebuffed: "I stick my neck out for nobody."

Bogart is great in the role of Rick, even better than Rick is in the role he has created for himself. Rick's performance as a cynical, self-centered rogue is undermined by his capacity for nobility and self-sacrifice, which our hero rediscovers, much to his great and grateful surprise, like someone finding valuables in the pocket of an old suit.

Blame it on Ilsa, the lost love who chooses to visit Rick's Café Americain out of all the gin joints in all the towns in all the world. She's not alone: Ilsa walks in on the arm of fugitive freedom fighter Victor Lazlo, her courageous (though somewhat stiff-backed) husband. Anxious to leave Casablanca before an imperious Nazi officer (Conrad Veidt) can contrive a reason for the local cops to arrest them, the couple seeks the stolen exit visas that everybody, even the local prefect of police, knows Rick has managed to obtain. But Rick — who was abruptly abandoned by Ilsa years earlier — isn't especially eager to help the woman he believes betrayed him. It requires some impassioned entreaties from Ilsa, along with some none-too-subtle guilt-tripping on the part of Victor, to make Rick realize that problems of star-crossed lovers "don't amount to a hill of beans" in a war-torn world.

Alas, almost all of the *Casablanca* players are dead now. And yet they linger — eternal in our memories, alive and well on film and home video. Ingrid Bergman remains radiant enough to melt the hardest of hearts, to reignite the worst burnt-out case. Paul Henreid still is the most eloquently persuasive and passionately debonair of rabble-rousers. Peter Lorre is the sleaziest — and most fatally ambitious — of sneak thieves. Conrad Veidt is the most repellently self-assured Nazi. Sydney Greenstreet is the most grandiloquent black marketer. Dooley Wilson — as Sam, the star performer at Rick's Café Americain — plays the dreamiest theme ("As Time Goes By") ever composed for movie romance. Better still, he plays it again and again.

Best of all, there is Claude Rains, stealing every scene that isn't bolted to the floor as the cheerfully corrupt Captain Renault, the Vichy-suave prefect of police. Just try to keep a straight face when this shameless hypocrite claims to be shocked — shocked! — to learn there is gambling in the back room at Rick's.

To be sure, some of the dialogue hasn't dated especially well ("Was that cannon fire, or is it my heart pounding?"). But even at its most melodramatic, *Casablanca* elicits smiles of pleasure, not giggles of disbelief or laughs of derision. Directed with consummate professionalism by Hungarian-born Michael Curtiz — who had more than sixty Hollywood productions to his credit before tackling this one — it is a movie with the courage of its corniness, the strength of its shameless contrivance, the power of its pulp-fiction redemption. They don't make them like this anymore. And even when they try, they lack certain key ingredients, such as Bogart and Bergman. And, just as important, an audience willing to suspend all disbelief for two hours of larger-than-life, bigger-than-self heroism. As time goes by, *Casablanca* just gets better and better.

SPECS:

Casablanca — Stars: Humphrey Bogart, Ingrid Bergman, Paul Henreid, Claude Rains. Conrad Veidt, Sydney Greenstreet, and Peter Lorre. Directed by Michael Curtiz. Screenplay: Julius J. and Phillip G. Epstein and Howard Koch, based on the play by Murray Burnett and Joan Alison. Running time: 103 minutes. Year of release: 1942. DVD distributor: Warner Home Video.

SUBJECTS FOR FURTHER RESEARCH:

To Have and Have Not (1944) — When Warner Bros. wanted a follow-up to *Casablanca*, Howard Hawks provided this marvelously entertaining comedy-drama starring Humphrey Bogart as an apolitical fishing-boat skipper who's drawn into helping the French Resistance. A va-va-voom Lauren Bacall (in her movie debut) provided romantic interest, on screen and off, for Bogie.

Havana (1990) — Sydney Pollack's seriously underrated riff on *Casablanca* stars Robert Redford as a roguish gambler who falls for the wife (Lena Olin) of a presumed-dead revolutionary (Raul Julia) during the last days of the Batista regime in Cuba.

Proof of Life (2000) — Russell Crowe tries to channel Bogie's romantic cynicism as a hostage negotiator who falls for the wife (Meg Ryan) of a kidnapped American businessman (David Morse) in Latin America. Unfortunately, the film fizzled, largely due to the lack of on-screen chemistry between the leads. (Ironically, Crowe and Ryan had a much-publicized *off-screen* romance during filming.)

LESSON FOR FILMMAKERS:

Love sells. When *Casablanca* was voted number one on the American Film Institute's list of 100 greatest movie love stories, filmmaker Sydney Pollack (whose own *The Way We Were* ranked No. 6 on the AFI list) said he wasn't surprised. "Many, many films haunt you," Pollack told the Associated Press, "but you get haunted in a way that's hard to shake off when you're watching star-crossed lovers who you really care about, and who get under your skin, like Bogart and Bergman. That's a story that's just irresistible."

P̲ILLOW T̲ALK

Whenever a film critic tries to disparage a romantic trifle by likening it to "a Doris Day movie," you can be sure the reviewer isn't referring to *Calamity Jane* or *With Six You Get Eggroll*. The belittling allusion is critic-speak shorthand for a specific type of glossy fluff that flourished between the late 1950s and the mid '60s, a genre best represented by *Pillow Talk*, the first and arguably best of some half-dozen movies that irreversibly established Day as the Virgin Queen of wholesome sex comedies.

Very much a pop-culture product of its time — and, as such, more enlightening than most historical or anthropological overviews of the period's mood and mores — *Pillow Talk* cast Day as... well, to use the quaint nomenclature of the time, a career girl. She was thirty-four years old when production began in early 1959, and already had more than twenty major movie credits on her resume. But on the advice of her agent-husband, Martin Melcher, the self-styled financial whiz who would eventually squander most of her millions on ill-advised investments, Day decided to jump-start her temporarily stalled career by not acting her age.

The first image we have of Day in *Pillow Talk* is an admiring close-up of her lovely legs as she arranges her stockings. But don't misunderstand: She's in her own bedroom, alone, getting dressed for work This bait-and-switch is typical of the tickle-and-tease that passed for sophistication in pseudo-risqué comedies of the era. (The DVD edition of "Pillow Talk" includes the original 1959 coming-attractions trailer, which promises "the most sparkling sex-capade that ever winked at conventions." Yeah, right.) Another distinguishing characteristic: The movie's depiction of single working women — whoops, excuse me, I meant to say "career girls" — as pitiably incomplete and unhappy creatures in desperate need of a good man, a lusty ravishing or, preferably, both.

Doris Day plays Jan Morrow, an interior decorator who's sufficiently successful to afford a stunning wardrobe, a spacious Manhattan apartment, and a housekeeper given to excessive drinking and wisecracking. Early on, however, *Pillow Talk* tips its hand by underscoring Jan's true worth in the world. When she complains about the playboy who monopolizes their shared party line, a phone company official makes sympathetic noises, but claims he can't do anything to solve the problem. Yes, he knows that Jan needs to use her phone for business purposes. But, no, she can't be placed any higher on the list of folks waiting for single lines. Unless, of course, some kind of emergency arose. "If you were to become pregnant," he explains, "you'd jump right to the top of the list." But — remember, this is 1959 — that would require a husband, right?

Actually, Jan does have a serious marriage proposal to contemplate: Jonathan Forbes (Tony Randall), a fabulously wealthy client, wants to make her his fourth wife. But Jan isn't interested, and not just because of Jonathan's matrimonial track record. She simply doesn't love the guy. And she doesn't want to marry anyone just for his money.

Could it be that Jan enjoys her independence? That's her story, and she's sticking to it. But Alma (Thelma Ritter), her cynical housekeeper, isn't convinced: "If there's anything worse than a woman being alone, it's a woman who says she likes it." Indeed, even the annoying playboy — played by Rock Hudson as the kind of guy who, in an updated remake, would likely read *Maxim* and *Playboy* — feels entitled to make snide remarks about Jan's unmarried status. If she doesn't like to hear his crooning sweet nothings to his many girlfriends every time she picks up the phone, well, that's her problem, not his. "Don't take your bedroom problems out on me," he snarls.

Naturally, these opposites are destined to attract. Brad Allen (Hudson) — who just happens to be a good friend of Jonathan — is intrigued when he fortuitously recognizes Jan in a nightclub. She doesn't know who he is, however, and he contrives to hide his true identity by posing

as a courtly Texas gentleman named Rex Stetson. He begins a meticulously chaste courtship, figuring the best way to lure Jan into bed is to
behave as though his intentions are purely honorable.

And just to have a little fun at her expense, he drops none-too-subtle
hints that any guy who's *this* polite must be — wink-wink, nudge-nudge
— very devoted to his mother. (One can only wonder what mixed emotions Hudson felt as the famously closeted gay actor played a straight
character who pretended to be effeminate.) Despite Rex's pronounced
"sensitivity" — or, more likely, because of it — Jan falls for his smooth
talk. But just before Brad can make his move — are you ready for this?
are you sitting down? — he realizes he has truly fallen in love with her.
And even then, he's forced to delay his gratification when she sees
through his role-playing.

Brad desperately woos her, apologizes to her, even hires her to redecorate
his Hugh Hefneresque apartment. When Jan gets even by turning his
love shack into a tacky faux bordello, Brad responds by smashing
through her door, grabbing her out of bed, and carrying her down the
street, back to his place. She squawks and complains, but, oddly enough,
no passer-by comes to her aid. Or maybe it's not so odd after all: As I
said, this is 1959, back when men were able to do this sort of thing with
impunity — in the movies, at least — and women, when they came to
their senses, really liked it.

The funny thing is, even as you recognize the smug (and frankly sexist)
assumptions on which the comedy is based, *Pillow Talk* remains inex-
plicably irresistible as a lavishly produced, campily retrograde guilty
pleasure. (In 2003, the makers of *Down With Love* paid it affectionate
homage by hiring Ewan McGregor and Renee Zellweger to channel
Rock and Doris.) It helps that Day and Hudson are such appealing
farceurs, and the supporting players are such scene-stealing scamps. It
helps even more that much of this particular "Doris Day movie" is undeniably funny, albeit in some of the most blatantly non-PC ways
imaginable.

SPECS:

Pillow Talk — Stars: Rock Hudson, Doris Day, Tony Randall, Thelma Ritter, and Nick Adams. Directed by Michael Gordon. Screenplay: Stanley Shapiro, Maurice Richlin. Running time: 103 minutes. Year of release: 1959. DVD distributor: Universal.

SUBJECTS FOR FURTHER RESEARCH:

That Touch of Mink (1962) — Just how far would filmmakers go to preserve Doris Day's on-screen virginity? Consider this: In her only co-starring vehicle with Cary Grant, she conveniently breaks out in hives just before she succumbs to the handsome smoothie's come-on. It's hard to top that as a method for delaying premarital gratification.

What's New, Pussycat? (1965) — The needle on the naughtiness meter veers toward the red zone in this indefatigably zippy sex comedy starring Peter O'Toole as a skirt-chasing fashion editor who wants to be monogamous, and Peter Sellers as an eccentric psychiatrist who wants to be a skirt-chasing fashion editor. This was as playfully raunchy as a movie could get in the final days of the old Production Code.

Caprice (1967) — When sex comedies started to become *really* sexy, Doris Day turned to another '60s genre, spy spoofs, to once again re-invent herself. Unfortunately, she fell flat on her cute little nose in this widely reviled comedy-drama about industrial espionage. She starred in only two more films before drifting into TV, then early retirement. Would-be superstars, take note: You make one kind of movie for too long, and you're never again accepted in anything else.

LESSON FOR FILMMAKERS:

Feel free to laugh with *Pillow Talk* — but don't be too quick to laugh *at* a glossy romantic comedy that many people take very seriously. One of the highest-grossing movies released during the 1950s, it edged out *Wild Strawberries*, *North by Northwest*, and *The 400 Blows* in the Oscar race for Best Original Screenplay. More than three decades later, producer Lynda Obst discovered during the casting of *How to Lose a*

Guy in 10 Days (2003) just how difficult it can be to find Mr. Right while manufacturing a modern-day equivalent of *Pillow Talk*. "These days," Obst says, "the hardest thing about making romantic comedies is casting the guy. Casting the woman? Easy. But you always have the same scripts chasing the same six guys — most of whom can't do it, won't do it, are afraid to do it, or can't get hired by the studio."

~5~
SONG AND DANCE

42ND STREET

Here they are, ladies and gents: Lads and lassies, sassy and brassy, singing and swaying as Broadway sensations of 1933 while they tap-tap-tap their way into your hearts.

There's Dorothy Brock (Bebe Daniels), the delightful diva who juggles a sugar daddy (Guy Kibbee) and a hunky hoofer (George Brent) while celebrating her own superstardom. There's Billy Lawler (Dick Powell), an all-American "juvenile" who's catnip to ladies of all ages. There's Ann Lowell (Ginger Rogers), a chorus girl with an eye for the boys and a naughty nickname — Anytime Annie — she bent over backwards to earn. There's Peggy Sawyer (Ruby Keeler), a starry-eyed novice who's ever-so-excited to be just another pretty face (and a pair of flashy gams) in the background of the big show.

And folks, we mean a really, *really* big show: the latest and greatest produced and directed by Julian Marsh (Warner Baxter), the living legend who's fading fast, and who's determined to score once last triumph before he takes his final bow. Always the most demanding of taskmasters, Marsh is even more unforgivingly ferocious than usual as he hand-picks his cast, nitpicks his material — "Sure, I liked that number! I liked it in 1905! What do you think we're putting on, a revival?" — and rants and raves through rehearsals that push everyone, including Marsh, to egregious extremes.

Through sheer force of will, Marsh bends everyone and everything to his design. Even when fate tosses him a nasty curve — Dorothy breaks her ankle just before opening night — he barely slows his breakneck progress. Left without a suitable star, he simply plucks a replacement from the chorus: Peggy, the fresh-faced first-timer. Is she nervous? Sure. Is she game? You bet. But just to make sure she's fully aware that it's not just a show she is shouldering — after all, there is a Great Depression going on — Marsh shoves her toward the spotlight with a last-minute pep talk:

"Miss Sawyer, you listen to me… and you listen hard! Two hundred people, two hundred jobs, $200,000, five weeks of grind and blood and sweat depend on you! It's the lives of all these people who've worked with you! You've got to go on, and you've got to give and give and *give*! They've got to like you — *got* to! You understand? You can't fall down, you can't! Because your future's in it, my future and everything all of us have is staked on you! All right now, I'm through! But you keep your feet on the ground and your head on those shoulders of yours! And Sawyer — you're going out a youngster, but you've got to come back a star!"

Cowabunga!

Lloyd Bacon's *42nd Street*, the exuberantly campy classic in which chorus girls become overnight sensations and Broadway extravaganzas are literally matters of life or death, is widely viewed as the mother of all backstage musicals, as well as the lexicon containing every cliché of the genre. As such, it's an easy target for cynics and satirists. But it's quite capable of raising your spirit and touching your heart if you give it half a chance, because even the moldiest clichés can be surprisingly potent when you confront them in their original context. To put it another way: The characters here are so intensely sincere, even when they're well aware of how silly they might seem, that it's almost inconceivably cruel not to take them seriously.

To be sure, audiences of the 1930s were inclined to take *42nd Street* very seriously indeed. As Martin Scorsese perceptively notes in his *Personal Journey Through American Movies*, the rise of the musical paralleled that of the gangster melodrama in early '30s cinema. And just as dire economic conditions and widespread unemployment often figured into the motives of movie mobsters, Scorsese writes, "The harshness of the times, the Depression, colored this most escapist of film genres… In those times, if one showed any ambition, one either became a gangster or a showbiz performer — at least in the fantasy world of Warner Bros. Broadway offered a metaphor for a desperate, shattered country. Director or chorus girl, your life depended on the show's success."

All of which helps explain why, even during the leanest and meanest years of the Great Depression, movie attendance remained remarkably steady as anxious masses sought Hollywood products that either promised escape from hard realities of the day, or encouraged audiences by reinforcing a sense of solidarity in the face of adversity. To its considerable credit, *42nd Street* did both.

Just as important — from a film historian's view, at least — *42nd Street* did much to define the movie musical as an art form separate and distinct from the stage-bound variety, by introducing an aesthetic of dance conceived for the camera. Like him or loathe him, cheer him or jeer him, dance master Busby Berkeley envisioned a vigorously spectacular form of choreography involving beautifully leggy chorus lines, machine-like precision, intricate geometric design, surrealistic excess — and, what the hell, as much sexually charged imagery as he could slip past the Production Code bluenoses.

Film historian David Thomson may have said it best: "Berkeley was a lyricist of eroticism, the high-angle shot and the moving camera; he made it explicit that when the camera moves it has the thrust of the sexual act with it. It is only remarkable that some viewers smile on what they consider the 'period charm' of such libertinage."

In the final third of *42nd Street* — and even more so throughout *Footlight Parade* (1933), *Dames* (1934), *Gold Diggers of 1935*, and other films that employed him as choreographer and/or director — Berkeley devised elaborate musical sequences that could never be contained in a Broadway production. Nor could they ever appear as impressive on the Great White Way as they do in one of Berkeley's trademark overhead shots. The grand and glorious irony of Berkeley's career is that he brought to backstage musicals the type of spectacle that could never be replicated on stage. (No, not even in the popular Broadway musical adapted from the 1933 film.) By doing that, he earned a place of honor in the pantheon of those visionaries who helped establish the wondrous ways that movies move.

SPECS:

42nd Street — Stars: Warner Baxter, Bebe Daniels, George Brent, Una Merkel, Ruby Keeler, Guy Kibbee, Ginger Rogers, Ned Sparks, and Dick Powell. Director: Lloyd Bacon. Screenplay: Rian James and James

Seymour, based on the novel by Bradford Ropes. Running time: 89 minutes. Year of release: 1933. DVD distributor: Warner Home Video.

SUBJECTS FOR FURTHER RESEARCH:

Gold Diggers of 1935 (1935) — Busby Berkeley's first solo effort as director-choreographer is a mostly frothy and funny escapade. But its most famous production number is one of the darkest that Berkeley (or anyone else) ever conceived for a Hollywood musical: "Lullaby of Broadway," a moodily-lit fantasia about a tap-dancing, hard-living party girl, ends with the "Broadway baby" taking a fatal plunge from a penthouse balcony.

All That Jazz (1979) — Taking his cue from the melancholy conclusion of *42nd Street*, Bob Fosse refuses to provide a happily-ever-after ending for its stressed-for-success Broadway director (Roy Scheider). Indeed, Fosse goes far beyond mere melancholy to spring something at once sublime and shocking in the final scene of his razzle-dazzling, semi-autobiographical musical.

A Chorus Line (1985) — In Richard Attenborough's uneven adaptation of the long-running Broadway hit, Michael Douglas plays a brutally demanding choreographer who makes Warner Baxter seem like a pussycat. While desperately eager dancers audition, Douglas — whose character remains largely unseen in the original stage version — decides which of the hopefuls he wants for an upcoming show.

LESSON FOR FILMMAKERS:

Critics don't always appreciate, or even understand, revolutionary innovation. Consider this snippy pan of *42nd Street*, written by an uncredited (and, apparently, unqualified) movie critic for the March 18, 1933 edition of *Newsweek*: "Busby Berkeley, the dance director, has gone to a lot of ineffectual bother about his intricate formations, not having been told that masses of chorus girls mean something only in the flesh. His talent is wasted in the films."

SNOW WHITE AND THE SEVEN DWARFS

Nearly seventy years after Walt Disney audaciously defied conventional wisdom to create the first full-length animated feature, *Snow White and the Seven Dwarfs* continues to enchant audiences of all ages. Even grumpy middle-aged film critics can't help falling under its spell. It's best enjoyed in a spacious movie theater with Dolby Stereo, or a comfy den with a world-class home theater system, alongside as many children as you can reasonably corral. But if you can't find any kids to watch it with, don't let that stop you: Do yourself a favor and enjoy it on your own.

What's that? You say you're too old for fairy tales? Well, that's a shame. But, okay, be that way: You can still admire Disney's *Snow White* for its sheer technique. In terms of depth, detail, and delicate play of light and shadow, the supple artistry of this must-see movie has seldom been equaled, even in an era of computer-generated imagery.

A few sequences are simply unforgettable: Snow White, racing through a shadow-streaked forest, sees threatening alligators in floating branches and wild-eyed monsters in rotting tree trunks. The Wicked Queen, transformed into a cackling crone, drifts through the gray fog of a pale dawn on her mission of murder. The height-challenged yet ever-hearty Seven Dwarfs, alerted at their mine by anxious forest animals, race back to their cottage to save Snow White while, thanks to crosscutting worthy of D. W. Griffith, we see our heroine being offered The Poisoned Apple.

Show *Snow White* to children of an impressionable age, and they'll never be satisfied with the corner-cutting animation of Saturday morning television. See it yourself, and you'll be reminded of the hand-made impressionistic beauty that prospered under Uncle Walt, long before animators at Disney and elsewhere discovered the magic of CGI. Indeed, the animation is so effective in *Snow White* that very small youngsters may be frightened by some scenes, especially when The Fairest of Them All runs through the seemingly haunted woods.

Granted, there's not much even the Disney animators can do to make Prince Charming appear anything but white-bread bland. (It always requires a leap of faith to believe that Snow White, or any other animated heroine, could ever live happily ever after with such a stiff.) On the other hand, it's not entirely the poor hero's fault: The Dwarfs — Doc, Grumpy, Sleepy, Dopey, Happy, Sneezy and Bashful — upstage everybody, even the radiant heroine, with highly individualized personalities that are the by-products of meticulously detailed artistry.

Nitpickers have a point when they complain that this precedent-setting classic — the mother of all animated movies — firmly established the convention of stuffing a slew of "original songs" into almost every Disney or non-Disney animated feature. Still, even Grumpy would have to agree that the wall-to-wall musical score in *Snow White* is cheerily pleasant, with some songs ("Whistle While You Work," "Heigh-Ho" and "I'm Wishing") as endearing and immortal as the movie that introduced them.

SPECS:

Snow White and the Seven Dwarfs — Supervising director: David Hand. Sequence directors: Perce Pearce, Larry Morey, William Cottrell, Wilfred Jackson, and Ben Sharpsteen. Story adaptation: Ted Sears, Otto Englander, Earl Hurd, Dorothy Ann Blank, Richard Creedon, Dick Richard, Merrill De Maris, and Webb Smith. Running time: 83 minutes. Year of release: 1937. DVD distributor: Walt Disney Home Video.

SUBJECTS FOR FURTHER RESEARCH:

Bambi (1942) — Arguably the most beautiful and definitely the most heart-wrenching of the animated features Walt Disney personally oversaw in the wake of *Snow White and the Seven Dwarfs*. Grown men have been known to get misty-eyed when they hear the bad news from Bambi's newly widowed father: "Your mother can't be with you any more."

Snow White and the Three Stooges (1961) — Disney's *Snow White* conclusively demonstrated that an animated cartoon could be stretched to feature length. Unfortunately, most features starring The Three Stooges prove that the slaphappy knuckleheads are best enjoyed in smaller doses. Walter Lang's ponderous musical fairy tale — which actually borrows quite a bit of imagery from the 1937 animated classic — calls for the original wild and crazy guys to be unusually restrained as they aid a perky Snow White (Olympic champion figure-skater Carol Heiss) who spends an inordinate amount of time dashing across frozen ponds.

The Color Purple (1985) — Steven Spielberg received more than a few well-aimed brickbats for sustaining a light, bright tone in his uneven adaptation of Alice Walker's dark, stark novel. At times, it's hard to shake the suspicion that he's operating under the influence of too many Disney movies. Take a close look at the sequence in which Celie (Whoopi Goldberg) magically transforms a grimy, cobwebby kitchen into something out of a *Country Living* photo spread. Looks like a scene from *Snow White*, doesn't it? All that's missing are the helpful birds and squirrels.

LESSON FOR FILMMAKERS:

If you make it real, they will believe. Woody Allen was five years old when his folks brought him to see his first movie: *Snow White and the Seven Dwarfs*. He was so enraptured that he wanted to rush toward the screen and touch the characters. "But I didn't get up there," Allen says. "I was intervened." Even so, the experience may have inspired his first crush on a movie star. In *Annie Hall* (1977), Allen — as Alvy Singer, his on-screen alter ego — admits that, during his childhood, he developed an unhealthy romantic fixation on the Wicked Queen.

SINGIN' IN THE RAIN

Okay, movie buffs, here's a quick pop quiz. The exhilarating magic of *Singin' in the Rain*, the greatest of all Hollywood musicals, must be credited to (a) the virile grace, infectious enthusiasm, and self-mocking good-sportsmanship of Gene Kelly; (b) the canny co-direction of Kelly and Stanley Donen, fortuitously teamed dance masters who warmed up with *On the Town* (1949) before ensuring their immortality with this masterwork; (c) the splendiferous supporting performances of antic Donald O'Connor and endearing Debbie Reynolds; (d) the scintillating screenplay by Betty Comden and Adolph Green, which artfully commingles spoofery, sentiment, and showbiz mythos; (e) the astute conceptualization of producer Arthur Freed, the brilliantly eclectic mastermind who supervised two decades' worth of musical extravaganzas during the golden age of Metro-Goldwyn-Mayer; or (f) all of the above.

If you chose (f), give yourself an A-plus. Better still, count yourself among the savvy film aficionados who recognize *Singin' in the Rain* as one of the more decisive exceptions to the *auteur* theory. A theory, it should be noted, that Stanley Donen himself has dismissed as simplistic. "Anyone who says that every picture is not a collaboration is an idiot," he insisted in a late '60s interview. "It's a question of how much you collaborate, and who you collaborate with."

In the case of *Singin' in the Rain*, producer Freed — a former vaudevillian who worked his way up from staff songwriter to Grand Kahuna of musical production at MGM — lays claim to the title of Most Valuable

Collaborator. After all, it was Freed who assembled the other members of the creative dream team for this classic, and whose multifaceted showbiz experiences informed both the story and the storytelling.

Long before Baz Luhrmann ransacked a half-century of pop music history to collect the playlist for his razzle-dazzling *Moulin Rouge* (2001), Freed commissioned a similar, smaller-scaled job of recycling: He directed Comden and Green to concoct a script that would incorporate several tunes Freed had written with composer Nacio Herb Brown for dozens of earlier MGM movies.

"Singin' in the Rain," the best of the lot, had been introduced in *The Hollywood Revue of 1929*, a patchwork of songs, sketches, and dances that was hurriedly thrown together at MGM during the early, awkward days of talking pictures. How appropriate, then, that the tune would provide a title — and cinema's grandest solo production number — for the smart and sassy Comden-Green scenario about the madcap misadventures that ensue as moviemakers make the transition from silents to talkies.

The fun begins at the Hollywood premiere of a silent swashbuckling epic, then segues to an extended flashback as superstar Don Lockwood (Kelly) gives a fawning interviewer a self-serving account of his salad days. Even as Don insists that he and best buddy Cosmo Brown (O'Connor) adhered to a simple motto — "Dignity, always dignity!" — the richly amusing montage shows how they barely made the grade as vaudeville song-and-dance men (like Freed, perhaps?) until Don stumbled into movies as a stuntman, and Cosmo tagged along as an on-set musical accompanist.

Singin' in the Rain maintains its puckishly playful tone as we're introduced to Lina Lamont (the great Jean Hagen), Don's frequent co-star and (according to the fan magazines, which Lina accepts as gospel) his off-screen love interest. Lina looks like a fetching goddess — and sounds like a screeching harpy. Like many others in the Hollywood firmament, she runs the risk of becoming a fallen star as talking pictures become the rage. Fortunately, the producers of her first talkie are able to disguise her vocal deficiencies: They arrange for Lina's singing and speaking to be dubbed by Kathy Seldon (Reynolds), an aspiring actress (and sometime chorus girl) who just happens to be the real off-screen apple of Don's eye. When she learns of the deception, however, Lina vows to keep Kathy behind the scenes — and away from Don.

Singin' in the Rain vividly conveys the heady atmosphere of panic, promise, and improvisation that prevailed in Hollywood at the dawn of the talkies, often alluding to real-life mishaps and missteps that have become the stuff of showbiz legend. (Note the hilarious struggles to camouflage microphones and record audible dialogue.) Indeed, this enduringly entertaining musical merits inclusion in the syllabus of any college-level film history course. But don't let that scare you off: Donen, Kelly, and company never allow facts to get in the way of telling a wonderfully entertaining story and casting an irresistibly captivating spell. For that, each member of the all-star creative team deserves a fair share of grateful praise.

SPECS:

Singin' in the Rain — Stars: Gene Kelly, Donald O'Connor, Debbie Reynolds, Jean Hagen, and Cyd Charisse. Directed by Gene Kelly and Stanley Donen. Screenplay: Adolph Green and Betty Comden. Running time: 103 minutes. Year of release: 1952. DVD distributor: MGM Home Entertainment.

SUBJECTS FOR FURTHER RESEARCH:

The Band Wagon (1953) — One year after *Singin' in the Rain*, Betty Comden and Adolph Green concocted another musical scenario with a satirical edge. Directed by Vincente Minnelli (*Meet Me in St. Louis*), *Band Wagon* merrily spoofs Cinemascope epics, pretentious theater "artistes" and hardboiled detective fiction while following the misadventures of a career-stalled movie star (Fred Astaire at his lightest and brightest) who attempts a Broadway comeback.

Nickelodeon (1976) — Peter Bogdanovich's nostalgia-laced comedy-drama is an affectionate ode to the pioneers of silent cinema. Ryan O'Neal is in top form as an attorney who lucks into filmmaking, and Burt Reynolds is perfectly cast as a journeyman actor who stumbles into stardom.

Shanghai Knights (2003) — During a cleverly choreographed fight scene, martial-arts master Jackie Chan pays witty tribute to Gene Kelly, one of his heroes, by using an umbrella to best a few bad guys in a not-so-veiled allusion to *Singin' in the Rain*. As in-jokey references go, it's a lot cheerier than Malcolm McDowell's rendition of the familiar tune while inflicting ultra-violence in Stanley Kubrick's *A Clockwork Orange* (1971).

LESSON FOR FILMMAKERS:

If you can, go to the source — and then, to the source of the source. When he audaciously transformed *Love's Labour's Lost* (2000) into a '30s-style movie musical, complete with recycled period tunes by Irving Berlin, George Gershwin, and other Tin Pan Alley greats, Kenneth Branagh looked to *Singin' in the Rain* for inspiration. And just to make sure he learned his lessons well, he asked Stanley Donen — and Martin Scorsese, a director who's been known to use a pop tune or two in his movies — to preview a rough cut. "Overall," Branagh says, "they were quite moved by the film. Particularly Mr. Donen — because he saw something that quite clearly had his influence all over it. He was a terrific supporter of it." So much so, in fact, that Donen, like Scorsese, agreed to be billed as a "presenter" in the movie's credits and advertising.

CABARET

Liza Minnelli is a megawatt superstar, no doubt about it, but you could never prove it by listing just the movie credits on her lengthy resume. During the thirty-plus years since her Oscar-winning turn in *Cabaret*, she has appeared in relatively few films, only two or three of which could be described as financially or artistically successful. Blame it, to a large degree, on bad timing: It was her considerable misfortune during the final quarter of the twentieth century to be a luminous, larger-than-life musical star at a time when luminous, larger-than-life musicals were in fretfully short supply. Indeed, you could persuasively argue that, until the release of *Chicago* in 2002, *Cabaret* was the last great American movie musical.

Ironically, Minnelli played Roxie Hart (the role eventually essayed by Renee Zellweger) during the original Broadway run of *Chicago* back in the mid-1970s. And she reportedly was eager to reprise her portrayal when Bob Fosse, director of the stage version, first announced plans for a movie adaptation. Unfortunately, Fosse didn't live along enough to bring his final Broadway success to the screen. (He died of a heart attack in 1987.) Even so, he merits honorable mention as one of cinema's most influential movie musical directors, thanks almost entirely to *Cabaret*, a once-in-a-lifetime confluence of audacious style and enthralling substance. And at the center of its razzle-dazzle dynamism is a performance that is the stuff of showbiz legend.

As Sally Bowles, a brazenly ambitious and aggressively flamboyant American entertainer in 1931 Berlin, Minnelli comes across as self-absorbed, recklessly impulsive — and more than a little trampy. In short, she is irresistible. Turning a willfully blind eye to all portents of the rising Nazi menace, Sally thrives in the spotlight each evening at the spectacularly seedy Kit Kat Klub. Sometimes, she goes home with a customer, in the hope of landing a movie audition or making a valuable contact. Other times, she goes home with a customer because — well, because that fits into her philosophy of "divine decadence."

Sally first appeared as a character in the *Berlin Stories* of Christopher Isherwood, and later took central stage in *I Am a Camera*, a play based on Isherwood's autobiographical tales of '30s life in Berlin. The play morphed into a popular Broadway musical, which served as the basis for Fosse's film.

Fosse tossed aside much of Joe Masteroff's book for the Broadway *Cabaret*, preferring to draw more from the original source material. In Jay Allen's screenplay, Sally falls for her boarding-house neighbor, Brian Roberts (Michael York), a sexually ambivalent would-be writer clearly modeled after Isherwood. But after the first blush of a tender romance — and a short-lived ménage a trois with a bisexual bon vivant (Helmut Griem) — Sally ultimately decides that, for a variety of reasons, she could never live happily ever after with Brian. Besides, there's always the chance that — somehow, some way — she'll be noticed by an important somebody at the cabaret.

Rather than strive for the "organic" style of traditional Broadway and movie musicals, Fosse maintains throughout *Cabaret* a firm line of demarcation between the big production numbers and the non-singing emotional scenes. At the Kit Kat Klub, where the ineffably demonic Master of Ceremonies (Oscar-winner Joel Grey) encourages the audience to "leave your troubles outside," the show-stopping song-and-dance interludes provide pointed commentary on what's happening to and around the lead characters. On at least one occasion — when a slaphappy comic number is intercut with Nazi brutality — the ironies are too obvious by half. For the most part, however, Fosse works with ingenious stealth. Using production-design imagery cribbed from German artists of the era — most conspicuously, George Groz — he creates within the confines of the Kit Kat Klub an animated caricature of a Weimar Germany in the final stages of rot and ruin. (Which explains why

Cabaret has become, almost by default, the touchstone for every later movie set in Germany between the world wars.) The film's last image makes it all too clear that, very soon, the deluge will engulf even those who insist "life is a cabaret, old chum."

All of which makes Minnelli's desperately charismatic performance all the more powerful. On stage and off, Sally Bowles wants to be loved — totally, unreservedly, and entirely on her own terms. Her naked yearning is often discomforting, sometimes embarrassing. She is, in short, too much. And yet, miraculously, the actress playing her gives us just enough to get that point across. Maybe that's the *real* reason why Minnelli has never been so effective, or used so effectively, in any subsequent film. She is so dead-solid perfect here, it's almost impossible to imagine her — or even want to see her — as anyone else.

SPECS:

Cabaret — Stars: Liza Minnelli, Michael York, Helmut Griem, Marisa Berenson, and Joel Grey. Directed by Bob Fosse. Screenplay: Jay Presson Allen, based on the musical play *Cabaret* (book by Joe Masteroff, music by John Kander, lyrics by Fred Ebb), the play *I Am a Camera* by John Van Druten, and stories by Christopher Isherwood. Running time: 124 minutes. Year of release: 1972. DVD distributor: Warner Home Video.

SUBJECTS FOR FURTHER RESEARCH:

Sweet Charity (1969) — Bob Fosse's overlooked and underrated debut as a filmmaker showcases one of Shirley MacLaine's finest performances as an unlucky-in-love dance-hall hostess. The choreography is extraordinary, of course, but the film overall plays like a warm-up for *Cabaret*, charting Fosse's tentative first steps away from traditional movie musical style.

Chicago (2002) — Rob Marshall's Oscar-winning adaptation of the Broadway hit originally conceived by Bob Fosse is unmistakably influenced by the latter's approach to musical moviemaking. Specifically, Marshall's *Chicago*, like Fosse's *Cabaret*, finds a dramatically satisfying way to introduce stylized production numbers (as fantasies, actually) within the context of a more "realistic" storyline.

Max (2002) — It's a darkly ironic drama, not a coolly brilliant musical, but Menno Meyjes' film about a fateful encounter between a cynical art dealer (John Cusack) and a young Adolf Hitler (Noah Taylor) proves just how difficult it can be to set any scenario in Weimar Germany without conjuring memories (if not expectations) of Sally Bowles.

LESSON FOR FILMMAKERS:

Be of your time, in your medium. While discussing *Cabaret* a few years after the film's release, Bob Fosse told New York Magazine: "I had to break away from movie musicals that just copy the Broadway show. Or movie musicals that copy conventions of the stage. *Singin' in the Rain*, *An American in Paris*, all the Gene Kelly, Fred Astaire musicals – they're classics. But they represent another era. Today I get very antsy watching musicals in which people are singing as they walk down the street or hang out the laundry... In fact, I think it looks a little silly. You can do it on the stage. The theater has its own personality — it conveys a removed reality. The movies bring that closer."

≈6≈
WESTWARD BOUND

S̲T̲A̲G̲E̲C̲O̲A̲C̲H̲

The disreputable doctor who cracks wise and drinks heavily, but sobers up to do the right thing when the chips are down. The golden-haired prostitute who brightens incandescently when a naïve cowpoke refers to her as a "lady." The shifty-eyed gambler with a gun at his side and, presumably, an ace up his sleeve. The bumptious stagecoach driver who twists his tongue into knots while politely addressing his passengers. And, of course, the square-jawed, slow-talking gunfighter who's willing to hang up his shootin' irons, who's even agreeable to mending his ways and moving to a small farm someplace with a good woman by his side — but not before he settles some unfinished business with the varmints who terminated his loved ones. Why? Because, as the gunfighter tersely notes, "There are some things a man can't run away from."

These and other familiar figures had already established themselves as archetypes by 1939, that magical movie year in which *Stagecoach* premiered. Even so, director John Ford's must-see masterwork arguably is the first significant Western of the talking-pictures era, the paradigm that cast the mold, set the rules, and firmly established the *dramatis personae* for all later movies of its kind. Indeed, it single-handedly revived the genre after a long period of box-office doldrums, elevating the Western to a new level of critical and popular acceptance. And unlike, say, Raoul Walsh's creaky and badly dated *The Big Trail* (1930) — John Wayne's first starring vehicle, but a career-stalling flop in its time — *Stagecoach* remains a lot of fun to watch.

Ford's film is a classically simple tale of strangers united in close quarters for a brief but intensely dramatic interlude. In this case, the characters are passengers aboard an Overland Stage Line coach during a dangerous trek through Indian Territory. The journey begins in the small town of Tonto, as two social outcasts — Doc Boone (Thomas Mitchell), a gleefully roguish alcoholic, and Dallas (Claire Trevor), a tearfully vulnerable prostitute — are forcibly exiled by the good ladies of The Law and Order League.

These pariahs board the stage to Lordsburg along with Mrs. Mallory (Louise Platt), a very proper — and very pregnant — Army wife; Hartfield (John Carradine), a courtly gambler who appoints himself as Mrs. Mallory's protector; Peacock (Donald Meek), a mild-mannered whiskey salesman whose sample case is progressively depleted by Doc Boone; and, at the last minute, Gatewood (Berton Churchill), a blustering banker who has absconded with the contents of his office safe. Buck (Andy Devine) is the driver, and Sheriff Wilcox (George Bancroft) rides shotgun.

Just outside of Tonto, the travelers are joined by The Ringo Kid, a boyishly handsome gunfighter who has broken out of prison to avenge his murdered father and brothers. As Ringo — the role that saved him from the professional purgatory of B-movies — John Wayne makes one of the greatest entrances in movie history: As he spins a rifle like a six-gun, the camera rapidly tracks toward him, then frames him heroically, almost worshipfully, in a flattering close-up. Ringo is a friendly and forthcoming fellow, even when dealing with Sheriff Wilcox. But he leaves no room for doubt that he's quite capable of minding his own bloody business at the end of the line.

If you're familiar with *Stagecoach* only through its reputation, or if you've seen nothing more than cut-and-paste highlights from Ford's classic, you may be surprised by the movie's intimacy. To be sure, the majestic landscapes of Monument Valley — to which Ford returned for several subsequent Westerns — are grandly impressive. And the much-imitated Indian assault on the speeding stagecoach, replete with breath-taking stunt work choreographed by the legendary Yakima Canutt, is every bit as exciting as its reputation attests. But what really makes *Stagecoach* so vital and memorable is the emotionally charged interaction among its vividly drawn characters.

Much of the movie consists of expressionistically lit interior scenes. And in many of its most memorable moments, the archetypes reveal unexpected depth and complexity. Even Carradine's ostentatious gambler turns out to be truly chivalrous in his fashion, redeeming himself gracefully under fire. And Wayne demonstrates that, long before his speech patterns and body language ossified into self-parody, he could give as soulfully affecting a performance as any hero who ever rode hard and shot straight in the most American of movie genres.

SPECS:

Stagecoach — Stars: John Wayne, Claire Trevor, George Bancroft, Andy Devine, John Carradine, and Donald Meek. Directed by John Ford. Screenplay: Dudley Nichols, based on the story by Ernest Haycox. Running time: 97 minutes. Year of release: 1939. DVD distributor: Warner Home Video.

RELATED FILMS:

My Darling Clementine (1946) — This highly romanticized, moodily photographed classic, featuring career-defining performances by Henry Fonda as Wyatt Earp and Victor Mature as Doc Holliday, is Ford's most eloquent statement about the struggle to establish the rule of law amidst the anarchy of lawlessness in the Old West.

She Wore a Yellow Ribbon (1949) — By turns exciting and autumnal, the second chapter of Ford's "Cavalry trilogy" (after *Fort Apache*, before *Rio Grande*) is a richly satisfying tale of duty, honor and tradition, with John Wayne perfectly cast as an aging Army officer in his final week of service on the frontier. French *auteur* Bertrand Tavernier has acknowledged the film's influence on his own *Life and Nothing But* (1989).

The Poseidon Adventure (1972) — The *Stagecoach* formula (take a cross-section of humanity, add life-threatening events, then shake vigorously) was transformed into a game plan for dozens of star-studded disaster movies throughout the 1970s. Ronald Neame's much-parodied (and much-imitated) *Poseidon Adventure* is the genre's emblematic masterwork.

LESSON FOR FILMMAKERS:

While preparing to direct *Citizen Kane*, his first and greatest feature, Orson Welles sought inspiration by screening *Stagecoach* nearly 40 times. "I wanted to learn how to make movies," Welles later told Peter Bogdanovich, "and that's such a classically perfect one, don't you think? Not by any means my favorite Ford, but what a textbook... A lot of people ought to study Stagecoach."

HIGH NOON

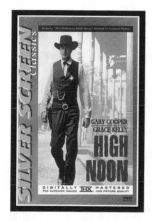

Everybody knows that *High Noon* is the Western saga of a noble marshal who must stand alone against vengeful outlaws while the cowardly citizens of his small town refuse to offer assistance. As often is the case with things that "everybody knows," however, Fred Zinnemann's must-see movie is appreciably more complex than conventional wisdom suggests.

Sure enough, Will Kane (Gary Cooper) does appear to be an icon of integrity when we meet him on what he figures to be the first day of a brand-new life. Judging from what he says, and what is said about him, he's been the well-respected marshal of Hadleyville for a number of years, dutifully turning a lawless Wild West town into an oasis of rectitude and family values. Now he's turning in his badge and tying the knot with Amy (Grace Kelly), a notably younger Quaker lady who wants her new husband to adopt a pacifistic approach to life.

But just before the newlyweds can depart on their honeymoon, Will gets bad news: Frank Miller, a surly killer Will helped send to prison years ago, is on his way back to Hadleyville to settle accounts with the lawman. Three of his gun-slinging goons are waiting at the depot, waiting for Frank to arrive on the noon train. And it's already 10:40 a.m. Uh-oh.

Being a reasonable fellow — and, more important, newly married to a beautiful Quaker lady — Will initially agrees with the townspeople who suggest that he and Amy should skedaddle. But he's barely past the Hadleyville town limits before our hero feels compelled to turn his buggy around and head back home because... well, you know, a man's got to do what a man's got to do.

Trouble is, Will can't find anybody to do it with him. For the next hour or so, he dashes from person to person, group to group, trying to rally support for his stand against the invading barbarians. Time and again, however, Will is rebuffed or betrayed.

Harvey Pell (Lloyd Bridges), his callow deputy, refuses to get involved because he blames Will for impeding his career advancement. (Harvey thought he would be a great replacement marshal; Will evidently thought otherwise.) Martin Howe (Lon Chaney Jr.), Will's mentor and predecessor, is too embittered — and, to be fair, too arthritic — to risk his neck once again for ungrateful townspeople. Mayor Henderson (Thomas Mitchell) actively discourages any assistance to Will, insisting that violent gunplay on the town's streets would be bad for business and worse for Hadleyville's image. Meanwhile, Amy sits and stews in the local hotel, threatening to leave town on the very train carrying Frank Miller to his date with destiny.

In the end, Will — with a little help from Amy, who decides to stick around and, better still, shoot one of the bad guys in the back — has to take care of business without any help from the lily-livered Hadleyvillians. He tosses his badge onto the street in a final gesture of disgust, and rides off with Amy to a better and presumably quieter life elsewhere. The End.

High Noon greatly upset some traditionalists when first released in 1952 — John Wayne and Howard Hawks were among its most vocal detractors — but many critics warmly praised the movie as a smart, sophisticated "adult Western." Audiences bought scads of tickets, and Academy voters honored Gary Cooper with a richly deserved Oscar for Best Actor. (Cooper — then fifty years old, but looking even older — stoically endured a bleeding ulcer during filming, partly accounting for the generally mournful and frequently pained expressions that enhance the credibility of his performance.) Oscars also went to the film's editing and musical score, and to the memorably mood-setting *High Noon* theme — a.k.a., *Do Not Forsake Me, Oh My Darlin'* — sung throughout the movie by Tex Ritter.

After more than a half-century of revivals, revisionist reviews, and made-for-TV remakes, *High Noon* continues to fascinate as a political allegory. It was written by Carl Foreman, who subsequently endured a long spate of blacklisting for alleged Communist sympathies. (He had to use an alias when he co-wrote *The Bridge on the River Kwai*, and couldn't accept his award when that 1957 movie earned an Oscar for Best Adapted Screenplay.) For those inclined to bother, the movie is easily interpreted as a metaphor for the climate of fear generated by McCarthyism in the 1950s, a period when many directors, writers, and actors were abandoned by old friends — were treated as pariahs, actually — because they had been branded as "subversives."

Aside from its politics, *High Noon* remains noteworthy because of its formal structure. The 85-minute movie is ingeniously paced and edited to sustain the illusion of its unfolding in "real time," methodically and inexorably counting down to the final showdown. To intensify the suspense, director Zinnemann and Elmo Williams, his Oscar-wining editor, occasionally cut away to close-ups of relentlessly ticking clocks, effectively underscoring Will's mounting desperation.

All well and good, of course. But what almost always goes unmentioned in discussions of *High Noon* are the glancing hints and subtle intimations that suggest maybe, just maybe, the entire situation isn't as black and white as it seems. Here and there, you can spot clear-cut signs that, for some people in Hadleyville, Will Kane has been a sanctimonious spoilsport who won't be missed or mourned. It's not so much that they're afraid to offer help — rather, it's more like they're eager to witness long-delayed payback. Or, as a hotelkeeper bluntly says of Will, "He's got a comeuppance coming." Obviously, Frank Miller still has friends and admirers throughout the town. Just as obviously, Will hasn't done nearly enough during his tenure as marshal to sway their allegiance.

And then there's the delicate issue of sexual intrigue. Delicate, that is, because a 1952 movie couldn't be terribly explicit about who might be sleeping with whom, and why they might not want anyone to know about it. Early on, *High Noon* none-too-subtly indicates that Will once had a major hankering for Helen Ramirez (Katy Jurado), a harshly beautiful and fiercely proud Mexican woman who used to dally with Frank Miller. Is that why Will arrested Frank in the first place? Was he eager to remove a romantic rival? The questions linger in the air, tantalizingly unanswered.

Given the exigencies of time, place, and local custom, Will more than likely felt he could never openly court, much less marry, someone like Helen. (A local businessman is grateful for her help as a silent partner — but she knows enough not to ever insist that he ever be seen in public with her.) Even so, that hasn't stopped Harvey, the swaggering and over-compensating deputy, from trying to replace Will in Helen's affections after the marshal attached himself to a respectably Anglo sweetheart. Unfortunately, a callow boy is no substitute for a mature (albeit image-conscious) man, and Helen tells Harvey as much the first time we see them together in *High Noon*. Which, of course, suggests that professional frustration isn't Harvey's only motivation in his refusal to help Will.

Late in the movie, the two men meet in a barn. Will briefly considers saddling a horse and riding away, and Harvey strongly encourages this tactical retreat. But no, Will just can't bring himself to cut and run. Harsh words are exchanged, accusations are made — and the upshot is a viciously brutal fistfight. The Oedipal undertones are unsettling, if not entirely unexpected. In fact, the testosterone-fueled slugfest is so purposefully protracted, and so charged with sexual jealousy, the final gunplay almost appears anti-climactic.

It just goes to show you: Even in a Western restricted by Production Code constraints, there may be more than one reason why a man's got to do what a man's got to do.

SPECS:

High Noon — Cast: Gary Cooper, Grace Kelly, Thomas Mitchell, Lloyd Bridges, Katy Juardo, Otto Kruger, Lon Chaney Jr., and Henry Morgan. Director: Fred Zinnemann. Screenplay: Carl Foreman, based on the story *The Tin Star* by John W. Cunningham. Running time: 85 minutes. Year of release: 1952. DVD distributor: Republic Entertainment.

SUBJECTS FOR FURTHER RESEARCH:

Once Upon a Time in the West (1968) — Sergio Leone offers a tip of the Stetson to *High Noon* during the opening minutes of his sprawling Western epic, as three mangy hired guns (including Jack Elam, who appears unbilled as a drunk in Zinnemann's film) wait at a train depot to ambush Charles Bronson. Not surprisingly, the depot turns out to be their final destination, not his.

Outland (1981) — *High Noon* in outer space, with Sean Connery effectively cast as a twenty-first-century marshal who awaits the arrival of bad guys on a mining planet where almost everyone else (except for a grizzled doctor played by Frances Sternhagen) is too corrupt or afraid to help.

Nick of Time (1995) — John Badham's modestly clever thriller unfolds in real time, a la *High Noon*. Johnny Depp stars as an innocent businessman whose daughter is kidnapped by villains (led by Christopher Walken) intent on forcing him to assassinate a troublesome politician. The plot owes more than a bit to Sidney J. Furie's *The Naked Runner* (1967), in which Frank Sinatra played a similarly beleaguered businessman.

LESSON FOR FILMMAKERS:

Jean-Luc Godard once claimed that the best way to criticize someone else's movie is to make one of your own. Maybe he was thinking of Howard Hawks, who made little secret of his contempt for *High Noon*, and *Rio Bravo*, which Hawks filmed partly as a response to Fred Zinnemann's Oscar-winning classic. "I didn't think a good sheriff was going to go running around town like a chicken with his head off asking for help," Hawks told film historian Joseph McBride, "and finally his Quaker wife had to save him. That isn't my idea of a good Western sheriff. I said that a good sheriff would turn around and say, 'How good are you? Are you good enough to take the best man they've got?' The fellow would probably say no, and he'd say, 'Well, then I'd just have to take care of you.' And that scene was in *Rio Bravo*."

SHANE

Although some detractors complain about its solemnity and self-consciousness, George Stevens' *Shane* remains one of the most widely revered and frequently plagiarized Westerns ever made. Indeed, many of the very elements most often derided by its critics — the Technicolor scenic splendor, the knightly sheen of the hero's buckskin attire, the stately parade of conventions and archetypes — are among the things that make this must-see movie so beloved by those who embrace "classic Westerns" (i.e., Westerns filmed before '60s revisionism complicated the genre) as inspiring, entertaining, and altogether unironic American myths.

Of course, if you define a myth as a movie that most people automatically assume they've seen, even if they haven't, because so many other movies have reprised its basic plot, then Stevens' saga certainly qualifies for that label. Faithfully adapted from a popular novel by Jack Schaefer, *Shane* spins a tale that already seemed whiskery back in 1952, when the movie first appeared in theaters. Even so, this particular telling of the oft-told tale has become the paradigm, partly because of Stevens' reverential approach — which, at times, borders on the ritualistic — and largely because at least two lead players offer definitive portrayals of their familiar characters.

Alan Ladd is spot-on perfect as Shane, a mysterious gunfighter who providentially appears in a Wyoming community just when the clash between homesteaders and cattle ranchers is turning uglier and bloodier. Shane finds himself impressed by the hearty industriousness of Joe Starrett (Van

Heflin), a farmer who's determined to work the land and protect his family. Just as important, Shane also finds himself drawn to the homesteader's wife, Marian (Jean Arthur), even though both of them are too noble to ever act on their obvious attraction. (In the 1960s, when *Shane* was turned into a short-lived TV series staring David Carradine, producers "solved" the problem of this taboo love by turning the wife into a widow.)

Eager to escape his never-discussed but clearly unpleasant past, Shane wants to settle down and, who knows, maybe work as a hired hand in this bucolic valley of "sodbusters." He's amused by the idolatry of young Joey (Brandon De Wilde), the Starretts' precocious son, who views the semi-retired gunfighter as a superhero. But Shane doesn't want to be a hero, rightly figuring that once he demonstrates his lethal talents, he'll have to exile himself from Eden.

For roughly the first half of the movie, Shane refuses to be pushed into gunplay or fistfights, even when he's confronted by a belligerent thug (Ben Johnson) employed by the Ryker brothers, the cattle kings who want the homesteaders to vacate their property. The Rykers don't take no for an answer, or even acknowledge it as an option. So when Shane finally starts to stand up for himself, and for the homesteaders, the brothers send for a hired gun — a bigger and badder than life hombre named Jack Wilson (Jack Palance in a career-defining performance) — to expedite the expulsion of the sodbusters and their savior.

Shane is the kind of myth that relies on the natural or temporarily willed innocence of its audience to achieve maximum impact. Stevens sorely tests your suspension of disbelief while introducing Wilson, a malevolent figure whose effortless ability to radiate bad vibes — dogs whimper and turn tail as he approaches — pushes the movie perilously close to self-parody. But the laughter catches in your throat when Wilson mercilessly goads a hopelessly outmatched homesteader (the perpetually put-upon Elisha Cook Jr.) into a showdown. Wilson draws first, then pauses — tauntingly, sadistically — while his opponent stands, abashed and afraid, in the middle of a muddy street. Then Wilson pulls the trigger, reveling in his own evil as he relishes the gratuitous slaughter.

After that, you know — you just *know* — that Shane will never find peace in this valley.

If you know anything about Ladd's unhappy off-screen life — chronically insecure, discontent, and self-critical, he died at age fifty after overdosing on alcohol and sedatives — you can easily be distracted by the pained melancholy of his performance (to say nothing of his character's near-suicidal actions in the final reel). Even so, that melancholy emerges as primary color in the movie's romanticized portrait of the gunfighter as a tragic hero, forever cursed by his own prowess to remain apart from less formidable but much happier mortals.

Despite his relatively short stature, Ladd never had trouble being persuasive as a movie tough guy. In *Shane*, however, that toughness is effectively undercut, and thereby enhanced, by the title character's wistful sense of longing for roads not taken, and his awareness of options no longer accessible. At the end, when Joey's famously mournful cry to the departing hero — "Come back, Shane!" — echoes throughout the valley, the *frisson* is all the more affecting as you realize the boy is, quite literally, asking for the impossible.

SPECS:

Shane — Stars: Alan Ladd, Jean Arthur, Van Heflin, Brandon De Wilde, Jack Palance, Ben Johnson, Edgar Buchanan, and Elisha Cook Jr. Director: George Stevens. Screenplay: A.B. Guthrie Jr. and Jack Sher, based on the novel by Jack Schaefer. Running time: 117 minutes. Year of release: 1952. DVD distributor: Paramount Home Video.

SUBJECTS FOR FURTHER RESEARCH:

Pale Rider (1985) — Clint Eastwood does double duty as director and star of this unofficial *Shane* remake, which plays like a more benign version of his own *High Plains Drifter* (1973). Eastwood's seemingly invulnerable gunman appears as the answer to a frightened child's prayer when gold miners are tyrannized by an evil land baron.

Soldier (1998) — *Shane* in outer space, with Kurt Russell well-cast as an obsolete fighting machine who defends a colony of intergalactic pioneers against an attack by DNA-enhanced warriors under the command of Jason Scott Lee.

The Negotiator (1998) — Are we meant to assume Shane is dying at the end of George Stevens' 1952 Western? The question fuels a lively ongoing debate between the central characters of F. Gary Gray's exciting action-thriller: a hostage negotiator (Samuel L. Jackson) framed for murder, and a colleague (Kevin Spacey) determined to talk him into surrendering.

LESSON FOR FILMMAKERS:

If Woody Allen ever decides to direct a Western — okay, wipe that smile off your face! — it very likely will be heavily influenced by *Shane*, one of his favorite American movies. No kidding. While discussing the 1952 classic with Rick Lyman of the *New York Times*, Allen sounded especially impressed by Stevens's skillful set-up for the final showdown between Shane and Jack Wilson. "Shane doesn't want to get back into gunfighting," Allen noted. "He's been trying the whole movie to put it behind him. But he knows that the only way to put an end to the violence in the valley is for him to do it. That's what makes the film great in my eyes. He knows. He's got to go in there and kill them. And sometimes in life — it's such an ugly truth — there is no other way out of a situation but you've got to go in there and kill them. Very few of us are brave enough or have the talent to do it. The world is full of evil, and rationalized evil, and evil out of ignorance, and there are times when that evil reaches the level of pure evil, like Jack Palance, and there is no other solution but to go in there and kill them."

THE SEARCHERS

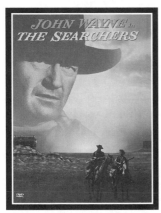

Back in 1979, long before Kevin Bacon was designated the center of the pop-culture universe, critic Stuart Byron argued in a much-discussed *New York* magazine essay that John Ford's *The Searchers* was the primary influence for an entire generation of American filmmakers. Indeed, according to Byron, everything from Martin Scorsese's *Taxi Driver* (1976) to George Lucas's *Star Wars* (1977), from Sergio Leone's *Once Upon a Time in the West* (1969) to Quentin Tarantino's *Kill Bill: Vol. 2* (2004), contain thematic and/or visual elements that could be traced to Ford's classic drama of obsession and pursuit.

You could argue, of course, that Byron overstated his case. What's beyond debate, however, is his judgment that *The Searchers* is one of the truly great American movies, an epic Western that expands and transcends the limitations of its genre by offering a darkly powerful counterpoint to the reassuring clichés of standard-issue horse operas. Even when viewed nearly a half-century after its initial theatrical release, Ford's masterwork seems fresh and vital — and, yes, surprisingly contemporary — as it undermines audience assumptions about what to expect from Westerns in general, and "a John Wayne movie" in particular.

Wayne gives one of his finest and most complex performances here as Ethan Edwards, a former Confederate soldier who returns to Texas in 1868 after a string of post-Civil War misadventures. (His favorite response to idle threats — "That'll be the day!" — inspired the signature song of '50s pop star Buddy Holly.) At first, Ethan is greeted with open arms by his brother, Aaron (Walter Coy), who lives with his family — wife Martha (Dorothy Jordan), son Ben (Robert Lyndon), daughters Lucy (Pippa Scott) and Debbie (Lana Wood) — on a remote homestead in an area where Indian raids are common. Gradually, however, long-simmering tensions between the two brothers bubble to the surface. More important, it becomes increasingly clear, to the audience if not to Aaron, that Martha secretly loves her errant brother-in-law.

Ethan's own feelings are indirectly revealed when, after he returns from a hunt for stolen cattle, he finds Aaron, Martha, and Ben have been massacred — and Lucy and Debbie have been abducted — by marauding Comanches. Fearing a fate worse than death for his nieces, Ethan gives chase, accompanied by Marty (Jeffrey Hunter), a "half-breed" orphan raised to adulthood by Aaron, and Brad (Harry Carey Jr.), Lucy's boyfriend. Early on, Lucy is found slain, and Brad dies while trying to avenge her. But Ethan and Marty survive to continue their quest for several years — for very different reasons.

Working from a sprawling yet engrossing script by Frank S. Nugent, Ford subtly hints that Ethan may in fact be Debbie's true father. And even if he isn't, he is implacably determined to find his last living blood relative, and to save her from becoming the "squaw" of the notorious Chief Scar (Henry Brandon). In most other Westerns, Ethan's obsession would be presented uncritically as a noble endeavor. But in *The Searchers*, Ford infuses his story with a troubling moral ambiguity by repeatedly emphasizing that Ethan is a fanatical racist who rarely hides his contempt for the "half-breed" Marty, and who likely will kill Debbie (played as a teen-ager by Lana's big sister, Natalie Wood) if he discovers she has been living as Scar's wife.

Which is why Marty continues along for the ride: The younger man knows that, if they ever do find Debbie, he may have to kill Ethan to save her.

The Searchers is not without flaws. The aggressively raucous "comic relief" scenes are even more intrusive here than in most other Ford movies, and the subplot involving Marty and Laurie (Vera Miles), the girl he leaves behind while riding with Ethan, is astonishingly silly. It doesn't help much that, whether he's seriously emoting or simply pratfalling, Jeffrey Hunter is, to put it charitably, overly intense. And it helps even less that Ken Curtis (as Marty's romantic rival) appears to have walked in from a *Beverly Hillbillies* rerun.

But these minor flaws are overshadowed by everything that is so stunningly right in *The Searchers*, a film justly famed for the extraordinary beauty and emotional impact of Ford's widescreen compositions. Of the movie's many striking images, two are especially worthy of note. In the first, during the opening minutes, a Texas Ranger (played with robust authority by Ward Bond) stands in the dining area of a frontier cabin, drinking a cup of coffee. Quite inadvertently, he spots Martha in the next room as she lovingly embraces Ethan's jacket. He quickly averts his eyes — and leaves no room for doubt that he will never reveal what he has seen.

Ethan, the movie's heart of darkness, figures prominently in another unforgettable image. Throughout *The Searchers*, Wayne gives a performance that is profoundly eloquent as both a concise summation and a skeptical critique of his entire career in Westerns. But he is never more affecting than in the closing moments, as Ethan is viewed through the doorway of another cabin, standing alone far away, not quite able to move, while Debbie is warmly welcomed back into civilization. The door closes. For Ethan, it will never open again.

SPECS:

The Searchers — Stars: John Wayne, Jeffrey Hunter, Vera Miles, Ward Bond, and Natalie Wood. Directed by John Ford. Screenplay: Frank S. Nugent, based on the novel by Alan Le May. Running time: 119 minutes. Year of release: 1956. DVD distributor: Warner Home Video.

SUBJECTS FOR FUTHER RESEARCH:

Hardcore (1979) — Paul Schrader, screenwriter of *Taxi Driver*, used the *Searchers* scenario as his roadmap for another walk on the wild side in this drama about a repressed Calvinist (George C. Scott) who obsessively wades through the porno underworld in search of his runaway daughter. Schrader "quotes" another John Ford classic by having a seedy private eye (Peter Boyle) routinely address Scott's character as "Pilgrim," John Wayne's nickname for James Stewart in Ford's *The Man Who Shot Liberty Valence* (1962).

Unforgiven (1992) — Nearly forty years after John Wayne purposefully tarnished his image as a straight-shooting hero in *The Searchers*, Clint Eastwood took an even more critical approach to debunking his own mythos while playing a remorseful yet relentless killer in this brutally violent revisionist Western.

Star Wars Episode II: Attack of the Clones (2002) — George Lucas tipped his hat to John Ford by presenting the first turning point in *Star Wars* (1977) — Luke's discovery of his murdered aunt and uncle in their burnt-out home — as a visual "quote" of the first turning point in *The Searchers*. A quarter-century later, Lucas continued to echo his mentor: Compare Anakin Skywalker's hunt for his abducted mother — he drops down a cliff, then stealthily enters an enemy camp — to strikingly similar activity near the end of Ford's Western.

LESSON FOR FILMMAKERS:

Great filmmakers learn from great films. Steven Spielberg told Stuart Byron in 1979 that he had watched *The Searchers* a dozen times, including twice while on location for *Close Encounters of the Third Kind* (1977), for instruction and inspiration. Spielberg started learning his lessons at a very early age: While he was a seventh-grader in the '50s, he filmed his own two-reel version of *The Searchers* in a friend's backyard, using a backdrop of Ford's beloved Monument Valley painted on a bedsheet.

R<u>IO</u> B<u>RAVO</u>

There's a cold-blooded killer in the small-town jail, and Sheriff John T. Chance aims to keep him there until the varmint gets a fair trial and a quick hanging. Unfortunately, the killer's brother is the most powerful man in the territory, with scads of hired guns to enforce his whim of iron. Even more unfortunately, Chance is seriously outmanned and outgunned as he holds out against the bad guys. During the sporadic siege, the sheriff's only allies are a discredited drunk with a trembling trigger finger, a crotchety and crippled old coot, and a naïve young gunslinger with a decidedly non-cowboyish coiffure.

Nerves fray and tempers flare as the unlikely heroes pass long hours in the jail. Tensions mount to near-unbearable extremes, until the drunk, the coot, and the gunslinger feel compelled to take drastic measures. And so, they… *sing*?

That's right. In the Wild West according to Howard Hawks' *Rio Bravo*, characters reveal themselves through meaningful gestures. And since two of those characters are played by famous singers — crooner Dean Martin as the heavy-drinking deputy, teen idol Ricky Nelson as the callow sharpshooter — Hawks felt the best way to demonstrate their grace under pressure would be to have them join voices in a flavorsome frontier ballad ("My Rifle, My Pony and Me"). The musical mood lightens as the duo becomes a trio: The gimpy crank played by grizzled character actor Walter Brennan (*My Darling Clementine*, *To Have and Have Not*) joins the fun while Sheriff Chance, played by Western icon John Wayne, grins approvingly.

Howard Hawks directed dozens of diverse movies — everything from musicals to war stories, gangster melodramas to screwball comedies — throughout a prodigious and prolific career that spanned from the silent era to the early '70s. But *Rio Bravo* stands apart from his other certifiable masterpieces as a uniquely revered cult fave, one that elicits rapturous praise from fans and filmmakers alike. (Quentin Tarantino famously declared: "When I'm getting serious about a girl, I show her *Rio Bravo*, and she better fucking like it.") Its stature has relatively little to do with its simple but serviceable storyline — which Hawks and co-screenwriter Leigh Bracket later recycled for *El Dorado* (1967) and *Rio Lobo* (1970) — and almost everything to do with its being a triumph of distinctive style over commonplace substance.

Hawks made *Rio Bravo* in 1959, a time when fully a third of the filmed series on prime-time network television were Westerns. (Brennan and Nelson were regulars on popular TV sitcoms — *The Real McCoys* and *The Adventures of Ozzie and Harriet*, respectively — when they strapped on their shootin' irons for Hawks.) As Todd McCarthy notes in his invaluable *Howard Hawks: The Grey Fox of Hollywood*, the director figured that, due to the sheer volume of broadcast horse operas, audiences were weary of overworked, formulaic plots. "But if you can keep them from knowing what the plot is," Hawks reasoned, "you have a chance of holding their interest." Which is why Hawks — justly famed for the snappy pacing and rapid-fire dialogue of his '30s and '40s movies — opted for a more deliberate and indirect approach while cantering through familiar territory.

In *Rio Bravo*, action is not nearly as important as reaction and interaction. That is, the movie is propelled by behavioral detail, not plot mechanics, as we savor a typically Hawksian scenario of isolated professionals who remain true to personal codes of honor and duty — even as they grapple with limitations, weaknesses, inner demons, and really nasty hangovers — while bound together for a common purpose (in this case, keeping a killer behind bars while trying to avoid being killed).

As often happens in a Hawks film, male characters express their unspoken and entirely platonic affection through the exchange of favors or inanimate objects. (Chance often rolls cigarettes for his drunken deputy, who's too trembly to complete the task himself.) Meanwhile, the most substantial female character — Feathers (Angie Dickinson), a leggy lady with a sordid past — proves her worthiness to the hero by making few demands, remaining self-sufficient, cracking wise just like the guys and, most important, not getting tediously teary when a man's got to do what a man's got to do. She also paraphrases the memorable come-on of the ultimate Hawksian heroine — Lauren Bacall in *To Have and Have Not* — by pointedly reminding Chance that he doesn't have to do much to have her.

During the first four minutes, Hawks returns to his silent-movie roots by vividly defining — with audacious precision, without a word of dialogue — the nature of the relationship between Chance and Dude (Martin), the depths of Dude's self-loathing, the viciousness of a casual killer (Claude Akins), Chance's unshakable devotion to justice, and Dude's fumbling first steps toward self-redemption. Then, with the premise of the piece sufficiently established, Hawks shifts his focus and slows his pace while rising to his self-imposed challenge. In the end, *Rio Bravo* isn't about capturing a killer or thwarting a jailbreak. Rather, it's about stealthily telling a story while events unfold with a randomness that is far more apparent than real.

SPECS:

Rio Bravo — Stars: John Wayne, Dean Martin, Ricky Nelson, Walter Brennan, Angie Dickinson, Ward Bond, and John Russell. Directed by Howard Hawks. Screenplay: Jules Furthman and Leigh Brackett. Running time: 141 minutes. Year of release: 1959. DVD distributor: Warner Home Video.

SUBJECTS FOR FURTHER RESEARCH:

El Dorado (1967) — Howard Hawks more or less reprises *Rio Bravo*, with Robert Mitchum subbing in the Dean Martin role and James Caan kinda-sorta filling in for Ricky Nelson, in a sturdily made Western with an affectingly melancholy undercurrent. Look for the scene in which Hawks, slyly acknowledging his deification by French film critics, makes a fleeting allusion to François Truffaut's *Shoot the Piano Player* (1960).

Support Your Local Sheriff (1969) — Burt Kennedy's amusingly tongue-in-cheeky Western incorporates several elements from *Rio Bravo* in its spoofy plot about an Australian-bound drifter (an immensely appealing James Garner) who reluctantly becomes the lawman in a town direly in need of one. Cast as the father of an imprisoned killer (Bruce Dern), Walter Brennan offers a comical riff on the dead-serious villain he portrayed back in John Ford's *My Darling Clementine* (1946).

Assault on Precinct 13 (1976) — There's a lot of *Rio Bravo* (and a hunk of *Night of the Living Dead*) in John Carpenter's low-budget, high-octane urban thriller about cops, convicts, and not-so-innocent bystanders holding out against street gangs in an isolated, inner-city police precinct house. Carpenter tips his hat to Hawks' classic by using the pseudonym of John T. Chance for his film editor's credit.

LESSON FOR FILMMAKERS:

"My favorite Western is *Rio Bravo*," says John Carpenter. "It's the situation and setup. I could remake that 100 times and be happy." Carpenter freely admits that he's already used Howard Hawks' classic twice as a template — for *Ghosts of Mars* (2001) as well as *Assault on Precinct 13* — and he'll likely be a repeat offender. As far as he's concerned, every movie Hawks ever made, in every genre, should be studied by all would-be filmmakers. But seeing *Rio Bravo* is especially instructive. When he was planning his own first films, Carpenter says, ""I kept asking myself, why did I go see *Rio Bravo* five times in 1959? Because it was an emotional film, and I love emotional films, films that get people emotionally involved, that manipulate people to feel something... When I was a kid, those were the types of films that took me away from my everyday life. Sitting in a theater made me a whole person. The more tension, suspense and emotion, the more I got into the film. And I knew that was the kind of film I wanted to make."

A FISTFUL OF DOLLARS

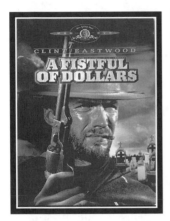

Looking very much like something the cat dragged in, thought twice about, and dragged outside again, the gritty, grimy stranger rides into the flyspeck border town. He passes a dead man who's been tied to the saddle of his cantering horse and adorned with a cryptic sign: "Adios, Amigo." The stranger tips his hat, then rides on.

Draped in a tatty serape and riding a woefully weary mule, he endures the derisive laughter of four thuggish cowboys who make rude remarks about his humble steed and threadbare attire. They fire their guns into the ground, spooking the mule into a terrified gallop. The stranger manages to dismount only by grabbing a makeshift streetlamp.

In a decrepit cantina, the barkeep brings the stranger up to speed: The town is dominated by two rival gangs, and each side uses hired guns to maintain an uneasy truce. To earn a job, however, an applicant must be a quick draw and a cold killer. The stranger appears intrigued by the employment opportunities.

Back on the street, the stranger walks over to the thuggish cowboys, pausing only to tell an industrious coffinmaker: "Get three coffins ready." He calmly confronts his tormentors, and advises them to apologize to his mule. They respond by laughing. So the stranger flips back his serape, revealing the six-guns at his sides, and the laughter stops.

The stranger rasps: "I don't think it's nice, you laughin'. You see, my mule don't like people laughing. He gets the crazy idea you're laughin'

at him. Now if you apologize, like I know you're going to, I might con-
vince him that you really didn't mean it..."

For a long, lingering moment, there is nothing but an ominous silence.
Then the thugs start to draw their guns. But not nearly fast enough. The
stranger fires repeatedly, hitting each mark. The local sheriff — who just
happens to be the employer of the newly deceased — appears from out
of nowhere to issue impotent threats. The stranger replies: "If you're the
sheriff, you better get these men in the ground." And then, as an aside to
the coffinmaker, he adds: "My mistake. Four coffins..."

All of which left movie audiences of the '60s gaping incredulously and
gasping: "Just what the hell kind of Western *is* this?"

Filmed in Spain by an Italian director inspired by a Japanese script, with
Italian and German supporting players backing an American TV star in
the lead role, *A Fistful of Dollars* represented an innovative twist in multicultural cross-pollination. Director Sergio Leone took the conventions
of traditional sagebrush sagas and pushed them to unprecedented
extremes of graphic violence and seriocomic cynicism. By doing so, he
more or less invented a new subgenre — the so-called "Spaghetti
Western" — in which old rules did not apply, and new attitudes propelled heroes and villains alike.

Inspired by *Yojimbo* (1961) — Akira Kurosawa's often darkly comical
samurai saga about a warrior who pits warring clans against each other
for fun and profit — *Fistful* stripped away the noble motives and altru-
istic heroism that had been hallowed hallmarks of the Western genre.
(Yojimbo itself obviously drew inspiration from vintage American cowboy flicks — and, perhaps not so obviously, from the 1929 crime novel
Red Harvest by Dashiell Hammett.) The protagonist is a steely-eyed
pragmatist who is driven by greed and self-interest, not justice and self-
denial, and who gets into trouble only when he impulsively aids a wife
and mother commandeered by a bandit chief. He shoots first — and last
— and rarely bothers to ask questions afterwards. He comes off as a
good guy primarily because the bad guys are much, much worse.

Critics debate whether Leone was ignorant of genre conventions or,
more likely, chose to ignore them. Whatever the reason, *A Fistful of*

Dollars violates almost all of the unwritten laws that had heretofore defined the American-made Western — including, most shockingly, the rule that mandated a character's gun and its lethal impact should never be shown in the same frame. In 1964, when this must-see movie first appeared in Leone's native Italy, and '67, when it finally appeared in America, the wanton slaughter was all the more startling because most of the bullets were fired by Clint Eastwood, the personable young star of *Rawhide*, a then-popular Western television series, in which the actor played a thoroughly conventional, uncomplicatedly amiable cowboy. *A Fistful of Dollars* turned Eastwood into an international star through the simple expedient of transforming Mr. Nice Guy into a down-and-dirty anti-hero who would become known throughout the world as The Man With No Name. Several other actors — including Ty Hardin, Edd Byrnes, John Phillip Law, Alex Cord and — no kidding! — Elvis Presley (in 1969's *Charro!*) would follow in Eastwood's hoofprints, attempting similar image makeovers during the heyday of "Spaghetti Westerns," but with considerably less success.

Eastwood often has claimed Leone "operacized" the Western. The description is apt, given the director's penchant for grandiose overstatement in *Fistful* and its two more ambitious sequels, *For a Few Dollars More* (1965) and *The Good, The Bad and The Ugly* (1966). Time and again, you see self-consciously ritualized gunfights that intercut immense wide shots of wary antagonists and intense close-ups of their squinty eyes. Everything is overlaid with Ennio Morricone's alternately twangy and thunderous music, and protracted by pauses sufficiently pregnant to produce quintuplets.

Leone's subsequent films — most notably, his magnificent *Once Upon a Time in the West* (1968) — display even greater degrees of operatic flamboyance. But his "Man With No Name" films have remained his most significant and enduringly influential legacy. Originally derided by some critics as blood-soaked pastiches and genre-defiling follies — the term "Spaghetti Western" originally was coined as a dismissive put-down — they long ago attained respectability for their own considerable merits, and for inspiring such action filmmakers as John Carpenter, Sam Peckinpah, John Woo, Walter Hill, Quentin Tarantino, and Robert Rodriguez. (Rodriguez admits that *Once Upon a Time in Mexico*

[2003], the follow-up to his *El Mariachi* [1992] and *Desperado* [1995], completes his own version of a "Spaghetti Western" trilogy.)

The only downside of that legacy, argues Leone biographer Christopher Fraying, has been the oversimplification — or, to be less diplomatic, the dumbing down — of many Hollywood action flicks produced for international consumption. Leone assumed "a low boredom threshold on the part of the audience," Fraying says, "and therefore jerked them to attention every eight or ten minutes with a major action climax that, in the old days, would have sustained an entire movie... (I)t was a series of electric shocks, really." Not unlike the rival Italian filmmakers who churned out copycat "Spaghetti Westerns" during the '60s and '70s, too many of Leone's acolytes have proven heavily addicted to high voltage, and far too fond of sounds and fury that signify nothing.

Speaking of influence: Without taking anything away from Sergio Leone's primary role as *auteur*, credit must be given to the advertising department of United Artists, the U.S. distributor of *A Fistful of Dollars* and its two sequels, for playing a key role in the creation of a mythos. Even though Eastwood's character is referred to by a different name in each film — Joe (*Fistful*), Monco (*Few More*), and Blondie (*Good, Bad and Ugly*) — the UA team chose to pique interest by dubbing him The Man With No Name in trailers, posters and newspaper ads while releasing English-dubbed versions of the three films more or less back to back between February 1967 and January 1968. The movies were hits, and the Man With No Name has remained part of the legend ever since.

SPECS:

A Fistful of Dollars — Stars: Clint Eastwood, Marianne Koch, Gian Maria Volonte (billed as John Wels), Wolfgang Lukschy, S. Rupp, and Joe Edger. Director: Sergio Leone. Screenplay: Victor A. Catena, G. Schock, Duccio Tessari, and Sergio Leone. Running time: 100 minutes. Year of release: 1964. DVD distributor: MGM Home Entertainment.

SUBJECTS FOR FURTHER RESEARCH:

Sabata (1970) — After Clint Eastwood, lean and mean Lee Van Cleef (who memorably appeared opposite Eastwood in Sergio Leone's *For a Few Dollars More* and *The Good, The Bad and The Ugly*) was the American actor who enjoyed greatest success as a grizzled anti-hero in "Spaghetti Westerns." In Gianfranco Parolini's violent drama, one of his best starring vehicles, Van Cleef credibly portrays a master gunslinger who covets the booty of Army payroll thieves. Parolini directed two sequels, including one (*Adios, Sabata*, 1971) in which Yul Brynner temporarily assumed the title role.

Mad Max Beyond Thunderdome (1985) — Even more than *The Road Warrior* (1981), the third chapter of George Miller's "Mad Max" franchise is heavily influenced by Sergio Leone's "Spaghetti Western" trilogy. Note the echoes of *A Fistful of Dollars* when Mel Gibson's Max strolls into Bartertown, and catch the reference to Max as "The Man With No Name."

Last Man Standing (1996) — Walter Hill's remake of *Yojimbo* and *A Fistful of Dollars* is a thoroughly ridiculous and improbably enjoyable melodrama set in 1930s Texas, where a taciturn stranger (Bruce Willis) positions himself between rival gangs of bootleggers. He plays both sides against each other, with predictably violent results.

LESSON FOR FILMMAKERS:

If you're going to make a remake, be sure you own the rights to the original film. Everybody knows that *A Fistful of Dollars* is a remake of Akira Kurosawa's *Yojimbo* (1961). What isn't so widely known, however, is that *Fistful* was an entirely *unauthorized* remake. After screening Leone's version, Kurosawa wrote the Italian filmmaker to complain: "It is a very fine film, but it is my film." Lawyers were hired, court papers were filed — and Leone's production company wound up paying a considerable sum to Kurosawa. Meanwhile, distribution of the movie in the U.S. and Great Britain was delayed for two and a half years during the protracted negotiations.

THE WILD BUNCH

pproximately ten minutes were trimmed from *The Wild Bunch*, Sam Peckinpah's career-defining magnum opus, during the early weeks of the film's 1969 theatrical release. Surprisingly, considering the revisionist Western's notoriety for slo-mo carnage and other graphic mayhem, the deleted scenes had more to do with character development than bloody violence. They were cut primarily to make the movie move faster — and, of course, to enable exhibitors to schedule an additional showtime each day.

When the missing footage finally was restored more than a quarter-century later, audiences could better appreciate the complexity of the relationship between characters played by William Holden and Robert Ryan. Just as important, the restoration allowed for a fairer judgment of Peckinpah's movie as a whole. It remains, then as now, a profoundly troubling masterpiece that is much better, and more ferociously magnificent, than the sum of its parts.

The sentimentality of some scenes comes dangerously close to self-parody. And the aggressively robust camaraderie of the outlaw anti-heroes — a dream-team ensemble that includes Holden, Ernest Borgnine, Ben Johnson, Warren Oates, Edmund O'Brien, and Jaime Sanchez — occasionally seems as synthetic as friendships romanticized in beer commercials.

And yet, ultimately, none of that really matters. Despite these excesses — maybe even *because* of them — *The Wild Bunch* is the most affecting American movie ever made about men who remain loyal to a private code of honor, and to each other, even as they engage in the most reprehensible criminal acts. "When you side with a man," Holden proclaims, "you stay with him. And when you can't do that, you're no better than an animal."

At the same time, *The Wild Bunch* is the Western that forever shattered our illusions about the genre. After it blazed into theaters, no one, not even John Wayne, could ever again get away with lulling us into accepting the convention of bloodless gunfights between white hats and black hats. For better or worse, Peckinpah almost single-handedly ended our Saturday matinee–informed innocence.

The story, co-written by Peckinpah and Walon Green, is set in and around the Texas-Mexico border country. The year is 1913, and time is running out for aging outlaws like Pike Bishop (Holden) and his gang.

(It might have been amusing, and enlightening, if Peckinpah had noted that these bad boys are still riding and robbing a full decade after the release of *The Great Train Robbery*, the first movie Western.)

All the outlaws want is one last big score, so they can retire. (Pike warns: "We've got to start thinking beyond our guns!") But when they try to rob a railroad payroll in the film's horrifyingly brilliant opening sequence, they nearly are killed by a vicious gang of bounty hunters reluctantly led by Pike's former ally, Deke Thornton (a dead-solid perfect Ryan). The shoot-out takes place on a crowded street, with various innocent bystanders tragically caught in the middle.

The Wild Bunch is even more violent during the outlaw gang's legendarily bloody final shoot-out with a rogue platoon of Mexican soldiers. But what makes the sequence truly extraordinary is its quietly intense prologue, as Pike and his men boldly march toward certain death in a gesture of loyalty to a captured comrade. Their unhurried stroll toward destiny is at once thrilling, suspenseful, and ineffably sad, a classic movie moment.

Peckinpah claimed in promotional interviews that he presented so much violence, in so much detail, in order to sicken the audience on the whole idea of violence. And maybe he was sincere in what he said. On the other hand, as critic Stanley Kauffmann noted in his 1969 review, the images speak louder than Peckinpah's rationalizations. Peckinpah, Kauffmann wrote, "is not an oblique puritan, he is a talented maniac who loves his bloody work. And his work is significant."

It still is. More than two decades after Peckinpah's death, directors as diverse as Martin Scorsese, Walter Hill, John Woo, and Quentin

Tarantino continue to evoke the kinetic fury of the most memorable scenes from *The Wild Bunch*. But the original has a melancholy savagery that is uniquely its own.

SPECS:

The Wild Bunch — Stars: William Holden, Ernest Borgnine, Ben Johnson, Warren Oates, Edmund O'Brien, Jaime Sanchez, Strother Martin, L.Q. Jones, Albert Dekker, Bo Hopkins, Dub Taylor, and Alfonso Arau. Directed by Sam Peckinpah. Screenplay: Sam Peckinpah, Walon Green. Running time: 145 minutes. Year of release: 1969. DVD distributor: Warner Home Video.

SUBJECTS FOR FURTHER RESEARCH:

Butch Cassidy and the Sundance Kid (1969) — Paul Newman and Robert Redford play mostly for laughs in a much lighter Western about past-their-prime outlaws. But they, too, are forced to confront the deadly serious consequences of violence in a couple of shattering scenes.

Soldier Blue (1970) — Ralph Nelson's well-meaning but borderline-unwatchable Western, all-too-obviously intended as a Vietnam War allegory, takes a sternly revisionist approach to Old West clichés by depicting U.S. Cavalry troops as genocidal monsters in their pursuit of Native Americans. The legendarily violent climax contains fare more carnage than any scene in *The Wild Bunch*.

The Wild Rovers (1971) — Among the many grittily realistic Westerns that appeared in the late '60s and early '70s, Blake Edwards' melancholy drama about aimless cowpokes (William Holden, Ryan O'Neal) who impulsively rob a bank is an underrated gem. Best scene: Holden bids farewell to a long-time friend. Edwards waits until he's finished to reveal that the buddy is dead.

LESSON FOR FILMMAKERS:

Burt Reynolds, an avid fan of *The Wild Bunch*, drew on vivid memories of the Peckinpah classic while co-starring with Bruce Dern in *Hard Ground*, a 2003 made-for-TV Western. "Bruce told me I gave him one of the best pieces of direction he'd ever received," Reynolds says. "We were shooting one night — actually, it was about 4 o'clock in the morning — and he'd taken a nasty spill off a horse a few days before, so he was hurting like hell. He wasn't going to take anything, he wanted to tough it out. But he was bent over double, just exhausted. So I said, "Think William Holden." And he knew exactly what I meant — William Holden, all beaten down but still walking proud, in *The Wild Bunch*. So he went on and did the take. And he was stunning."

≈7≈
CINEMA-
FANTASTIQUE

MᴇTROPOLIS

Call it the mother of all science-fiction movies, and you won't be far off the mark.

To view *Metropolis*, Fritz Lang's deliriously extravagant allegory of dehumanized masses and applied cybernetics, is to marvel at its profound influence on later generations of filmmakers (and their production designers). The crowning achievement of German silent cinema, it survives and thrives as the visual and thematic template for hundreds, maybe thousands, of films, comic books, teleplays — and MTV clips. No kidding: When Madonna immersed herself in "Express Yourself," director David Fincher (*Seven, Fight Club*) filmed a music video for the 1989 pop song as an elaborate, ultra-glossy, sepia-toned homage to Lang's 1927 sci-fi classic.

But wait, there's more: Lang's darkly grandiose vision of a time-warped dystopia — a teeming, sprawling cityscape where retrograde fashions and artifacts are juxtaposed with futuristic technology, mountainous skyscrapers and soulless Modernism run amok — continues to inspire such contemporary visionaries as Terry Gilliam (*Brazil*), Luc Besson (*The Fifth Element*), and Steven Spielberg (*Minority Report*).

Remarkably, none of the aforementioned acolytes who directed under the influence of *Metropolis* has ever seen Lang's film in its entirety. Tragically, neither has anyone else under the age of seventy-five. Indeed, even the justly praised 2001 restoration of *Metropolis*, which incorporated long-missing footage from archives throughout the world, is not the *Metropolis* viewed by audiences during its brief theatrical run in

Berlin and Nuremberg three-quarters of a century ago. As an on-screen title in the restored version notes: Over a quarter of the original film has to be considered lost.

What remains, however, constitutes a unique and electrifying extravaganza, an ambitiously conceived and audaciously executed epic charged with alternating currents of cautionary fabulosity, Expressionistic imagery, kitschy melodrama, pseudo-religiosity, and anything-goes razzamatazz.

Scripted by Thea von Harbou, then Lang's wife, the film pivots on escalating tensions between the pampered oligarchy that rules Metropolis from atop the immense skyscrapers, and the downtrodden workforce that toils far, far below the city streets. Lang's theatrical background is reflected in his memorable (and much-imitated) depiction of shift changes, as solid blocks of workers — heads bowed, devoid of distinguishing characteristics — march into and out of elevators, forming symmetrical arrangements like those employed by legendary stage director Max Reinhardt.

The broad silent-movie performances are frequently amusing, especially when displays of wanton lust are called for. But many of the main characters — especially Rotwang (played by Rudolph Klein-Rogge), a gleefully mad scientist with an artificial hand (shades of *Dr. Strangelove*) and the most dangerous fembot this side of an *Austin Powers* misadventure — are so indelibly vivid, they long ago evolved into archetypes.

Freder (Gustave Frohlich), the ever-so-sensitive son of Metropolis ruler Joh Fredersen (Alfred Abel), falls madly in love with Maria (Brigitte Helm), a spiritual advisor for the exploited workers, and follows her below the surface, where he witnesses a horrific industrial accident. (During one of the film's many feverish fantasies, Freder imagines the workers as human sacrifices, marching into the maw of the great god Moloch.) Fredersen doesn't want his son hanging with the wrong crowd. And he doesn't want Maria stirring up the masses. So he asks Rotwang to transform the fembot into a faux Maria, to instigate unrest that he can quell with an iron fist. Not surprisingly, nothing good comes of this.

What does it all signify? Well, what do you *want* it to signify? In 1927, German leftists were quick to condemn *Metropolis* as implicitly fascistic; at the same time, the right attacked the film as Communist rabble-rousing.

Even now, Lang's masterwork remains one of the most provocative Rorschach tests ever conceived for the cinema: You can read almost any motive or meaning into its action and imagery.

Which is not to say, however, there is no method to the apparent madness. In truth, there is an underlying foundation of mirror images and counterbalances throughout *Metropolis*. The brave new world according to Fritz Lang is a place where ancient religious imagery (both Christian and pagan) can be glimpsed amid the high-tech futurism, where totalitarian control of the overworked masses is disrupted by the equally dangerous dynamic of anarchy and mob violence.

While the dehumanized workers are transformed into automatons, Rotwang seeks to replace a lost love — who left him years earlier to marry Joh — with his "feminine" robot. As critic A.O. Scott has noted, *Metropolis* "stands between *Frankenstein* and (Steven Spielberg's) *A.I.* as an expression of the defining modern preoccupation with machines that blur the boundary between the human and the mechanical."

For decades, unfortunately, audiences have had access to only bits and pieces of Lang's magnum opus. In an ironic foreshadowing of what happened decades later to Ridley Scott's *Blade Runner* (1982) — which was drastically altered, and outfitted with voiceover narration, after disastrous preview screenings — the original three-hours-plus *Metropolis* was withdrawn from release shortly after its 1927 premiere, and whittled down to a more audience-friendly length. More cutting was mandated by Paramount, the film's U.S. distributor, which hired dramatist Channing Pollock to write new English title cards and, while he was at it, rearrange scenes to suit his own narrative designs. So many other versions were cut-and-pasted that Lang eventually resigned himself to the permanent loss of his original epic. When asked about *Metropolis* during his sunset years, he usually would reply: "Why are you so interested in a film that no longer exists?"

In the early '80s, movie music composer Giorgio Moroder (*Flashdance, Midnight Express*) devoted $2 million to restoring much of *Metropolis*. When he was finished, however, he switched on his synthesizer, hired some rock vocalists — including Pat Benatar and Freddie Mercury — and prepared a soundtrack that turned the reconstituted classic into something that looked and sounded like... well, the oldest music video in the MTV playlist. Trouble is, until the 2001 restoration, anyone who wished to savor *Metropolis* had to settle for the Moroder folly. Either that, or endure the incomprehensibly incomplete public-domain versions available only in scratchy 16mm prints (or muddy-looking VHS and DVD editions).

It speaks volumes about the bravura genius of Lang's visual stratagems and hyperbolic melodrama that, even in bastardized and/or borderline-unwatchable forms, *Metropolis* managed to inspire so many major (and minor) filmmakers, and established itself so firmly in our collective pop-culture consciousness. Most classics merely are immortal. But *Metropolis* has proven to be indestructible as well.

SPECS:

Metropolis — Stars: Brigitte Helm, Alfred Abel, Gustave Frohlich, Rudolph Klein-Rogge, Fritz Rasp, and Heinrich Georg. Directed by Fritz Lang. Screenplay: Thea von Harbou. Running time: 124 minutes. Year of release: 1927. DVD distributor: Kino Video.

SUBJECTS FOR FURTHER RESEARCH:

Batman (1989) — Thanks to the gloomy-and-doomy Expressionistic production design of Tim Burton's comic-book classic, Batman bounds through a Gotham City that appears modeled on the blueprints of *Metropolis*.

Dark City (1998) — There's actually a logical reason for the *Metropolis*-like mix of anachronisms in the costume and production design of Alex Proyas' ingenious sci-fi thriller: Inquisitive extra-terrestrials have thrown together an improvised environment for their human test subjects.

Minority Report (2002) — Steven Spielberg's cautionary sci-fi parable is set in a day-after-tomorrow Washington, DC where the crazy-quilt of futurism and antiquity suggests *Metropolis* writ large. Artfully commingling the modern and the mystical, the plot focuses on "Pre-Crime" cops who pre-emptively arrest potential killers based on tips by visionary "Pre-Cogs."

LESSON FOR FILMMAKERS:

Novelist and scriptwriter Robert Bloch (*Psycho*), who wrote several episodes of *Star Trek*, *Night Gallery*, and *Alfred Hitchcock Presents*, viewed *Metropolis* as the primary source for all subsequent sci-fi movies and TV dramas. In an '80s essay, Bloch wrote: "Lang was among the first filmmakers to foresee, and daringly dramatize, the coming conflict of Man vs. Machine, the growing schism between the new industrialist elite and the manipulated masses. The message he stated... rings even more true today: Science alone is not our savior."

FRANKENSTEIN

It is a dark and stormy night. Suddenly — amid the roar of generators, the crackling of lightning, and the feeble rustling of a reanimated corpse — a crazed scientist triumphantly wails: "It's alive! It's alive! In the name of God — now I know what it feels like to *be* God!"

Yes, Virginia, there really was a time — long ago in a distant, pre-ironic era — when audiences could listen to that kind of dialogue with a straight face. It was the same time when the actors speaking those lines weren't kidding around, or emphasizing anything with a wink-wink, nudge-nudge twist. Both they and the movies in which they appeared were — pardon the pun — deadly serious.

It was 1931 when Universal Studios scored the diabolical double play of releasing *Dracula*, the broodingly atmospheric account of the undead gent from Transylvania, and *Frankenstein*, the monster melodrama about the dangerous folly of messing around with things that man wasn't meant to mess with. For more than seven decades, both films have inspired countless sequels, remakes, parodies, and mondo-bizarro hybrids. (Anyone remember *Billy the Kid vs. Dracula*? Okay, how about *Frankenstein Meets the Space Monster*?) Even so, rarely has either film ever been equaled in influence or impact.

To be sure, most cinematic purists insist that F.W. Murnau's *Nosferatu* — which predates *Dracula* by nine years — is the first movie version of Bram Stoker's classic novel, and therefore has greater claim to being the paradigm for all subsequent vampire misadventures. (Never mind that, when it comes to choosing a necking partner, most damsels in distress would pick Bela Lugosi over *Nosferatu* star Max Schreck any night of the week.) But *Frankenstein*, James Whale's visually flamboyant version of Mary Shelley's immortal novel, is surpassed only by Whale's own *Bride of Frankenstein* (1935) as the definitive man-made-monster opus.

But wait, there's more: Whale's original go-for-baroque horror show also deserves a place in the history books as the movie that helped save a studio.

In 1931, Universal found itself on the verge of financial meltdown. The wolves were temporarily banished from the door when *Dracula* was a surprise box-office smash. But even that fortuitous windfall was not enough to sustain the status quo: Shortly after the vampire melodrama opened in New York, Universal pink-slipped 350 employees and shut down for six weeks. Then as now, conventional Hollywood logic dictated that, if at first you do succeed, try the same thing — or something very similar — again. And so, once Universal resumed full operations, the studio brass green-lit an effort to make lightning strike twice with more scary stuff.

After filmmaker Robert Florey (*Murders in the Rue Morgue*) completed some initial spadework, director James Whale — the unabashedly gay British émigré played to Oscar-worthy perfection by Ian McKellen in *Gods and Monsters* (1998) — took control of the project. When Bela Lugosi passed on playing the non-verbal monster, Whale made the inspired choice to cast Boris Karloff as the grotesque creation of scientist Henry Frankenstein (Colin Clive) after spotting the then-unknown Brit actor at a table in the studio commissary. (Karloff was grateful for his good fortune — but understandably miffed that a director might take one look at him and think: "There's my monster!") Just as important, Whale drove his production designers to literally electrifying extremes.

Take another peek at Mary Wollstonecraft Shelley's 1818 novel, and you'll notice the author avoided any explanation of how her modern-day Prometheus worked his miracles. Whale and company opted to fill in the gaps by providing the last word in a "mad scientist" laboratory, complete with spinning dials, industrial-size switches, sparking electrodes, and the mother of all operating tables. The same set later turned up in dozens of other movies, including — no kidding! — Mel Brooks' *Young Frankenstein* (1974).

Karloff doesn't appear as Frankenstein's Monster until a half-hour into the picture, but he's well worth the wait. A hulking behemoth in his undersized suit and asphalt spreader's boots, Karloff — with, of course, immeasurable help from make-up wizard Jack Pierce — is a singularly poignant bogeyman, a lost child driven to homicidal rages after being rejected by his "father." His iconographic portrayal has become the measure for all imperfect products of hubristic scientists, on screen and off.

Frankenstein set the standard for many other Universal horror movies of the 1930s and '40s, most of which appear, like Whale's original, to be set in some Middle European fantasyland where peasants swill beer and tramp around in leiderhosen, upper-class toffs speak in snooty British accents — "Perhaps you know what all this tommyrot is all about!" — and everybody is forever ready to moonlight as a member of a torch-wielding mob. The pace is amusingly zippy, the body count is surprisingly low. And while some of the lead performances haven't aged very well, that, too, is part of the fun. Colin Clive's wild-eyed Henry Frankenstein — yes, he's the one with the above-noted God complex — is a campy archetype that must be seen to be adequately disbelieved. And Dwight Frye's preternaturally creepy Fritz remains the most exuberantly loathsome of all hunchbacked assistants.

SPECS:

Frankenstein — Stars: Colin Clive, Mae Clarke, John Boles, Boris Karloff, Dwight Frye, and Edward Van Sloan. Directed by James Whale. Screenplay: Francis Edward Faragoh, Garrett Fort, and John L. Balderston, based on the play by Peggy Webling and the novel by Mary Shelley. Running time: 71 minutes. Year of release: 1931. DVD distributor: Universal.

SUBJECTS FOR FURTHER RESEARCH:

Bride of Frankenstein (1935) — James Whale's deliriously rococo sequel to his own monster smash suggests that, even before the term "high camp" was coined by critics and commentators, Whale instinctively appreciated the entertainment value of perfectly balancing shivery scares and sly self-parody.

Frankenstein 1970 (1958) — Unlike fellow bogeyman Bela Lugosi, Boris Karloff never plumbed the lowest depths of B-movie hell. (You don't see any Ed Wood movies on his resume, do you?) But he came perilously close to the bottom of the barrel in this futuristic cheapie-creepie, which cast him as a distant relative of the original Dr. Frankenstein. While a TV crew films a documentary in his castle, the good doctor tries to create life in a nuclear-powered lab. Nothing good comes of this.

Van Helsing (2004) — While concocting his revisionist monster mash, writer-director Stephen Sommers felt obligated to reprise the basic look of Boris Karloff's original bogeyman. "I knew," Sommers said, "that Frankenstein *had* to have a flat head and wear Doc Martens."

LESSON FOR FILMMAKERS:

In order to make an indelible impression with a horror movie, the fantastic must seem at least temporarily plausible. At least, that's the attitude expressed by James Whale while promoting *Frankenstein* in a 1931 *New York Times* interview: "I consider the creation of the monster to be the high spot of the film, because if the audience did not believe the thing had been really made, they would not be bothered with what it was supposed to do afterward. To build up to this I showed Frankenstein collecting his material bit by bit. He proves to the audience that he actually did know something about science, especially the ultraviolet ray, from which he was expecting the miracle to happen... Frankenstein puts the spectators in their positions, he gives final orders to Fritz, he turns the levers and sends his diabolic machine soaring upward to the roof, into the storm. He is now is a state of feverish excitement calculated to carry both the spectators in the windmill and the spectators in the theater with him. The lightning flashes. The monster begins to move. Frankenstein merely has to believe what he sees, which is all we ask the audience to do."

PLAN 9 FROM OUTER SPACE

ome people are born to be punchlines for bad jokes. Edward D. Wood Jr. — World War II veteran, Hollywood fringe-dweller, and uncloseted cross-dresser — wanted to make movies in the worst way. Unfortunately, that is precisely what he did.

Long before the term "high camp" conjured images of anything other than a mountaintop military base, Wood labored indefatigably in the 1950s netherworld of no-budget, fly-by-night film production. Among his most notorious credits: *Glen or Glenda*, a fervently sincere but dizzyingly incoherent defense of transvestitism as a way of life; *Jail Bait*, a forlornly sleazy crime melodrama notable only for an early, pre-*Hercules* appearance by a beefcakey Steve Reeves; and *Bride of the Monster*, a stark and stupid cheapie-creepie that climaxes with an irradiated Bela Lugosi battling frantically, albeit unconvincingly, with a rubber octopus.

Each of these Z-movies is of a mind-frying, jaw-dropping awfulness that must be seen to be disbelieved. And yet, at the same time, each clearly is the work of someone who passionately believes in the seriousness of his endeavor, whose intensity of purpose surely is no less than that of the people who made *Citizen Kane* or *The Seventh Seal*. Wood may have been one of the most incompetent filmmakers — if not *the* most incompetent — to ever darken a soundstage, but there's something engaging, even endearing, about the exuberance that informs his ineptitude. By virtue of his threadbare *oeuvre*, he merits canonization as the patron saint of anyone who has all of the drive and ambition, and none of the talent, to become a true artist.

And like a true artist, Wood actually did achieve a kind of immortality through his work — though not quite the kind he no doubt craved.

His awesomely awful *Plan 9 from Outer Space*, widely acknowledged as the worst movie ever made, is the yardstick by which all cinematic fiascoes are measured, a title that has become shorthand for critics, academics, and plain-vanilla movie buffs to demarcate the lowest of the lowest depths. It is, in its uniquely perverse fashion, a genuine classic. Better still, even after repeated revivals throughout the decades since its understandably limited theatrical release, it continues to live down to its reputation.

Just about everything you've ever heard about *Plan 9 from Outer Space* is true. Yes, this is the sci-fi extravaganza that Wood fancifully stitched together to utilize random footage of his idol, Bela Lugosi, that he shot shortly before the actor's tragic death in 1956. And, yes, in order to give his slapdash narrative some slight semblance of continuity, Wood really did cast his chiropractor — not-so-artfully disguised with a black cloak drawn across his face — as Lugosi's stand-in for scenes filmed much later with other actors. (Look closely, and you see the same snippets of Lugosi, pathetically resplendent in his trademark Dracula attire, used over and over *and over...*) The switcheroo is laughably ineffective, and not just because the chiropractor was a foot or so taller than Lugosi. But, then again, *Plan 9* is a movie in which the sun often appears to rise and fall several times during the course of the same scene, in which mismatched shots are conjoined with a logic that usually prevails only in a fever dream. In this context, Wood's failure to persuasively double a stand-in for a dead "guest star" is a relatively minor gaffe.

There is a plot, of sorts: Campy extraterrestrials invade California's San Fernando Valley to launch a pilot program of mass destruction, intending to raise the recently deceased to dispose of the troublesome living. Why? Well, the extraterrestrials want to nip a problem in the bud by obliterating Earthlings before they perfect a potentially catastrophic weapon that... but never mind. Such niceties as logic and motivation have little if anything to do with the movie's appeal.

Any sane individual who willingly submits himself to *Plan 9 from Outer Space* doesn't seek traditional sci-fi thrills and chills. Instead, we peruse Wood's *magnum opus* to savor ludicrously melodramatic dialogue, much of which is delivered by Criswell, a phony-baloney oracle, as narrator and master of ceremonies. ("We are all interested in the future, because that is where you and I are going to spend the rest of our lives.")

Just as important, we want to gawk in bug-eyed wonderment while bit players inadvertently jostle rubber headstones in graveyard scenes, or while two guys in military mufti stand in front of a bare wall and pretend to oversee the firing of heavy artillery at wobbly flying saucers. (Is it just me, or does one of these faux soldiers resemble a very young Steve Buscemi?) We want to snicker while actors flub their lines, or clumsily read from cuecards, or distractedly scratch their foreheads with gun barrels, while Wood damns the retakes and moves full speed ahead.

And while we're doing all of this, we are transfixed — no, mesmerized — by Edward D. Wood Jr.'s singular triumph of will over incompetence.

SPECS:

Plan 9 from Outer Space — Stars: Gregory Walcott, Mona McKinnon, Duke Moore, Tom Keene, Paul Marco, Tor Johnson, Dudley Manlove, Joanna Lee, Lyle Talbot, Vampira, and Bela Lugosi. Directed and written by Edward D. Wood Jr. Screenplay: Running time: 78 minutes. DVD distributor: Image Entertainment.

SUBJECTS FOR FURTHER RESEARCH:

Night of the Lepus (1972) — Okay, you have these giant killer rabbits, see? And they hop through the desert – ears twitching and paws pounding *in slow motion* — accompanied by creepy-spooky electronic music, until they reach a small town where they proceed to munch on…. No, I swear, I'm not making this up. And, no, despite every indication to the contrary, Ed Wood had nothing to do with it. In fact, it was cast with not-half-bad actors (including Stuart Whitman, Janet Leigh, Rory Calhoun and a pre-*Star Trek* DeForest Kelly), and released by a major Hollywood studio (MGM) as a dead-serious horror flick. Oh, the horror! The hilarity! An instant camp classic!

Ed Wood (1994) — Tim Burton's hugely entertaining and sweetly sympathetic tribute to the notoriously inept *auteur* (vividly played by Johnny

Depp) is something truly unique: A compassionate farce that evolves into a heartfelt celebration of self-delusion. Martin Landau received a richly deserved Oscar for playing Wood's partner in cinematic crimes, a decrepit but intrepid Bela Lugosi.

Battlefield Earth (2000) — Cheesy special effects. Boneheaded plotting. Bargain-basement costumes. Inadvertently hilarious dialogue. Alien invaders led by John Travolta in a fright wig and platform shoes. Ladies and gentlemen: Welcome to *Plan 9 from Outer Space* for the twenty-first century.

LESSON FOR FILMMAKERS:

Never, never, *never* get too cocky during production. You know how great you might feel on certain days? How you think everything is coming together, falling into place, working perfectly? How every performance is dead-solid perfect, or at least competent enough to be "saved" in the editing room? Well, consider this: Ed Wood doubtless felt the very same way some days on the set of *Plan 9 from Outer Space.*

2001:
A SPACE ODYSSEY

If you accept the conventional wisdom regarding the late Stanley Kubrick, your worst suspicions will be confirmed by his crowning achievement, *2001: A Space Odyssey*.

You think Kubrick was an egomaniacal control freak? Okay, maybe he was. But it's hard to see how a modest Mr. Nice Guy could have convinced a major Hollywood studio — Metro Goldwyn Mayer, no less! — to bankroll something this intellectually ambitious, tauntingly ambiguous *and* budget-bustingly expensive back in 1968. As Norman Kagan notes in *The Cinema of Stanley Kubrick*, the director spent a year and a half shooting 205 special effects shots, "many of them possible only because of technical processes Kubrick himself invented." Compared to this guy, even James Cameron seems like a meek under-achiever.

You say you've always heard Kubrick was a dour misanthrope with a sour view of humankind? Then check out the scene that signals the dawn of civilization: Man-apes learn how to kill more efficiently by reconfiguring animal bones as lethal weapons. And while you're at it, fast-forward a bit, and contemplate the insufferable blandness of supposedly more advanced homo sapiens. Time and again, *2001* underscores the ironic contrast between the miraculous and the mundane, between the panoramic splendors of outer space and the narrow-focused behavior of smaller-than-life humans. There's something borderline-sadistic about the way Kubrick caricatures a white-bread, charm-free scientist who gets his first glimpse at hard evidence of intelligent life on other planets. "Well," he remarks with the empty cheer of a Kiwanis Club luncheon speaker, "I must say – you guys have certainly come up with something."

Do you find yourself agreeing with Calder Willingham, co-screenwriter of Kubrick's *Paths of Glory*, who accused the director of "a near-psychotic indifference to and coldness toward the human beings" in his movies? Then consider this: HAL 9000, the soft-spoken super-computer, seems a lot more human than its flesh-and-blood traveling companions aboard a Jupiter-bound spacecraft. It's so affecting, even tragic, when an astronaut (another personality-challenged human, played by Keir Dullea) disables HAL, that you're almost willing to forgive the digital paranoid for causing the deaths of every other crew member. Indeed, with the arguable exception of Tom Cruise's obsessive seeker in *Eyes Wide Shut*, Hal is the closest thing to a genuinely charismatic and sympathetic character in any movie Kubrick made after *Spartacus* (1960).

Despite the absence of a significant human protagonist to generate a rooting interest, *2001* was a huge commercial success during its first theatrical run. (And not just because many chemically-enhanced viewers repeatedly savored it as a widescreen head trip.) More than three decades later, it is widely viewed as a masterpiece, even by some critics who expressed serious misgivings in their initial reviews. That it was, and continues to be, one of the past century's most influential films is beyond dispute. And it is so firmly affixed in our collective pop-culture consciousness that even people who have never actually seen *2001* get the joke when someone makes a wink-wink, nudge-nudge allusion to the opening notes of Richard Strauss' *Thus Spoke Zarathustra* (perhaps the most inspired musical choice ever made by a filmmaker) or the arrival of those imposing black Monoliths that encourage human beings to transcend themselves.

Trouble is, much of *2001* hasn't aged very well. The mystifying climax of what one critic described as the film's "shaggy God story" seems more than ever like a precocious sophomore's idea of deep-dish philosophizing. (It doesn't help that, when Dullea awakens after a dazzling sound-and-light show, he finds himself trapped inside what looks like the spectacularly garish luxury suite of a Las Vegas hotel.) Worse, Kubrick's intricately and interminably detailed depiction of extra-terrestrial travel — meant to convey shock and awe at the miracle of space flight — now seems, compared to more recent displays of high-tech wizardry, almost quaint.

Of course, some things — titles, for instance — never go out of date. And just as *1984* continues to serve as shorthand for a dystopian vision of technologically-enhanced totalitarianism, *2001* retains its mythic resonance — an optimistic prediction of first contact with other, presumably wiser, life forms — long after people stopped scribbling that cluster of numbers in checkbooks. Instead of inspiring awe, however, the film itself now is more likely to evoke a kind of wistful melancholy that Kubrick never intended. It's sad, but true: These days, we simply don't view interstellar exploration with the same wonder-fueled enthusiasm shared by Kubrick and millions of others back in 1968.

To be sure, there's the occasional media frenzy about images beamed from Mars by unmanned spacecraft. And there's always a ready audience for every new chapter of the *Star Wars* franchise. But with each passing year, it's increasingly more difficult to imagine that anything short of a real-world appearance by a beckoning Monolith would re-ignite our intergalactic wanderlust. All you have to do is read news accounts of petty Congressional squabbling over NASA funding, and you'll realize that, never mind what the calendar might tell you, we're still a long, long way from the bold new age of discovery we were promised all those years ago.

SPECS:

2001: A Space Odyssey — Stars: Keir Dullea and Gary Lockwood. Directed by Stanley Kubrick. Screenplay: Stanley Kubrick, Arthur C. Clarke. Running time: 139 minutes. Year of release: 1968. DVD distributor: Warner Home Video.

SUBJECTS FOR FURTHER RESEARCH:

Solaris (1972) — Russian filmmaker Andrei Tarkovsky responded to what he viewed as the soulless technology of *2001* with an equally mystifying but appreciably more humane drama about a psychiatrist who investigates inexplicable events aboard a distant space station. (Steven Soderbergh's 2002 remake is, depending on your point of view, a transcendent improvement or a mushy-minded simplification.)

2010 (1984) — Working from a novel by *2001* writer Arthur C. Clarke, writer-director Peter Hyams tried to "explain" Kubrick's masterwork with a relatively straightforward sequel. Most fans of the original did not appreciate the enlightenment.

Mission to Mars (2000) — Cult-fave director Brian De Palma aped Kubrick's dead-serious, deliberately vague approach to sci-fi storytelling in this drama about a rescue team seeking errant astronauts on the Red Planet. Unfortunately, De Palma found himself pummeled with unflattering comparisons: Critics used Kubrick's film much like the *2001* man-apes utilized animal bones while delivering their unforgiving attacks.

LESSON FOR FILMMAKERS:

Tom Hanks and James Cameron are among the notables who have credited *2001* as a seminal influence. (Cameron says he first viewed the film in his mid-teens, "and sparked my interest in filmmaking.") It's worth noting, though, that one man's cautionary parable is another man's vocational guide. Stanley Kubrick harbored a profound mistrust of modern technology, which explains a lot about his depiction of Hal 9000. Even so, Microsoft co-founder Bill Gates has said that *2001* inspired his vision of the potential of computers. Which, of course, may explain a lot about Microsoft.

STAR WARS

ilm is a mongrel medium in which masterpieces are, much more often than not, mixed-breed mutts. For all the talk about singular sensations or one-of-a-kind achievements, the fact remains that most movies — including most of the greatest ever made — tend to be artfully apportioned fusions of elements appropriated from other media (theater, literature, opera, comic books, pulp fiction, ancient myth, rock 'n' roll, whatever) and, yes, other movies.

Art and artifice routinely commingle. The sacred complements the profane. Grand spectacle is undercut — yet also complemented — by low comedy. Multitudes of borrowings are at once instantly recognizable and inextricably entwined.

And in the end, even the most dedicated deconstructionists are hard-pressed to completely calculate each source, every influence, that goes into the making of an amalgamation that's bigger, better, and altogether more amazing than the sum of its parts.

Consider George Lucas' *Star Wars*, one of the most splendiferous patchworks ever to gain near-universal acceptance as a classic motion picture. The 1977 movie is voraciously eclectic, incorporating everything from *Beowulf* to *Buck Rogers*, John Ford to J.R.R. Tolkien, samurai epics to seafaring swashbucklers, ancient Greek dramas to Saturday matinee cliffhangers. It imagines extraterrestrial warfare in terms of WWI-era aerial dogfights — establishing a stylistic convention for scores of later sci-fi action-adventures — and celebrates its protagonists in a climactic ceremony that echoes (visually if not thematically) *Triumph of the Will* (1934), Leni Riefenstahl's notoriously Nazi-worshipping documentary. And speaking of Nazis: The white-clad minions of dastardly Darth

Vader (the black-clad villain whose chronic wheezing suggests a sleep apnea patient in desperate need of a CPAP breathing machine) just happen to be called Storm Troopers, even though they appear to take sartorial advice from Ku Klux Klansmen.

Lucas has freely acknowledged that while preparing *Star Wars* — and, later, *The Empire Strikes Back* (1980) and *Return of the Jedi* (1983), the second two chapters in his original trilogy — he was heavily influenced by *The Hero with a Thousand Faces*, anthropologist Joseph Campbell's seminal study of patterns and stages of mythology throughout the ages. ("It is possible," Lucas said of Campbell in 1985, "that if I hadn't run across him, I'd still be writing *Star Wars* today.") And he admitted to biographer Dale Pollock that "The Force" — the much-discussed, multifaceted energy field created and shared by all living things, for better or worse, in all *Star Wars* movies — is a variation of the "life force" described by a Mexican Indian sorcerer in *Tales of Power*, author Carlos Castaneda's 1974 installment in his *Don Juan* cycle.

But Lucas has been equally upfront about crediting far less esoteric influences: *Flash Gordon* (from which he borrowed, among other things, the Ming the Merciless character as inspiration for his own villainous emperor), *The Sea Hawk* (the classic 1940 pirates-and-plunder adventure with Errol Flynn flaunting his action-hero expertise), Frank Herbert's *Dune* (the immensely popular sci-fi novel set on a parched planet not at all unlike Luke Skywalker's desert homeworld), E. E. "Doc" Smith's celebrated *Lensmen* saga (in which bad guys outdo Lucas' planet-killing Grand Moff Tarkin by destroying entire *galaxies*) and on and on and on.

"You have opinions, you are curious, you have a rich fantasy life — and you are able to create stories," Lucas explained in a 1999 interview. "You start combining things that you like, and you start to tell a story. In (*Star Wars*), I was interested in mythology and so I set out to create a modern myth. But I also wanted it to be an action adventure serial."

His success at striking the perfect balance — indeed, at offering the best of both worlds — was immediately apparent to most of us who encountered *Star Wars* when it was still just a movie, not yet a mythos. A long time ago, in a galaxy far, far away... Well, okay, it was actually back in

1977, at a multiplex in Shreveport, Louisiana. That's when and where I previewed *Star Wars* as critic for a local newspaper. The closing credits were still flicking on the screen when I raced to the parking lot, so I could speed back to the office and hastily type an unabashed rave:

"*Star Wars* is a wonderfully rousing adventure, filmed with unbridled imagination and enthusiasm, inspiring a sense of wonder which appeals to the child in all of us. It is one part space opera, one part *Wizard of Oz*, one part swashbuckler and all parts fun. Writer-director George Lucas (*American Graffiti*) may have set out to simply pay homage to the films he enjoyed as a youngster, but what he has come up with is a classic."

And, mind you, mine was one of the more subdued hosannas that greeted this epochal movie.

The plot by now is much too familiar to require a lengthy synopsis. Suffice it to say that, long before it evolved into a pop-culture phenomenon and a multi-billion-dollar industry, spawning sequels and prequels, academic analysis and McDonald's merchandizing, *Star Wars* quickened pulses and raised spirits as a frankly old-fashioned, compellingly picaresque adventure about an ordinary farmboy, Luke Skywalker (Mark Hamill), who rises to the challenge of an extraordinary quest.

Summoned by the distress call of the captured Princess Leia (Carrie Fisher), Luke seeks spiritual advice and warrior training from the mystic Obi-Wan Kenobi (Alec Guinness), a semi-retired Jedi Knight; finds formidable allies in Han Solo (Harrison Ford), a roguish smuggler, and Chewbacca (Peter Mayhew), Solo's hefty and hirsute companion; and zips to the other side of the galaxy to join the rebel forces pitted against Darth Vader (played by David Prowse, but voiced by James Earl Jones) and Grand Moff Tarkin (Peter Cushing). And, oh yeah, I almost forgot: A couple of robots — C-3PO (Anthony Daniels) and R2-D2 (Kenny Baker) also figure into the mix.

A mix, it should be noted, that some film critics and filmmakers found, and still find, utterly distasteful. For these contrarians, *Star Wars* — or, more specifically, the astounding and unprecedented box-office success of the 1977 release — signaled the end of a fabled era in which Hollywood studios and mainstream audiences were unusually open to risk-taking, envelope-pushing cinema. Noted screenwriter (*Raging Bull*, *Taxi Driver*) and director (*Affliction*, *Auto Focus*) director Paul Schrader spoke for many like-minded folks when he complained: "*Star Wars* was the film that ate the heart and soul of Hollywood. It created the big-budget comic-book mentality."

Maybe so, but Lucas never apologized for ushering in a new era of escapism. As he told me in 1988:

"Coming out of film school, I looked at the world and said, 'This isn't the way they told me it was going to be. This is terrible. We aren't what we thought we were.' And that, to a young person, is a revelation. It's like, hey, it isn't a wonderful place — it's a horrible place. And so you spend a lot of your time saying, 'I'm going to spring this on the rest of the world.'

"But, really, anybody over thirty is well aware of what kind of a world this is. And these kinds of revelations — the fact that the world is not what we think it is — I've discovered, in my making movies, that they don't really help the society very much, ultimately. What helps is to sort of promote the human spirit, to say, 'Let's think of ourselves as those good people that we were, brought up in the fairy-tale of adolescence, of childhood, to believe we were. And let's promote *those* ideas, and believe in that.

"Because it's that kind of faith that makes that happen in reality. If we believe we're a terrible society, then that will overcome all of us. And it will just be anarchy and death and horror."

Two decades after he unveiled his trendsetting, genre-redefining epic, Lucas couldn't resist the temptation to improve upon perfection by retroactively adding more lavish special effects to a reissued *Star Wars* (which he re-titled *Star Wars Episode IV: A New Hope* to designate its rightful place in a multi-chapter saga). Nor could he later resist the urge to make increasingly lavish, ever-more-grandiose prequels that have polarized faithful fans of the original trilogy. (Insert joke about the law of diminishing returns here.) But never mind: *Star Wars* remains, as a single film as well as a cinematic myth, one of the most magnificent mongrels ever spawned in a medium where interbreeding is an art form. The Force, of course, is still with it.

SPECS:

Star Wars — Stars: Mark Hamill, Harrison Ford, Carrie Fisher, Peter Cushing, Alec Guinness, Anthony Daniels, Kenny Baker, Peter Mayhew, and David Prowse. Written and directed by George Lucas. Running time: 125 minutes. Year of release: 1977. DVD distributor: Fox Home Entertainment.

SUBJECTS FOR FURTHER RESEARCH:

The Hidden Fortress (1958) — George Lucas has gratefully acknowledged Akira Kurosawa's epic adventure as an inspiration for *Star Wars*. The bickering bumpkins who accompany a fugitive princess (Misa Uehara) and her loyal general (Toshio Mifune) clearly are precursors of R2-D2 and C-3PO. And the princess herself is the model for the feisty Princess Leia. It requires a bit more of a stretch to see Mifune's sardonic general as Han Solo, but never mind: Lucas learned many important lessons from the master of samurai cinema that enabled him to create his own masterwork.

Star Trek: The Motion Picture (1979) — Producer Gene Roddenberry wasn't able to launch a big-screen adventure franchise based on his 1966–69 TV series until Paramount got a look at the *Star Wars* box-office grosses. The first installment, directed by Robert Wise, is a stiff and stilted piece of work, but a few sequels — especially *Star Trek II: The Wrath of Khan* (1982) and *Star Trek: First Contact* (1996) — are satisfyingly exciting as first-rate popcorn movies.

E.T.: The Extra-Terrestrial (1982/2002) — Five years after George Lucas re-issued his original *Star Wars* trilogy with CGI enhancements, Steven Spielberg tried something similar with his own sci-fi classic. In addition to improving the special effects, however, Spielberg pointlessly revised his 1982 film by digitally removing the guns brandished by government agents, and altering the soundtrack to delete a fleeting reference to "terrorist." Why? Presumably, to make the movie more suitable for children. Or something like that.

LESSON FOR FILMMAKERS:

If somebody can't (or won't) understand what kind of movie you want to make, maybe it's better to make that movie for somebody else. As Dave Pollock reports in *Skywalking: The Life and Films of George Lucas*, Universal Pictures passed on producing *Star Wars* just a month before Lucas' *American Graffiti* (1973) became the studio's biggest hit in years. Ned Tanen, president of Universal during this fateful miscalculation, insisted years later that he had no regrets about the turndown. "I had a very tough time understanding (Lucas') treatment," Tanen said, adding that anyone else in his position would have been equally hard-pressed "to visualize what C-3PO means from reading a 13-page treatment of *Star Wars*." On the other hand, Pollock wrote, "Universal had only to pay Lucas $25,000 to develop a screenplay from his obtuse treatment, but the studio decided to save the money. The decision ultimately cost it more than $250 million."

HALLOWEEN

uring the final, frantic minutes of *Halloween*, John Carpenter's seminal slasher thriller, baby-sitter Laurie Strode (Jamie Lee Curtis) tells the grade-schoolers in her care that they shouldn't worry, that she has slain the masked murderer who has been slicing and stabbing his way through the neighborhood. But one of her young charges isn't easily convinced. As he puts it: "You can't kill the bogeyman." No kidding.

Sure enough, Michael Myers, the menace in the mask, quickly reappears. Laurie runs, but she cannot hide. Michael is impeded, but never quite defeated. It takes a few gunshots from Dr. Samuel Loomis (Donald Pleasence), a psychiatrist who aptly diagnoses Michael as "purely and simply evil," for Laurie to avoid a grisly quietus. But in the very last moments before the closing credits, the movie once again illustrates a basic tenet of the *Halloween* mythos: You can't keep a bad man down.

Throughout six of seven sequels — the totally unrelated *Halloween III: Season of the Witch* (1983) doesn't count — Michael Myers has periodically resurrected himself to make the world unsafe for oversexed teens and innocent bystanders. Unfortunately, even the best of these sequels have been formulaic fright fests, and the worst have been scarcely better than the repetitive rampages of Jason Voorhees and Freddy Krueger.

But never mind: Carpenter's 1978 original has lost none of its power to fascinate and frighten, even after a quarter-century of follow-ups and rip-offs. The fluid, premonitory camera movements and the sinister-sounding electronic music may seem almost self-satirical these days. But that's only because these and other elements were so potent – and, yes, so influential — when Carpenter concocted the formula.

Halloween relies heavily on the power of suggestion, the logic of a wide-awake nightmare — and the engagingly androgynous charisma of the nineteen-year-old Jamie Lee Curtis as Laurie. Unlike most other examples of slasher cinema — what Roger Ebert astutely dismisses as "dead teen-ager movies" — *Halloween* actually devotes some time to character development, so that the brainy and tomboyish Laurie comes across as a resourceful and sympathetic individual, rather than just another bosomy co-ed on the business end of a sharp object.

Indeed, *Halloween* is all the more disquieting because it seems so unfair, so absurd, that such a nice person would be threatened with the same fate that befalls her sexually precocious and vaguely unpleasant friends. The audience can't help wondering: Why her? What did *she* ever do to deserve this?

Unfortunately, Carpenter and co-screenwriter Debra Hill opted to diminish their mystery in the first sequel, *Halloween II* (1981), a more graphically violent horror show directed by Rick Rosenthal (who would later perpetrate 2002's *Halloween: Resurrection*). Mad Mikey set his sights on Laurie, we're told, because she's a blood relation. But wait, there's more: By the time they got around to *Halloween: The Curse of Michael Myers* (1995) — which Carpenter had nothing to do with — someone had the bright idea to "explain" Michael's remarkable resilience: The masked bogeyman was supernaturally-enhanced by modern-day Druids. Or something like that.

Things are much simpler, and scarier, in the original *Halloween*, the classic that set the standards and established the ground rules for an entire subgenre of horror thriller.

Much as he did in his creepy cult-fave *Assault on Precinct 13* (1976), Carpenter throws the audience off-balance early on by thumbing his nose at B-movie conventions. In the earlier film, he began with a familiar child-in-peril scene — then capped it off by actually killing the tyke. In *Halloween*, things begin — on Halloween night, appropriately enough, in the sleepy little town of Haddonfield, Illinois — with a skillfully sustained, single-take sequence in which we see, from an unidentified voyeur's point of view, an attractive teen-age girl's tryst with her hunky boyfriend, followed by her fatal stabbing at the hand of her disapproving observer. Only after the bloodshed do we learn that the observer — and the killer — is the slain girl's six-year-old brother: Michael Myers.

Flash-forward fifteen years: Michael escapes from the mental hospital that has been his home ever since he dispatched his sibling. Dr. Loomis follows his trail all the way back to Haddonfield, where — hey, wouldn't you know it! — it's Halloween night, and Michael wants to cut up just like old times.

Once again, Mad Mikey evidences a zero-tolerance policy toward teen sex. Indeed, three of his fresh kills are young people who die either just before or immediately after doing the wild thing. Lynda (P. J. Soles) practically courts death when she mistakes a camouflaged Mad Mikey for her boyfriend, and taunts the bogeyman with her nude body. ("See anything you like?") Meanwhile, in the house across the street from the carnage, Laurie keeps watch over the children in her care, all the while remaining chaste and vigilant.

Which, in the world according to *Halloween* and its lesser imitators, isn't just good behavior: It's a survival tactic.

SPECS:

Halloween — Stars: Jamie Lee Curtis, Donald Pleasence, Nancy Loomis, and P.J. Soles. Directed by John Carpenter. Screenplay: John Carpenter, Deborah Hill. Running time: 93 minutes. Year of release: 1978. DVD distributor: Anchor Bay.

SUBJECTS FOR FURTHER RESEARCH:

Friday the 13th (1980) — Kevin Bacon gets an arrow shoved through his throat and Betsy Palmer (not a hockey-masked bit player) plays the homicidal culprit in the first major *Halloween* knock-off. The best you can say about it: The sequels are worse.

Halloween H20: 20 Years Later (1998) — Audiences cheered when the long-suffering Laurie Strode (an older-and-wiser Jamie Lee Curtis) finally got medieval on her big brother in this surprisingly satisfying sequel. Unfortunately, producers cheated long-time fans by doing Laurie dirty in the despicable *Halloween: Resurrection* (2002)

The Blair Witch Project (1999) — Another amazingly successful no-budget indie, this shrewdly atmospheric horror flick is the work of people who learned an important lesson from *Halloween*: Sometimes, the scariest elements of a movie are those things that aren't explained, or even seen.

LESSON FOR FILMMAKERS:

Halloween was filmed for $300,000 — and grossed nearly $50 million. Which is why Joel and Ethan Coen combined trick-or-treating with bait-and-switching when they sought investors for *Blood Simple* (1984), their debut feature. "If we took advantage of people," Joel told me, only half-jokingly, in a 1985 interview, "it was by our glossing over the differences between what we were trying to do and horror movies... We'd say, 'Other independent movies have done successfully — like *Halloween*.' And we were sort of saying, 'Generically, this is like that. It's a murder thriller. And people like thrillers. We're not going to go off and make a movie about the mating habits of loons or anything like that. And it's not an art film.'"

BLADE RUNNER

Legend has it that *Blade Runner* was radically reconstituted — and, in the process, dumbed down for the masses — after failing to impress preview audiences. Violence was snipped and/or sanitized. A happier ending was filmed. Harrison Ford recorded hard-boiled narration to make the plot more comprehensible — and his character, Rick Deckard, more sympathetic.

These may seem like acts of desperation, if not vandalism. But trust me: As someone who fortuitously attended one of those disastrous previews, at a Dallas multiplex, I can easily understand why Warner Bros. might have urged director Ridley Scott to try *anything* to make his expensive sci-fi drama more audience-friendly. Never before and never again have I sensed so much seething hostility emanating from a group of moviegoers. Not only did they not get it — they most assuredly didn't want it.

Even so, the revised version of *Blade Runner* finally released in 1982 was almost universally recognized, even by people who detested it, as a groundbreaking achievement. In the second paragraph of her vituperative pan, critic Pauline Kael went so far to concede that the $30-million spectacle "has its own look, and a visionary sci-fi movie that has its own look can't be ignored – it has its place in film history."

Kael's words have proven astutely prophetic: Scott's extraordinarily vivid evocation of a noir-shadowed, rain-splattered, retro-futuristic metropolis — a dystopian landscape overrun by teeming polyglot multitudes, illuminated by commercial neon and police searchlights — immediately established *Blade Runner* as one of the century's most influential movies. Indeed, with the arguable exception of Fritz Lang's *Metropolis*, it continues to be the most frequently imitated of all sci-fi extravaganzas. Just about every subsequent fantasy or sci-fi spectacle — from *Brazil* and *Batman* to *The Fifth Element* and *Mystery Men* — has borrowed freely from its stunningly detailed production design.

But wait, there's more: Ten years after *Blade Runner* generated mixed reviews and unspectacular grosses during its initial theatrical run, Scott finally was able to find an audience for his original "Director's Cut" in a much-hyped — and modestly profitable — re-release. By then, the "original" version (i.e., the audience-friendly edition released in 1982) had already attracted a devoutly loyal cult following. The "new" version — minus the narration and the happy ending tacked on after the fact — increased the size of that cult and, more important, demonstrated the profit potential in re-releasing newly restored (and, in some cases, never-before-seen) versions of classic films. Even more than Steve Spielberg's reworked *Close Encounters of the Third Kind*, the restored *Blade Runner* set the precedent for releasing "Director's Cuts" of *The Third Man*, *Touch of Evil*, *Juliet of the Spirits*, and other masterworks.

Does all this mean *Blade Runner* — either the audience-friendly version or the "Director's Cut" — must be adjudged, on its own merits, a truly great film? Not really. Look beyond the dazzling production values, and you're left with a not-terribly-exciting neo-noir thriller about a cynical ex-cop who isn't as tough or smart as he pretends to be. The plot — adapted from a Philip K. Dick novel, *Do Androids Dream of Electric Sheep?* — is at once simplistic and abstruse. And while the narration in the audience-friendly version frequently is intrusive, it does help to humanize a lead character who is off-puttingly cold-blooded in the "Director's Cut."

In 2019, highly advanced humanoids known as Replicants are manufactured to labor in Off-World colonies. If a Replicant escapes to sample life on Earth, he or she is hunted down and "retired" (i.e., killed) by specially trained cops known as Blade Runners. Rick Deckard (Ford) is an L.A. Blade Runner who's tired of killing Replicants; trouble is, he's very good at his job. So when top cop Bryant (M. Emmet Smith) needs help in tracking down four rogue Replicants – Roy Batty (gleefully over-acted by Rutger Hauer), Pris (Darryl Hannah), Leon (Brion James), and Zhora

(Joanna Cassidy) – he sends Gaff (Edward James Olmos), his favorite flunky, to draft Deckard back into service.

Deckard does what a man's got to do, but that doesn't mean he's happy about it. Come to think of it, he isn't noticeably jolly even when he's placing a lip-lock on Rachel (Sean Young), a drop-dead gorgeous *femme fatale* he meets at the Tyrell Corporation, the place where Replicants are designed and built. (The company motto: "More human than human.") But, then again, Deckard is bound to be less than overjoyed about his attraction to Rachel. After all, it's not exactly a good career move for a Blade Runner to fall for a Replicant.

Some die-hard fans of *Blade Runner* insist that, at strategic points throughout the movie, Scott drops subtle hints to indicate Deckard himself is, unwittingly, a Replicant. For example, there's the matter of the unicorn: During a drunken daydream that appears only in the "Director's Cut," Deckard has a fleeting vision of the mythical creature; much later, near the very end of the movie, Deckard finds a paper-doll unicorn that Gaff has left behind as an ambiguous parting gesture. Maybe, just maybe, Deckard's fantastical daydream is something implanted in the mind of every Replicant.

But if that were the case, how would Gaff know about it? Is he, too, a Replicant? Or did he locate this information in a *Blade Running for Dummies* paperback? And if he's *not* a Replicant, why doesn't Gaff, a licensed Blade Runner, run a blade through Deckard? Does this fall under the heading of professional courtesy?

Such are the questions that obsess cultists who cling to a cult-fave like *Blade Runner*.

SPECS:

Blade Runner — Stars: Harrison Ford, Rutger Hauer, Sean Young, Edward James Olmos, M. Emmet Walsh, Daryl Hannah, William Sanderson, Brion James, and Joanna Cassidy. Directed by Ridley Scott. Screenplay: Hampton Fancher and David Peoples, based on Philip K. Dick's *Do Androids Dream of Electric Sheep?* Running time: 117 minutes. Year of release: 1982. DVD distributor: Warner Home Video.

SUBJECTS FOR FURTHER RESEARCH:

Total Recall (1990) — Another Philip K. Dick story about the deceptiveness of appearances (and the unreliably of memory) inspired Paul Verhoeven's violent sci-fi adventure about a twenty-first-century working stiff (Arnold Schwarzenegger) who uncovers the fearsome reality behind his fantasies of life on Mars.

The Crow (1994) — The multicultural casting, the grim-reaping manhunts and the urban-hell production design strongly recall *Blade Runner*. Even so, Alex Proyas' darkly stylish comic-book adaptation is more twisted fantasy than neo-noir sci-fi, with a back-from-death rock musician (Brandon Lee) violently avenging his untimely demise. Unfortunately, the movie always will be remembered best for an off-screen tragedy: Lee was accidentally killed by a loaded gun during filming.

The Fifth Element (1997) — Appreciably cheerier than *Blade Runner*, Luc Besson's jaw-dropping, mind-blowing pop epic mixes polyglot characters, sprawling cityscapes, and retro-futuristic sets and props to spin an exciting seriocomic story about a twenty-third-century cabdriver (well-cast Bruce Willis) who saves Earth by kicking ass at an extra-terrestrial entertainment resort.

LESSON FOR FILMMAKERS:

Should some mysteries ever be solved? Judging from their refusal (so far) to fully explain the mythos of their *Matrix* movies, the Wachowski Brothers obviously think that a little ambiguity — well, okay, a lot of ambiguity — is a good thing. But maybe the evasive artists should take a tip from Ridley Scott, who freely admitted in a 2000 interview that, yes, the suspicious fans were correct: Deckard really *is* a Replicant. Did Scott do himself and his film a disservice by being so truthful? Probably not. More than likely, he simply figured that, after nearly two decades of heated debates and fanciful speculation, fans deserved a definitive answer.

≈8≈

THE MASTER
OF SUSPENSE

NOTORIOUS

Alfred Hitchcock's *Notorious* may well be the most perverse love story to have ever slipped past the old Hollywood Production Code. Indeed, even in this supposedly more open and less censorious era, when all manner of once-unmentionable kinkiness is routinely referenced in PG-13 fare, Hitchcock's classic 1946 cloak-and-dagger romance can still unsettle audiences with its psychosexual undercurrents. Working from a shrewdly crafted screenplay by Ben Hecht, Hitchcock applies dark shadings of motive and emotion to transform a conventional thriller plot — a not-so-innocent bystander is recruited for spy games by a cynical handler — into a compelling drama of desire, deception, and sadomasochism.

Shortly after the end of World War II, T.R. Devlin (Cary Grant), a purposefully charming federal agent, offers Alicia Huberman (Ingrid Bergman), a hard-drinking good-time girl in Miami, an opportunity to make amends for her immigrant father's recent bad behavior as a spy for Germany. (Dad is convicted of treason during the movie's opening minutes, then conveniently commits suicide.) He brings her to Rio, where a group of unreconstructed Nazis are just itching to go to *heil* again. Alexander Sebastian (Claude Rains), the bon vivant who has opened his home to these undesirable aliens, just happens to be an old friend of Alicia's father. More important, he's still carrying a flaming torch for the lovely daughter of his fallen comrade. So when Alicia appears out of the blue at his riding club one afternoon....

Hitchcock often contrived to make his villains sympathetic — one of many methods he employed to upend expectations — and so, right from the start, there's something downright pitiable, if not wholly appealing, about Sebastian. Sure, he's conspiring with Nazi refugees to establish a possible Fourth Reich with processed uranium (a textbook example of what Hitchcock called a "McGuffin," the almost entirely irrelevant item that propels a plot into motion). But Sebastian also is a middle-aged, height-challenged fellow who's hopelessly smitten with a taller, younger beauty. He's witty, courtly, sophisticated — and, alas, chronically intimidated by another woman in his life.

Sebastian still lives with his domineering mother — though you get the feeling that, if anyone would ask, he'd insist that *she* lives with *him*. And while she won't admit she feels threatened by the younger woman, Madame Anna Sebastian (Leopoldine Konstantin) isn't at all shy about offering catty criticisms and pointed observations about Alicia. When Sebastian impulsively defies his mom by proposing to the elusive object of his desire, his bold romantic gesture seems nothing less than courageous.

(Some critics, academics, and pop-psychologists theorize the mother-son relationship in *Notorious* — like the mother-son relationship in *Psycho* — was informed by Hitchcock's ambivalent feelings about his own domineering mom.)

And how does Alicia respond to this unexpected offer of marriage? She's flummoxed, but not for the reasons you might expect.

Very early in *Notorious*, Alicia falls madly in love with Devlin. And Devlin, true to his conniving nature, exploits her feelings while grooming her to do her patriotic duty in Rio. (Grant is almost too persuasive for comfort as a cold-blooded bastard with a serious streak of self-loathing.) This is where things really start to get kinky: The more distant and elusive he remains – the more he questions her ability to stop drinking, behave responsibly, and generally mend her ways — the more eagerly she abases herself in shameless appeals for his affection.

At one point, Alicia fleetingly turns feisty by wondering aloud if Devlin's stand-offishness is *his* problem, not *hers*. "You're sore," she says accusingly, "because you're falling for a little drunk... and you don't like it. It makes you sick all over, doesn't it? People will laugh at you. The invincible Devlin, in love with someone who isn't worth even wasting the words on. Poor Dev, in love with a no-good gal. It must be awful." Rather than bother with denials, he merely silences her tirade by kissing her hard on the mouth. Which, naturally, is just what she wants.

And *that* eventually triggers one of the most famous romantic interludes in movie history. At the time, the Production Code enforced restrictions against "passionate kissing" by setting strict time limits on each individual lip-lock. So Hitchcock slyly choreographed his two stars in a kind of wink-wink, nudge-nudge mating dance: Alicia and Devlin just can't get enough of each other as they repeatedly kiss, draw apart, then kiss some more while wandering around Alicia's Rio apartment. Censors couldn't complain, because no single smooch lasts more than a couple of seconds.

But the kiss-a-thon is rudely interrupted when duty calls: Devlin's superiors want Alicia to obtain valuable info by allowing Sebastian to woo her. And when Sebastian pops the question, the spymasters encourage her to accept his offer, even though that means she'll have to work, ahem, undercover. (Thanks to the aforementioned Production Code, Hitchcock had to imply rather than announce what Alicia's conjugal duties might entail.) By agreeing to the wedding, however, Alicia lives down to Devlin's expectations, and becomes a whore in his disapproving view. What he refuses to recognize, of course, is that she's sleeping with another man only to prove her love for him. Worse, Devlin isn't grateful for her sacrifice until it's nearly too late.

Notorious has been hailed in many circles as Hitchcock's crowning achievement. French filmmaker Francois Truffaut embraced it as "truly my favorite Hitchcock picture," and critic Roger Ebert applauds it as "the most elegant expression of the master's visual style." You can find many scenes that support Ebert's appraisal, but two will suffice.

First, there's the famous scene in the ballroom of Sebastian manor, where Hitchcock begins with an overhead shot of a party in progress, then slowly brings his camera down — way, *way* down — to focus on a key Alicia surreptitiously grips in her hand. A key, by the way, that permits Alicia and Devlin to locate, in the wine cellar, bottles filled with — remember? — processed uranium.

Much later, during the brilliantly sustained climax, Devlin storms into Sebastian's home before Alicia succumbs to arsenic poisoning. He more or less carries her down a long staircase while warning Sebastian not to impede their progress. Sebastian can't do anything, primarily because his co-conspirators are within earshot — are in the foyer below, actually — and he knows he'll be shot if they discover that he's inadvertently brought an American spy into their midst (which is why he and his mother tried to poison Alicia in the first place). Even so, Sebastian feels compelled to do *something* – despite his mother's frantic warnings, despite the extreme danger he's stumbled into – so he remains near Devlin during each slow, steady step toward the front door. Will the humiliated husband blurt some damning remark about his duplicitous wife? Will his Nazi collaborators realize on their own what's going on? The suspense intensifies as Hitchcock stealthily delays the downward progress with fluid cinematography and effective crosscutting.

In the end, Devlin and Alicia make their getaway. But you can enjoy this ending as a happy one only if you ignore some nagging questions raised by the rest of the movie: What if Alicia is right to assume the worst about the man she hopelessly, helplessly loves? What kind of future can she expect with someone who may indeed hate himself for loving her?

SPECS:

Notorious — Stars: Cary Grant, Ingrid Bergman, Claude Rains, Louis Calhern, and Leopoldine Konstantin. Director: Alfred Hitchcock. Screenplay: Ben Hecht. Running time: 102 minutes. Year of release: 1946. DVD distributor: The Criterion Collection.

SUBJECTS FOR FURTHER RESEARCH:

The Year of Living Dangerously (1983) — Prior to directing Mel Gibson and Sigourney Weaver in a scene of passionate lip-locking, Peter Weir advised his stars to prepare by studying Cary Grant and Ingrid Bergman in *Notorious*. Obviously, they learned their lessons well.

The Net (1995) — Irwin Winkler pays homage to *Notorious* by having a charming but deadly villain named Jack Devlin (Jeremy Northam) tie an oversized handkerchief around the bare midriff of heroine Angela Bennett (Sandra Bullock), just as Cary Grant's T.R. Devlin ties a kerchief around Ingrid Bergman's Alicia Huberman. (In 2001's *Enigma*, Northam again channels Grant's Devlin while playing a glib British Intelligence agent.)

Mission: Impossible II (2000) — Superspy Ethan Hunt (Tom Cruise) encourages his beautiful lover (Thandie Newton) to get horizontal with a bad guy (Dougray Scott) who's plotting to use uranium to... er, wait a minute, that's not right. Actually, the villain is armed with a genetically-created disease. Even so, it's impossible to miss how director John Woo blatantly "quotes" the romantic-triangle plot of *Notorious*.

LESSON FOR FILMMAKERS:

When asked to name a classic film that has greatly influenced his own work, director Stephen Frears (*The Grifters*, *Dirty Pretty Things*) cites *Notorious* for its perverse romanticism: "It's all about sexual complexity, isn't it? One of the most interesting things about it is the whole business of whether Ingrid Bergman is betraying Cary Grant — quite simply, whether she's going to bed with another man when she's in love with him. And the whole business of Claude Rains being so sympathetic — she's sent in to spy on a man who breaks your heart because he's so touching and so clearly in love with Ingrid Bergman. If you make films around sexual complexity, which I have done in my life, it's a theme close to your heart."

VERTIGO

Most audiences were puzzled and disappointed by *Vertigo* when it first appeared in 1958. Ticket-buyers of the time likely wanted a roller-coaster ride much like other Alfred Hitchcock classics of the 1950s (*North by Northwest, To Catch a Thief, The Man Who Knew Too Much*). What they got instead was something much darker and more complex, even though the movie's plot seemed — in synopsis, at least — the perfect blueprint for a straight-ahead, standard-issue popcorn flick.

Ex-cop John "Scottie" Ferguson (James Stewart) is asked by an old friend to watch over the friend's wife, Madeleine (Kim Novak), a beautiful but troubled woman who fears she is possessed by the spirit of a mad ancestor. Ferguson is fascinated by Madeleine, and can't help falling in love with her. But he's unable to stop her suicide because of his own weakness: His fear of heights, the "vertigo" of the title, prevents him from reaching her before she throws herself from a church tower.

Guilt-ridden and devastated, Ferguson suffers a nervous breakdown. While recovering, he meets a woman who is (pardon the expression) a dead ringer for his late beloved. Judy (Kim Novak again), a department store clerk, is wary of Ferguson's attentions, but agrees to date him — and, eventually, to be supported by him. She objects, though not very strenuously, when he tries to remake her in Madeleine's image, changing her clothes, her shoes, even the color of her hair.

Ferguson is overjoyed and grateful that he's found someone who resembles Madeleine so strongly. Unfortunately, there's a very good reason why there's such a strong resemblance....

Don't worry: No spoilers here, even though Hitchcock himself spills the beans well before the final scene. For those who prefer to enjoy *Vertigo* merely as a clever melodrama, and who haven't seen any of its innumerable imitations, the surprise may come as a modestly satisfying jolt. But there's much more to this must-see movie than an ingenious plot twist.

At heart, *Vertigo* is not so much a neo-gothic thriller as a moody meditation on sexual obsession. On one level, the film is a metaphor for the filmmaking process itself — or, more specifically, Hitchcock's approach to that process. Ferguson represents the director who tries to shape reality to his own ends, and Judy represents the actor who's asked to simply serve as a color in the director's palette. (Remember: Hitchcock is the filmmaker who claimed actors should be treated like cattle.)

But *Vertigo* also can be viewed as a study of sadomasochistic symbiosis, with Ferguson single-mindedly struggling to re-create a "perfect" relationship, and Judy reluctantly agreeing to be stripped of all identity to please the man she loves. You could argue that Judy is the more deranged of the pair, in that every action she takes hints at a bottomless self-loathing. You could also argue, however, that Judy gradually emerges in the movie's final reel as the more sympathetic character.

James Stewart is at the top of his form here, brilliantly playing Ferguson as a discontent, resolutely practical man who's swept away by grand passions that are not unlike madness. (There's a bitter irony at work: Ferguson, the man who's afraid of falling, allows himself to be drawn into a different but equally dangerous vortex.) Stewart's subtly nuanced and profoundly affecting performance provides the perfect counterpoint for Kim Novak's fatalistic intensity as Madeleine and her skittish, anxious submissiveness as Judy.

Vertigo is a fever dream of a romantic tragedy, with elegantly graceful passages – particularly the long, silent sequence that shows Ferguson following, and falling for, Madeleine — and foreboding undercurrents. Bernard Herrmann's score is at once lush and ominous, the perfect balance of musical moods. And cinematographer Robert Burks bathes San Francisco in an eerie glow that intensifies the lyrical beauty of key images, but also hints at hidden deceptions.

SPECS:

Vertigo — Stars: James Stewart, Kim Novak, Barbara Bel Geddes, Tom Helmore, and Henry Jones. Directed by Alfred Hitchcock. Screenplay: Alec Coppel and Samuel Taylor, based on the novel *D'Entre Les Morts* by Pierre Boileau and Thomas Narcejac. Running time: 128 minutes. Year of release: 1958. DVD distributor: Universal.

SUBJECTS FOR FURTHER RESEARCH:

The Legend of Lyla Clare (1968) — Kim Novak landed another dual role in Robert Aldrich's high-camp hoot, playing a legendary Old Hollywood star who died under mysterious circumstances *and* the beautiful unknown who's hired to play the star in a lavish biopic. During the filming — are you ready for this? are you sitting down? — the newcomer feels she is "possessed" by the spirit of the late legend.

Obsession (1976) — The first of Brian De Palma's many *Vertigo* variations is a relatively restrained (by De Palma standards) but none-too-subtly perverse thriller about a businessman (Cliff Robertson) whose wife and daughter are lost during a botched kidnapping. Years later, he meets a beautiful art expect (Genevieve Bujold) who just happens to look like his late spouse. Bernard Herrmann provides the musical score.

9 1/2 Weeks (1986) — Adrian Lyne's obviously *Vertigo*-influenced drama about a steamy S&M affair is appreciably more upfront about the kinkiness of its extreme-makeover plot. Mickey Rourke repeatedly degrades Kim Basinger, and she really, *really* likes it — for a while.

LESSON FOR FILMMAKERS:

Writer-director Atom Egoyan (*The Sweet Hereafter*) admires the stealthiness of against-type casting in *Vertigo*. "I love the way it introduces the theme of sexual obsession and perversity through the benign and identifiable all-American persona of Jimmy Stewart," Egoyan told the *London Telegraph*. "He gets himself worked into a state, which is very touching... because you can't believe it's Jimmy Stewart; you can't believe he would deconstruct his own persona so magnificently and so movingly. It's a recent phenomenon where we see actors play against type, but at that time, Hollywood was about leading men being leading men — and to have Jimmy Stewart in such a vulnerable place was breathtaking."

NORTH BY NORTHWEST

Alfred Hitchcock's celebrated contempt for "the plausibles" — his derogatory term for literal-minded spoilsports who carp about coincidence and logical inconsistency — infuses almost every frame of *North by Northwest*, a perpetual-motion machine geared to move faster than the speed of thought.

The impossibly complicated scenario of this 1959 must-see movie has something to do with a New York businessman who's mistaken for an FBI agent, and something else to do with a cross-country chase from Manhattan to Mount Rushmore. For the most part, however, the plot concocted by Hitchcock and screenwriter Ernest Lehman is little more than a gossamer thread, or a wispy excuse, to link a series of dazzling and audacious set pieces intended to surprise and delight.

Get a load of this: The hero is forcibly inebriated, then sent down a winding mountain road in a brakeless Mercedes. Look at that: The same hero arrives in the lobby of the United Nations building, just in time to be framed — and, worse, photographed — as a knife-wielding assassin. Check it out: The poor sap keeps an appointment near an open field in the middle of nowhere, standing precisely where he can be a sitting target for a crop-dusting plane armed with a machine gun.

There's more — much more — here, there, and everywhere. A luxury apartment where expensive accoutrements are stocked for a man who never was. An auction house where a fugitive desperately bids to save his life. A passenger train where an alluring woman is suspiciously eager to assist. An airport where a government agent explains the entire plot in thirty seconds — only we can't hear him over the sound of whirring propellers.

And, of course, a Mount Rushmore precipice where a spiteful villain stomps on the fingers of a dangerously dangling hero.

The template for countless other fleet and flashy action-adventures — including many, if not most, of the James Bond films — *North by Northwest* is propelled along the fast track by the megawatt star power of Cary Grant, one of Hitchcock's favorite collaborators. The funny thing is, even Grant was mystified by the knotty plot throughout much of the production. At one point, Hitchcock told François Truffaut, the actor complained: "It's a terrible script. We've already done a third of the picture, and I still can't make head or tail of it." Hitchcock couldn't help laughing. "Without realizing it," he said of Grant, "he was using a line of his own dialogue."

Grant plays Roger O. Thornhill, a carefree advertising executive who stumbles into the adventure of a lifetime when enemy agents wrongly identify him as an FBI operative named Kaplan. Thornhill actually is an ordinary fellow — at one point, he admits his ex-wife divorced him because he was so dull — but the chief villain of the piece, Phillip Van Damm (James Mason), suspects otherwise. As it turns out, Kaplan doesn't really exist — the imaginary agent was invented by a cunning spymaster (Leo G. Carroll) to distract Van Damm from a very real mole in his organization. So Thornhill repeatedly finds himself dodging bullets engraved with someone else's name.

Lehman frequently described *North By Northwest* as his one big chance to write "the Hitchcock picture to end all Hitchcock pictures." Strictly speaking, he didn't quite succeed: Hitchcock went on to make seven more films, including one — *Family Plot* (1976), his swan song — that Lehman also scripted. But Hitchcock did indeed express a special fondness for this classic thriller, if only because the crop-duster scene allowed him to realize his long-cherished goal of generating pure terror in broad daylight. "No darkness, no pool of light, no mysterious figures in windows," Hitchcock crowed. "Just nothing. Just bright sunshine and a blank open countryside with barely a house or tree in which any lurking menaces could hide."

Of course, this wouldn't be a *true* Hitchcock picture without a hint of aberrant psychology, or a smidgen of sexual tension. There's an ineffably kinky undercurrent to the relationship between Mason's villain and his wild-eyed right-hand man (Martin Landau). And Thornhill himself appears to have issues with a domineering mother (played by Jessie Royce Landis, even though she was ten months *younger* than Grant). But the most obvious Hitchcockian touch is Thornhill's wary bonding with Eve Kendall (Eva Marie Saint), the mysterious blond beauty working as an undercover agent. Not unlike the FBI operative Grant played in *Notorious*, Thornhill turns frosty and judgmental when his leading lady feels duty-bound to sleep with the elegant bad guy. Almost as if to punish our hero for his presumptuous moralizing, Hitchcock sends him racing through that open field, pursued by that bullet-belching crop-duster, and later forces him to dangle from Mount Rushmore. Serves him right, too.

SPECS:

North by Northwest — Stars: Cary Grant, Eva Marie Saint, James Mason, Jessie Royce Landis, Leo G. Carroll, Josephine Hutchinson, Philip Ober, and Martin Landau. Director: Alfred Hitchcock. Screenplay: Ernest Lehman. Running time: 136 minutes. Year of release: 1959. DVD distributor: Warner Home Video.

SUBJECTS FOR FURTHER RESEARCH:

From Russia With Love (1963) — The stylistic influence of *North by Northwest* on the James Bond series has never been more obvious than in this second 007 movie, which features an attack-helicopter sequence (not found in Ian Fleming's original novel) unmistakably inspired by the crop-duster scene in Hitchcock's classic.

Silver Streak (1976) — Arthur Hiller's lightly enjoyable mystery-romance borrows a few elements from *North by Northwest* (and a few more from Hitchcock's *The Lady Vanishes*) while spinning a seriocomic plot about a mild-mannered fellow (Gene Wilder) who's innocently ensnared in murder and conspiracy while on a long-distance train trip.

Enemy of the State (1998) — Tony Scott's glossy chase melodrama offers a clever variation of Hitchcock's trademark "wrong man" scenario, with Will Smith well cast as a cocky D.C. lawyer who's desperate to clear his name after being framed as an enemy agent by a ruthless National Security Agency chief (Jon Voight).

LESSON FOR FILMMAKERS:

Sometimes a "Hitchcockian" film is one that Alfred Hitchcock himself would never have considered making. Although *Paycheck* (2003) was a sci-fi action-adventure, a genre chronically avoided by the Master of Suspense, director John Woo intended the warp-speed chase melodrama as a homage to Hitchcock in general, and *North by Northwest* in particular. Woo explained: "Since they had so many clever designs and so many good gags and so many big surprises, and the whole story was about finding the truth, it made me feel ... I could make a movie (in) Alfred Hitchcock's style." Take note of the scene where hero Michael Jennings (Ben Affleck) is pursued by a subway train in a darkened tunnel. Woo intentionally shot the spectacle to echo Cary Grant's close encounter with the crop-duster.

P SYCHO

Alfred Hitchcock continues to entertain us, and sometimes astonish us, decades after his death. But that doesn't mean he ever really liked us. Indeed, there is ample evidence to the contrary — which, all things considered, might not be such a bad thing. François Truffaut, the French filmmaker who famously interviewed and occasionally emulated the Master of Suspense, once spoke of his idol as "the man whom we are glad to be despised by." And, mind you, Truffaut meant that as a compliment.

Throughout his prolific and prodigious life, Hitchcock repeatedly preyed upon our ambivalent responses to violent death. In doing so, he slyly pandered to our baser instincts, implicating us in the machinations of his characters by exploiting our voyeuristic impulses. Thanks to him, we want James Stewart to be right when he thinks he witnessed a murder in *Rear Window*. We really want Farley Granger's slatternly wife to get what's coming to her in *Strangers on a Train*.

And we really, *really* want Anthony Perkins to dispose of that car with the fresh corpse inside its trunk behind the Bates Motel in *Psycho*.

Do we blame Hitchcock for bringing out the worst in us? Quite the contrary: We're greatly amused, and grateful, for being so effectively worked over. And yet, when you remember the haughtily droll raconteur who quipped his way through countless interviews, promotional shorts, and wrap-around segments for his long-running TV series, you may find yourself reading something like contempt in Hitchcock's insolent smirk. He knew what his audiences wanted and, just as important, how to make them want more of it. And he made no secret of the ruthless methods he might employ to achieve his aims.

"My love of film," Hitchcock admitted in his book-length interview with Truffaut, "is far more important to me than any consideration of morality." Which is part of the reason why he was ready, willing, and able to make *Psycho*, arguably his most amoral movie. "I don't care about the subject matter, I don't care about the acting," Hitchcock said. "But I do care about the pieces of film and the photography and the soundtrack and all the technical ingredients that made the audience scream. I feel it's tremendously satisfying for us to be able to use the cinematic art to achieve something of a mass emotion. And with *Psycho*, we most definitely achieved this. It wasn't a message that stirred the audiences... They were aroused by pure film."

Or, perhaps more accurately, impure film. At once the granddaddy of all slasher movies and one of the blackest comedies ever concocted, *Psycho* was conceived and executed as something of a down-and-dirty stunt. Hitchcock wanted to see if he could make a feature film as quickly and cheaply as the B-movie moguls who produced low-budget, high-profit drive-in fare during the late 1950s. So he borrowed a production crew from his *Alfred Hitchcock Presents* TV show, drew upon impolitely lurid source material — a Robert Bloch novel very loosely based on the life and crimes of serial killer Ed Gein — and made a no-frills black-and-white thriller that overcame mixed-to-hostile reviews to become the second-highest grossing film (after *Ben Hur*) of 1960.

Psycho is one of Hitchcock's most enduring and influential masterworks. It also is the most cold-blooded and mean-spirited prank that any major filmmaker has ever pulled on an audience. The graphic violence of the infamous shower scene is more apparent than real because, thanks to Hitchcock's celebrated genius for montage, we're tricked into thinking we see much more than we're actually shown. But there's an even more significant sleight-of-hand to consider: *Psycho* is a movie that scores its most devastating impact by playing on assumptions and expectations informed by other movies.

Hitchcock blindsided moviegoers in 1960 by daring to switch gears from sexy crime story to shocking gothic horror, by insidiously luring the audience into sympathizing with a homicidal maniac — and, even more audaciously, by daring to kill off a well-known leading lady (Janet Leigh) fifty minutes into his story.

When asked to explain why he was drawn to Bloch's novel in the first place, Hitchcock claimed he found the central gimmick — Norman, is that you? — only modestly clever. What really sold him on the story, he said, was "the suddenness of the murder in the shower, coming, as it were, out of the blue." Obviously, he immediately recognized the sudden savagery as more than just a terrific device for scaring the yell out of people. The sequence also allowed him to pull the rug, and then the floor, out from under the audience.

Ever since Hitchcock opened this trap door, dozens of other filmmakers have tried, with mixed success, to match the Master of Suspense in narrative duplicity. And yet, as good or great as these other films might be, they cannot match the master's work. Two generations after its premiere, *Psycho* continues to loom imposingly large in our collective pop-culture conscious. So much so, in fact, that Gus Van Sant's 1998 remake never really had a chance to be judged on its own dubious merits, not even by people who never saw the original. Since *everybody* already knows what happens in *Psycho*, a shot-by-shot reprise isn't merely redundant — it's pointless.

For better or worse, *Psycho* is the title most people think about when they hear Hitchcock's name. The association is more than a little ironic — in many respects, the film is the least typical of Hitchcock's works — but maybe inevitable. The Master of Suspense prided himself on his ability to manipulate audiences. And he was never more masterful than when he checked us into the Bates Motel.

SPECS:

Psycho — Stars: Anthony Perkins, Vera Miles, John Gavin, Martin Balsam, John McIntire, and Janet Leigh. Directed by Alfred Hitchcock. Screenplay: Joseph Stefano, based on the novel by Robert Bloch. Running time: 109 minutes. Year of release: 1960. Distributor: Universal.

SUBJECTS FOR FURTHER RESEARCH:

The Crying Game (1992) — Maybe *The Lying Game* would be closer to the mark. At first, you assume you're seeing a political thriller about a reluctant IRA kidnapper (Stephen Rea) who bonds with a captive British soldier (Forest Whitaker). But then something unexpected happens, causing the movie to carom off in an entirely different direction. And then... Well, let's just say that appearances, like crafty and well-crafted movies, can be deceiving.

Malice (1993) — For the first half hour or so, you're convinced that you're watching a serial-killer thriller, and Bill Pullman is the prime suspect. But the victims are red herrings, the killer is a minor nuisance — and the villains of the piece give a whole new meaning to the term "lawsuit abuse." Alec Baldwin, Nicole Kidman, and Bebe Neuwirth co-star in director Harold Becker's ingeniously twisty thriller.

The Usual Suspects (1995) — Who is Keyser Soze? Or, perhaps more to the point, what is he? Apocryphal bogeyman? Fearsome criminal mastermind? The Prince of Darkness? You may answer "All of the above" after seeing this ingeniously plotted thriller, which slyly exploits our reflexive willingness as moviegoers to accept anything dramatized in a flashback as a "real" event. Alfred Hitchcock himself might have envied director Bryan Singer's brazen subversion of cinematic convention.

LESSON FOR FILMMAKERS:

Imagine this scenario: Forty minutes into a thriller, the female lead, played by Julia Roberts or Rene Zellweger, is suddenly and savagely murdered. After that, it's up to the character's sister — played by a lesser luminary, perhaps Joan Cusack or Kyra Sedgwick — to wrap up the plot. How do you think audiences might respond to this wrenching turnabout? Well, that's the impact Hitchcock achieved with *Psycho*. If you want to play in his league — that is, if you want to make a thriller that truly deserves the "Hitchcockian" label — think about doing something *that* audacious.

∞9∞
CRIMES AND MISDEMEANORS

M

While planning his first talking picture in 1930, German filmmaker Fritz Lang was distracted by news coverage of Peter Kurten, a mass murderer dubbed "The Monster of Düsseldorf" by the tabloid press. Lang was particularly intrigued by an item in the *Berliner Tageblatt*, which detailed how various underworld figures in Düsseldorf were furious because their "legitimate" criminal activities were disrupted during the intense police manhunt for "The Monster." So the thieves, pickpockets, and safecrackers offered to stalk and arrest the killer on their own.

Lang couldn't help himself: He set aside all previously considered plots and seized upon the sordid anecdote as source material. Today, we might refer to the fruit of that inspiration as a docudrama. Seven decades ago, Lang preferred to call it *M*.

Like many other influential classics of world cinema, Lang's masterwork is at once vividly evocative of its time and enduringly timeless. The movie may seem fancifully satiric, if not borderline outrageous, in its depiction of a decadent city where beggars band together in guilds for self-regulation and mutual protection, and where the criminal underworld has organized itself into clubs resembling trade unions. But these clubs and unions — which also figure prominently in Bertolt Brecht and Kurt Weill's *The Threepenny Opera* (1928) — actually did exist in Weimar-era Berlin.

During this same period throughout Germany, respectable newspapers and lurid tabloids attracted sensation-seeking readers with grisly stories about mass murderers, many of whom — like Karl Denke, a Münsterberg shopkeeper who peddled his victims as "smoked pork," or Berlin's own Carl Wilhelm Grossman, who eviscerated two dozen servant girls — make even contemporary fictional bogeymen such as Hannibal Lecter and Jason Voorhees seem like timorous under-achievers.

A masterpiece of cunning suspense and allusive terror, *M* is the gripping tale of a compulsive child-killer (Peter Lorre) who inspires fear and loathing on both sides of the law. It has been imitated so many times that, even if you've never seen it, you may assume you have, simply because it seems so familiar. (Producer Michael Mann brazenly recycled its criminals-as-vigilantes plot for an '80s episode of — no kidding! — *Miami Vice*.) But when you finally do see the original, or see it again several years after your first encounter, you can't help being startled by its undiminished impact.

The movie seizes you during its opening moments, as Lang mercilessly cuts back and forth between a shabby apartment, where a mother anxiously awaits her child's return from school, and vaguely menacing street scenes, as the little girl strolls with an aggressively pleasant stranger you know — you just *know* — is the child killer mentioned in police posters plastered on advertising columns. (The killer makes his first appearance, appropriately enough, as a dark shadow cast on one of those posters.)

Later, Lang reprises the cross-cutting technique for an equally arresting but more darkly ironic sequence, as he shows how a group of the city's police officials are considering the same options — and, quite often, using the very same language — as a band of underworld leaders while each group meets, separately yet simultaneously, to discuss strategies for tracking down the mass murderer. Amusingly enough, Lang doesn't appear to make many distinctions between either gathering.

There's something almost quaint about the movie's documentary-style depiction of "modern" investigative techniques (fingerprint comparisons, handwriting analysis, et cetera) in scenes that have served as templates for later generations of police procedurals and TV cop shows. But the striving for verisimilitude doesn't end there. While preparing their script, Lang and Thea von Harbou, his screenwriter wife, interviewed members of the Berlin criminal class to ensure accuracy of behavioral and linguistic detail. The director went so far as to hire real criminals as extras for the famous kangaroo court sequence, where the mass murder is tried by a jury of his "peers."

(Take a close look at the English subtitles, and you'll discover that, even though Lang originally was inspired by the "Monster of Düsseldorf," the unnamed setting of his movie is unmistakably Berlin. Each time a police detective orders the arrest of a suspect, the subtitler translates "Alex" as "headquarters." And rightly so: The original German gangster slang refers to the Berlin police headquarters on the Alexanderplatz.)

To a large degree, however, the most impressive aspects of *M* are those elements that are conspicuous by their absence. The killer, here known as Hans Beckert, never commits an act of violence on camera. In fact, during most of the film, Peter Lorre plays him as a sweaty and pathetic nonentity who is easily spooked by unwanted attention, who is almost pitiable in his anguish as he defends himself during his "trial." It's shockingly easy to sympathize with this murderer of innocents when he wails: "Always... Always, there is this evil force inside me... It's there all the time, driving me to wander through the streets... It's me, pursuing myself, because I want to escape... But it's impossible... *I have to obey it...* Who will believe me? Who knows what it is like to be me?"

Lang chillingly implies unspeakable horrors by focusing on mundane details. This indirect approach is especially effective during the aforementioned opening scenes, as we see and hear relatively little, but much more than enough. A little girl's ball rolls out from a bush. A balloon floats upward, to be entangled in electrical wires. A mother's plaintive cry for her missing daughter reverberates on the soundtrack as Lang cuts to an empty place at the kitchen table.

Here and elsewhere, the impact of the imagery is intensified by the almost complete absence of unnecessary sounds. *M* doesn't need an overbearing orchestral score to tell us what to think or how to feel; Lang was one of the first directors of talking pictures who fully appreciated the dramatic power of *silence*. The only music he provides is the killer's anxious whistling of the "Hall of the Mountain King" theme from Edvard Grieg's *Peer Gynt* during moments of emotional duress. It's worth noting, by the way, that Lang wasn't satisfied with Lorre's efforts, so he dubbed the whistling himself, deliberately striving for an off-key, tuneless sound to indicate madness.

It's also worth noting that, despite the ambiguity of the film's final scene, in which three grieving mothers remind us that no sentence passed by judges could ever bring back their dead children, some of Lang's contemporaries insisted on reading a law-and-order message into *M*. Joseph Goebbels, soon to be propaganda minister of the Third Reich, saw the movie during its initial theatrical run. On May 21, 1931, he noted in his diary: "Fantastic! Against humanitarian sappiness. For the death penalty. Well made. Lang will be our director one day." Two years later, however, Lang declined Goebbels' offer to head the German industry, and fled to the United States.

SPECS:

M — Stars: Peter Lorre, Ellen Widmann, Inge Landgut, Otto Wernicke, Theodor Loos, and Gustaf Grundgens. Directed by Fritz Lang. Screenplay: Thea von Harbou, Fritz Lang. Running time: 110 minutes. Year of release: 1931.

SUBJECTS FOR FURTHER RESEARCH:

Fury (1936) — In his first American movie, Fritz Lang took another dim view of mob hysteria while once again blurring the lines between cop and criminal, justice and revenge. Spencer Tracy plays a drifter who's wrongly accused of kidnapping in a small town, and very nearly lynched.

Shadow of a Doubt (1943) — Working from a script by Thornton Wilder (yes, that's right, the guy who wrote *Our Town*), Alfred Hitchcock concocted this classic thriller about beguiling evil lying low in a cheery small town. Joseph Cotten gives one of his best and creepiest performances as a charming gentleman with an unfortunate habit of wooing and murdering wealthy widows. His family greets him with open arms when he arrives for a visit. But then his favorite niece (Teresa Wright) reads about the manhunt for "The Merry Widow Murderer," and starts to suspect the worst about her beloved uncle.

The Silence of the Lambs (1991) — In sharp contrast to Peter Lorre's anguished portrayal of the tortured and self-loathing Hans Beckert, Anthony Hopkins goes for silken, insinuating menace, with just a soupcon of bloodthirsty ferocity, as the cannibalistic Hannibal Lecter in Jonathan Demme's Oscar-winning thriller. Different approaches, similar results: A monster responsible for unspeakable crimes becomes, if not entirely sympathetic, worthy of rooting interest.

LESSONS FOR FILMMAKERS:

Silence can speak volumes, as Fritz Lang repeatedly demonstrates in *M*. On the other hand, it may be a good idea to ask questions — if not express yourself nonverbally — should you be greeted with hostile responses every time you describe a proposed project. Lang originally planned to call his serial-killer drama *Murderers Among Us*. Time and again, however, he encountered negative reactions to this title. Indeed, while negotiating to rent an unused zeppelin hangar as a filming location, Lang was told by its caretaker that the hanger would never be available for a movie with such a title. "Without realizing it," Lang told an interviewer many years later, "I had grabbed him by the shirt and said, 'Why shouldn't I make this film?' And all of a sudden, I saw that there, on his lapel, was the (Nazi) Party insignia with the swastika." Lang instantly realized that the caretaker — and, perhaps, everyone else who had bristled upon hearing the title — had assumed his movie would be some sort of cautionary diatribe against Adolf Hitler and his rabid followers. When the caretaker was informed that Lang's movie was about a mass murderer — that is, an apolitical mass murderer — the hangar suddenly became available to the director.

THE PUBLIC
ENEMY

Despite what you've heard from three of four generations of nightclub comics and impressionists, James Cagney always insisted that he never really said "You dirty rat!" in any of his movies. Not even in William Wellman's *The Public Enemy*, where such verbal belligerence typified his portrayal of Tom Powers, a cocky and crafty bootlegger whose unbound id, hair-trigger temper, and insatiable appetites have enduringly defined the character as a prototype for cinema's most memorably monstrous gangsters.

On the other hand, Cagney most certainly *did* shove a grapefruit into the face of co-star Mae Clark during a key moment of Wellman's 1931 classic. Decades after the movie's first release, this celebrated scene remains shocking in the sheer casualness of its brutality. Cagney's bantamweight thug tires of nonstop nagging by his increasingly annoying girlfriend during breakfast, so he simply grabs the first object at hand to silence her yapping. It's not merely a spontaneous gesture, it's a wielding of absolute power — he does it because, dammit, he's *entitled* to do it. You won't find a scarier example of nonchalant sociopathy this side of Martin Scorsese's *GoodFellas* (1990), wherein Joe Pesci's demented Mafioso matter-of-factly shoots a troublesome waiter, then kills the poor guy for complaining.

Cagney didn't merely become a star, he established himself as an icon in *The Public Enemy*. With showboating displays of mannerisms that would forever define his on-screen persona — the frightfully ambiguous smile, the insolent curl of his lip, the staccato delivery of dialogue, the chronic hitching of his pants with clenched fists — he gives a performance at once theatrically stylized and persuasively naturalistic. And if that sounds contradictory, well, that's also part of his magic. As actor Malcolm McDowell, a Cagney admirer, perceptively noted, "The point is that you believed him — and he was *real*, but not *realistic*. They're different worlds altogether."

Cagney was the right man in the right role at the right time. During Wellman's must-see movie, his Tom Powers traverses an arc that begins with increasingly violent juvenile delinquency — he's betrayed by a Fagin-like crime boss, Putty Nose (Murray Kinnell), who later pays dearly for his treachery — and reaches an apogee with spectacular success as a mid-level mobster. Along with Matt Doyle (Edward Woods), a childhood friend and long-time partner in crime, Tom makes his mark as sales representative for a bootlegger with unforgiving rules regarding product placement. Tom enjoys fast women (including a sexy young Jean Harlow) and big money, much to the mounting concern of his saintly mother (Beryl Mercer) and Mike (Donald Cook), his honest brother.

Much of the violence in *The Public Enemy* — including the shooting of the traitorous Putty Nose, and the vengeance killing of a horse that may have inspired similar animal cruelty in *The Godfather* (1972) — occurs off-camera. But there's never any attempt to soft-peddle the unadulterated joy Tom takes in dishing out rough stuff. When Mike dares to complain about Tom's murderous business methods, Tom sneers at his sibling, a decorated WWI vet, and sarcastically snaps: "You didn't get those medals for holding hands with the Germans!"

In the end, of course, crime can't pay and the criminal must die: The final scene has Tom deposited as a bandage-wrapped corpse on his poor mother's doorstep. But that grisly quietus does relatively little to dim the attractive glow of earlier scenes that tend to glamorize strutting outlawry and conspicuous consumption. Those elements were potently symbolic, and politically charged, in an era before the Production Code curtailed violence and other antisocial behavior in movies. Many Depression Era audiences, enduring unemployment and deprivation in the wake of the stock market crash, dreamed of revenge against a system that had failed them. As a result, gangsters of the sort essayed by Cagney, Edward G. Robinson (*Little Caesar*, 1930), Paul Muni (*Scarface*, 1932), and Humphrey Bogart (*The Petrified Forest*, 1936) frequently were greeted as fantasy fulfillments.

Even now, Tom Powers' nose-thumbing disregard for convention (to say nothing of his lack of impulse control) is echoed in the protagonists of contemporary crime stories — *Casino*, *The Sopranos*, et cetera — and gangsta-rapper music videos. Robert Warshaw insightfully illuminated the phenomenon in *The Gangster as Tragic Hero*, his seminal 1949 essay, when he noted that a character such as Cagney's natural-born killer "appeals to that side of all of us which refuses to believe in the 'normal' possibilities of happiness and achievement; the gangster is the 'no' to the great American 'yes' which is stamped so big over our official culture and yet has so little to do with the way we really feel about our lives... And the story of his career is a nightmare inversion of the values of ambition and opportunity."

SPECS:

The Public Enemy — Stars: James Cagney, Jean Harlow, Edward Woods, Joan Blondell, Beryl Mercer, Donald Cook, Mae Clark, and Murray Kinnell. Director: William Wellman. Screenplay: Harvey Thew, based on a story by Kubec Glasmon and John Bright. Running time: 84 minutes. Year of release: 1931. VHS distributor: Warner Home Video.

SUBJECTS FOR FURTHER RESEARCH:

Get Carter (1971) — Michael Caine channels the tightly-coiled ferocity of James Cagney's Tom Powers throughout his superb performance as Jack Carter, a Brit mob hit man who kicks ass and takes lives while hunting for his brother's killer in Mike Hodges' classic neo-noir gangster drama. Scariest moment: Carter pulls out a knife after grilling an informant, then coolly announces: "You *knew* what I was going to do..."

Scarface (1983) — Although technically a remake of Howard Hawks' 1932 classic, Brian De Palma's deliriously overstated cult-fave melodrama about a Cuban-born cocaine kingpin owes at least as much to *Public*

Enemy. Al Pacino's swaggeringly flamboyant Tony Montana may be more of a cartoonish caricature than Cagney's snarlingly streetwise Tom Powers, but it's safe to say each character would recognize in the other the same cutthroat entrepreneurial spirit.

Miller's Crossing (1990) — On two occasions in Joel and Ethan Coen's stylish gangster drama, a weaselly hood (John Turturro) echoes the plaintively plea of Murray Kinnell's doomed Putty Nose in *Public Enemy*. "Look in your heart," he cries while begging for mercy from a stern-faced mob enforcer (Gabriel Byrne). Unfortunately, the ploy works only once.

LESSON FOR FILMMAKERS:

Don't be afraid to admit you've made a casting mistake even after the cameras have started rolling. A few days into the production of *Public Enemy*, director William Wellman and studio production chief Darryl Zanuck realized that Edward Woods, originally cast in the title role, simply didn't seem tough enough on screen. In sharp contrast, James Cagney, originally cast as Woods' sidekick, dominated every scene in which he appeared. So the two actors were told to exchange roles, and the rest is movie history.

THE MALTESE FALCON

Even purists who routinely oppose cinematic recycling concede the 1941 film version of Dashiell Hammett's *The Maltese Falcon* merits special dispensation from any Thou Shalt Not Remake admonition. The Warners Bros. brass okayed two earlier adaptations of Hammett's classic private-eye yarn — including *Satan Met a Lady* (1936), with Bette Davis cast as a conniving vixen — before screenwriter John Huston got a crack at the property for his directorial debut. The third time proved to be the charm, as Huston delivered a briskly paced, enormously entertaining melodrama, the perfect big-screen translation of Hammett's terse, tough-as-nails prose.

The dialogue, much of it lifted intact from Hammett's book, is deliciously hard-boiled. ("Keep on riding me — they're gonna be picking iron out of your liver!" "The cheaper the hood, the gaudier the patter!") And the actors are so perfectly matched with their roles that, more than six decades later, they continue to define the archetypes: Mary Astor as a seemingly helpless beauty with ice in her veins and crime on her mind; Sydney Greenstreet as a suave criminal mastermind who coyly toys with the hero; Peter Lorre as a fey supporting villain given to mincing murmurs and outraged hissy fits; and Elisha Cook Jr. as a cocky hired gun whose bold talk is undermined by ineffective actions.

The wild card in the deck is Humphrey Bogart as Sam Spade, a San Francisco detective who's driven to find the eponymous artifact — variously referred to as "the falcon," "the black bird" or, less reverentially, "the dingus" — after his partner is killed by someone seeking the legendary prize. Think you know what to expect of such a character? Well, guess again. As Spade, the breakthrough role that solidified his stardom, Bogart isn't the noble knight-errant of pulp fiction legend. (He played *that* role five years later, as Raymond Chandler's Philip Marlowe in Howard Hawks' *The Big Sleep*.) Nor is he the melancholy romantic hero he later essayed in *Casablanca*.

In *The Maltese Falcon*, Bogart plays Hammett's private detective as an aggressively anti-heroic SOB fueled with industrial-strength cynicism. Whenever he pummels Lorre's effeminate Joel Cairo or viciously taunts Cook's easily disarmed gunman, he reveals flashes of a barely contained savagery that, even in twenty-first-century cinema, more image-conscious action heroes rarely dare to display. ("When you're slapped," he snarls at a cringing Cairo, "you'll take it and like it!") But, then again, brutality is a way of life for Bogart's Sam Spade. Mere hours after his partner's untimely demise, the shameless shamus instructs his spunky secretary (Lee Patrick) to remove said partner's name from the office door and windows. He also rebuffs the dead man's not-so-grieving widow — with whom, it's worth noting, Spade has been having an affair.

By turns a sadistic little bully and a single-minded sociopath, Spade ultimately turns a seductive *femme fatale* over to the cops to prove — more to himself than anyone else — what a badass he is. Granted, he makes a token stab at claiming a slightly loftier motive. ("When a man's partner is killed, he's supposed to do something about it!") But even he can't believe what he's saying. Pressed by the murderess to give her a break, he growls: "I won't — because all of me wants to, regardless of the consequences!"

He won't play the sap for anyone, Spade insists. And you believe him, without question, because it's so obvious that he's already cast himself as the brightest, toughest, and coldest bastard you'd never want to meet. Indeed, he sounds as though he's delivering a well-rehearsed line from a self-prepared script when he caresses the *femme fatale* with his frigid sarcasm: "I hope they don't hang you, precious, by that sweet neck."

The Maltese Falcon has served as inspiration for hundreds of later private-eye melodramas, from *The Big Sleep* to *Chinatown* (1975) and beyond. But very few of the shamuses in subsequent movies have ever seemed so unremorseful — so unhinged, really — as Bogart does at his fearsome best in Huston's masterwork. All of which raises a couple of questions: Were audiences more willing to accept surly anti-heroes sixty-plus years ago? Or, more likely, are contemporary filmmakers simply too timorous when it comes to smoothing out the rough edges of potentially unsympathetic characters?

SPECS:

The Maltese Falcon — Stars: Humphrey Bogart, Mary Astor, Gladys George, Peter Lorre, Barton MacLane, Lee Patrick, Sydney Greenstreet, Ward Bond, and Elisha Cook Jr. Written and directed by John Huston, based on the novel by Dashiell Hammett. Running time: 100 minutes. Year of release: 1941. DVD distributor: Warner Home Video.

SUBJECTS FOR FURTHER RESEARCH:

Kiss Me Deadly (1955) — As Mike Hammer, author Mickey Spillane's legendarily hardboiled private eye, Ralph Meeker blunders and blusters his way through Robert Aldrich's cult-fave *film noir* on the trail of a stolen nuclear bomb. Unfortunately, he finds what he's looking for, in a scene later referenced by *Repo Man* (1984) and *Pulp Fiction* (1994).

The Black Bird (1975) — The laughs are few and far between throughout David Giler's grievously unfunny "sequel" to *The Maltese Falcon*, in which George Segal struggles as Sam Spade Jr. Even so, the alleged comedy is worth watching to see Elisha Cook Jr. and Lee Patrick reprise their characters from the original 1941 classic.

Night Moves (1975) — Purloined artifacts figure into the plot of Arthur Penn's classic neo-noir thriller (which, alas, was criminally underrated by critics during its original theatrical run). But the drama pays closer attention to the *Sturm und Drang* of private eye Harry Moseby (Gene Hackman at his finest), a troubled anti-hero who divides his time between shadowing his unfaithful wife (Susan Clark) and searching for a sexy runaway (Melanie Griffith).

LESSON FOR FILMMAKERS:

Some actors really should be allowed to make up their own dialogue. Humphrey Bogart (encouraged by a cannily indulgent John Huston) dreamed up the memorable final line for *The Maltese Falcon* — "It's the stuff that dreams are made of!" — perhaps the most fortuitous improvisation in movie history. He was referring to the "dingus" of the title, of course, but he also was paraphrasing a line from Shakespeare's *The Tempest*: "We are such stuff as dreams are made on..."

DOUBLE INDEMNITY

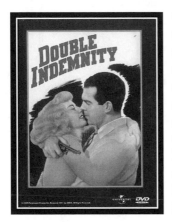

Okay, stop me if you've already heard this one. There's this guy who thinks he knows all the right angles, and this dame who knows she has all the right curves. He takes one look at her — the same kind of admiring appraisal a starving man might give to a Big Mac — and decides to detour from the straight and narrow path. Unfortunately, she's bad news. Even more unfortunately, he doesn't care. By the time he realizes how far he's in over his head, she's in precisely the right position to keep him immersed in hot water.

Sound familiar? It should. The scenario sketched above has long been a template for steamy dramas of crime and passion, some impressive (*The Postman Always Rings Twice, Criss Cross, Scarlet Street*), most not (*Palmetto, China Moon*, countless made-for-video movies starring Shannon Tweed). For discerning movie buffs, however, the most effective and indelible telling of the oft-told tale is *Double Indemnity*, Billy Wilder's cunningly well-crafted masterwork.

Of course, part of the fun associated with watching *Double Indemnity* today comes from being, in essence, witness at creation. The 1944 release is credited by most cinema scholars as one of the very first examples of *film noir*. Long before French film critics coined that term to describe those robustly hard-boiled and expressionistically stylized products of post-WWII Hollywood, *Double Indemnity* introduced the artifices and archetypes that would come to typify the genre: The prevailing mood of doom-laden cynicism; the deeply flawed, self-deluding anti-hero who willingly falls from grace; the seductive *femme fatale* who lures him beyond the point of no return; the seemingly foolproof plan that goes terribly, fatally wrong.

In Wilder's fiendishly clever drama — which he adapted, with an often contentious Raymond Chandler, from a novel by James M. Cain — the star-crossed chump who's drawn into danger is played by, of all people, Fred MacMurray. Even back in the 1940s, the casting of this affable lightweight in such a seamy role came as an unsettling surprise. Contemporary viewers who remember MacMurray only as the genial father figure from Disney comedies and TV's *My Three Sons* may be even more shocked. The good news is, MacMurray's performance, perhaps the finest of his long career, has a lot more than novelty value going for it.

Some classic noirs (*D.O.A.*, *Detour*) focus on anti-heroes who stumble into damnation almost by accident. But MacMurray offers the definitive portrayal of a more common *noir* archetype: A smart-mouthed cynic who isn't nearly as bright as he thinks, who's driven by roiling passion, or raging hormones, to plunge headlong into the lower depths.

MacMurray plays Walter Neff, a smooth-talking insurance agent who's undone by his fatal attraction to a client's sexy wife. In the movie's opening minutes, Neff makes a late-night visit to his downtown office, to spill his guts into a co-worker's dictation machine. That he's also spilling blood makes his activity all the more attention-grabbing.

Neff's "confession" cues an extended flashback that details his misadventure with Phyllis Dietrichson (Barbara Stanwyck), an alluringly leggy temptress whose tremulous vulnerability is far more apparent than real. When Neff drops by to extend her husband's auto-accident coverage, Mrs. Dietrichson drops transparently obvious hints that she'd be very happy, and extremely grateful, if she could secretly purchase a hefty life insurance policy for Mr. Dietrichson.

To his credit, Neff sees right through her beguiling come-on, and walks out the door. To his everlasting remorse, he reconsiders his initial response, and agrees to help the widow-to-be spin her web. "How could I know," he later asks himself, "that murder sometimes smells like honeysuckle?"

Mindful of Production Code restraints, Wilder works wonders with the power of suggestion. There's little doubt that Neff and Phyllis are getting horizontal whenever the camera isn't peeking, but the most revealing thing we ever see is a provocative shot of Phyllis clad only in a clingy towel. ("I was taking a sun bath," she insinuatingly coos, greatly perking the insurance agent's interest.) Later, when Neff rises from behind to murder Mr. Dietrichson in the passenger seat of the latter's car, we don't see anything of the actual strangulation. Instead, Wilder cuts away to a close-up of Phyllis, silently smiling and calmly driving while her partner in crime does the dirty work.

Perfectly cast as the blond and brazen Phyllis, Stanwyck is at her best in the movie's second half, as she and MacMurray are undone by their worst suspicions of each other. ("We're both rotten," he admits. "Only you're a little more rotten.") Thanks to the indefatigable efforts of Neff's co-worker and surrogate father, a claims investigator played with blustering gusto by Edward G. Robinson, it doesn't take long before the "accidental" death is revealed as a cold-blooded murder. The more Robinson digs, the more Stanwyck and MacMurray sweat. Savage ironies abound, poetic justice is served — and the viewer appreciates every moment of a grandly entertaining classic.

SPECS:

Double Indemnity — Stars: Fred MacMurray, Barbara Stanwyck, and Edward G. Robinson. Directed by Billy Wilder. Screenplay: Billy Wilder and Raymond Chandler based on the novel by James M. Cain. Running time: 107 minutes. Year of release: 1944. DVD distributor: Universal.

SUBJECTS FOR FURTHER RESEARCH:

Out of the Past (1947) — Jacques Tourneur's exemplary *noir* (remade as 1984's *Against All Odds*) stars droopy-eyed Robert Mitchum as a hard-luck anti-hero who's hired to find the errant girlfriend (Jane Greer) of a vicious gangster (Kirk Douglas), and makes the mistake of falling in love.

The Lady from Shanghai (1948) — Orson Welles does triple duty as director, screenwriter and star of this baroque melodrama about an Irish sailor who's drawn into a murder plot while cruising with a beautiful woman

(Rita Hayworth) and her handicapped husband (Everett Sloane). Woody Allen spoofed the movie's celebrated climax — a chase through a funhouse hall of mirrors — in his own *Manhattan Murder Mystery* (1993).

Body Heat (1981) — Lawrence Kasdan updates (and undresses) the standard-issue *noir* scenario in a steamy drama about a none-too-bright lawyer (William Hurt) who's easily manipulated by a hot-to-trot beauty (Kathleen Turner in a career-defining performance) with an inconvenient husband (Richard Crenna).

LESSON FOR FILMMAKERS:

"*Film noir* revealed the dark underbelly of human life," Martin Scorsese writes in his *Personal Journey Through American Movies*. "Its denizens were private eyes, rogue cops, white-collar criminals, *femmes fatales*. As Raymond Chandler put it, 'The streets were dark with something more than night.' After *Double Indemnity*, you couldn't take anything for granted anymore. Not even suburbia." Maybe so. But whenever he was asked about *film noir*, Billy Wilder himself always insisted that he "never heard that expression" back in the 1940s. "I just made pictures that I would have liked to see. And if I was lucky, it coincided with the taste of the audience."

DETOUR

Film rarely gets more *noir* than Edgar G. Ulmer's *Detour*, a wide-awake nightmare of unforgiving fate and dead-end fatalism that may be the cruddiest great movie ever made. Filmed in six days on a bare minimum of locations for Producers Releasing Corporation, the most impoverished of the Old Hollywood B-movie outfits known collectively as Poverty Row, it fairly reeks of grungy, sweaty desperation on both sides of the cameras. Indeed, it's tempting to imagine this 1945 must-see movie actually was written and directed by its own protagonist, a paranoid loser who's furiously anguished, but not terribly surprised, as his hard-knock life devolves into a worst-case scenario.

We meet Al Roberts (Tom Neal) in a dingy roadside diner that, like most of the movie's other claustrophobic interiors, does not appear to be a studio set so much as a hasty rough sketch for one. Unshaven and socially maladroit, if not borderline psychotic, Al almost immediately alienates everyone around him. Which means, of course, he must resort to voiceover narration — a classic *film noir* device, used to underscore the inevitability of an anti-hero's destiny — when he's stirred to spill his tale of woe.

Trouble is, it's not easy to feel sorry, or even remain patient, while Al regales us in a tone pitched somewhere between a pathetic whine and a self-justifying snarl. And, truth to tell, it's more than a little difficult to believe everything he says as he blames everyone but himself for his dire condition. "Whichever way you turn," he complains, "fate sticks out a

206

foot to trip you." Maybe so, but Al appears quite capable of stumbling into damnation without any outside assistance.

The extended flashback begins with Al speaking of happier days, when he was a pianist, and his girlfriend Sue (Claudia Drake) was a singer, at a New York nightclub. Even here, however, Al sounds like a chronic malcontent — and not just because the nightclub looks only slightly more lavish than the aforementioned roadside diner. When someone slips him a ten-dollar tip, he's underwhelmed: "What was it? A piece of paper, crawling with germs." And when Sue suggests that — somehow, some way — he'll be a great classical pianist, he snaps: "Yeah, someday! If I don't get arthritis first!"

Sue eventually announces her plan to leave town, to try her luck in Hollywood. (At least, that's her story, and she sticks with it.) Al decides to follow the only way he can afford — as a hitchhiker. He fortuitously finds a soul mate when he climbs into the convertible of Charlie Haskell (Edmund MacDonald), a glad-handing high-roller who seems, if such a thing can be imagined, even more misanthropic than Al. Asked about unsightly scratches on his hand, Haskell boasts: "I was tussling with the most dangerous animal in the world — a woman!" Al sympathizes: "There ought to be a law against dames with claws."

Unfortunately, the budding friendship between like-minded fellows is cut short during a heavy rainstorm. While Al tries to open the convertible top, a slumbering Haskell falls out of the door — and fatally bumps his head. Naturally, since Al is a *film noir* patsy and not a reasonably sentient human being, the poor lug decides that, since nobody would ever believe he didn't kill Haskell, he should dump the body, plant his own I.D. on the corpse, and drive away with the dead man's amply-stuffed wallet.

And then, as if to fully demonstrate his limitless capacity for self-destructive behavior, Al stops to pick up a hitchhiker a little further down the road. Yes, that's right: He's driving a dead man's car, on his way to see a girlfriend he simply can't live without, and he still can't resist slowing down for a hottie with, as he puts it, "a beauty that's almost homely because it's so real." Unfortunately, Vera (Ann Savage) — perhaps the most hard-bitten *femme fatale* in the entire pantheon of *noir* shady ladies — is the "dame with claws" who scarred Haskell. Even more unfortunately, she doesn't buy Al's story about Haskell's untimely demise. ("What did you do? Kiss him with a wrench?") And even if he is innocent, she doesn't give a damn: She's ready to blow the whistle on him anyway, unless he co-operates in her dubious scheme to fleece big bucks from Haskell's long-estranged family.

Vera doesn't appear until midway through this 68-minute movie, and she doesn't get to stick around until the final scene. (Big surprise, right?) But never mind: Once she sashays into the story, she dominates *Detour* like slumming royalty, bullying and browbeating the hapless, helpless Al for the sheer fun of it.

Having sunk even deeper into the lower depths than her reluctant companion — if you can believe her, she's dying of consumption – Vera is viciously eager to make a killing so she can finance her final days. But the more time she spends with Al inside the cramped quarters of a low-rent hotel room, the more energy and attention she diverts to a sadomasochistic relationship that, at its nastiest, makes the toxic byplay between George and Martha in *Who's Afraid of Virginia Woolf?* seem like conjugal bliss. (A typical taunt: "I'd hate to see a fellow as young as you wind up sniffin' that perfume Arizona hands out free to murderers!") Vera's telling response to Al's whiny pleading — "Stop making noises like a husband!" — intensifies the impression that, intentionally or otherwise, the second half of *Detour* plays like a perverse parody of a deeply troubled marriage.

And speaking of perversity: *Detour*, a squalid Poverty Row quickie that only gradually gained acceptance as a classic, turned out to be the high point in the lives of almost everyone involved.

Edgar G. Ulmer began his career at the heart of German Expressionism, working as a set and production designer for such notables as F.W. Murnau, Fritz Lang, and Ernst Lubitsch. After immigrating to the United States, however, he toiled mostly as a director of low-budget genre films, often disguising his threadbare production values with artful applications of light, shadow, and camera movement. (Peter Bogdanovich once marveled: "Nobody ever made good pictures faster or for less money than Edgar G. Ulmer.") He maintains a loyal cult following for a few other works — most notably, *The Black Cat* (1934), a seriously creepy thriller featuring Boris Karloff, Bela Lugosi, and striking Bauhaus-inspired sets — but remains best known for this single, singularly bleak B-movie.

Likewise, Ann Savage had a fleeting career as a minor Hollywood contract player, but never found a better or showier role than the virulent Vera. Even so, she enjoyed more happily-ever-aftering than the seemingly cursed Tom Neal, a quick-tempered ex-boxer who spent most of his final years in prison for the "involuntary manslaughter" of his wife. Although prosecutors originally sought a first-degree murder conviction, Neal always claimed the fatal shooting was accidental. Much as his character in *Detour* insisted that Haskell died because of a fall — and that Vera just happened to wind up in the wrong place at the wrong time when Al yanked on a telephone chord.

Knowing what happened to Neal two decades after *Detour*, you may be even more skeptical of Al's account, and more inclined to interpret the improbabilities of the plot as unconvincing testimony by a guilty party. In many ways, however, the movie is more potent, more devastating, if every word Al tells us is — God help him — absolutely true. Because if he *isn't* lying, it's all the more difficult to shake the chill evoked by his final line: "Fate, or some mysterious force, can put the finger on you or me for no good reason at all."

SPECS:

Detour — Stars: Tom Neal, Ann Savage, Claudia Drake, and Edmund MacDonald. Director: Edgar G. Ulmer. Screenplay: Martin Goldsmith, based on his novel. Running time: 68 minutes. Year of release: 1945. DVD distributor: Image Entertainment.

SUBJECTS FOR FURTHER RESEARCH:

D.O.A. (1950) — Almost as *noir* as *Detour*, Rudolph Mate's ruthlessly downbeat drama focuses on an accountant (Edmond O'Brien) who spends his final, frantic hours desperately seeking the reason why someone spiked his drink with a slow-acting poison.

Carnival of Souls (1962) — A cult-fave ghost story filmed on a cut-rate budget. Herk Harvey's stripped-to-essentials thriller provides a nifty final twist to its tale of a woman haunted by phantom figures in a bleak cityscape. (A random thought: Did M. Night Shyamalan see this before he scripted *The Sixth Sense*?) Minimalist production values somehow enhance the spooky atmosphere.

El Mariachi (1992) — Robert Rodriguez famously filmed his brashly self-assured debut feature for only $7,000. Not surprisingly, it *looks* like a $7,000 movie. Very surprisingly, it's also a genuinely exciting and impressive action-adventure, about a musician who's forced to improvise when he's mistaken for a murderous criminal.

LESSON FOR FILMMAKERS:

While filming *The Thin Blue Line* (1988), his mesmerizingly *noir*-like nonfiction feature about a hitchhiker wrongly convicted of murder, documentarian Errol Morris found himself thinking a lot about Edgar G. Ulmer's classic *film noir*. "I used to joke," Morris said, "that my films would get made when I became as desperate as the characters in them. Well, *Detour* becomes the prime example of this sort of thing... I like to think that all movies contain some kind of documentary element, but this is something far stranger, or if you like, something deeply weird. The movie became a prefiguration, a kind of prescient vision, of what was going to befall (Tom Neal) later in real life." Morris' own movie prefigured a more upbeat real-life ending: It sparked a judicial review that led to the exoneration of its unjustly imprisoned subject.

BONNIE AND CLYDE

So many decades after the fact, it's difficult, maybe impossible, to fully appreciate the impact *Bonnie and Clyde* had on movie-goers. Indeed, even if you're old enough to have seen Arthur Penn's violent folk ballad during its initial theatrical release, more than three decades' worth of subsequent cinematic slaughter very likely has immunized you against the shock value of this film's groundbreaking bloody mayhem.

To be sure, *Bonnie and Clyde* still can make you flinch, particularly when Warren Beatty's Clyde Barrow shoots a bank employee in the face during the panicky chaos of a high-speed getaway. (Clyde's horror is palpable: This is the first time he's ever had to actually kill anyone.) And the extended slo-mo carnage of the famously bloody finale, which has Bonnie Parker (Faye Dunaway) and her partner riddled with dozens of bullets in a police ambush, is all the more devastating because of the empathy we inevitably feel for these Depression-era desperadoes.

Even so, violence is no longer the most provocative element of this must-see movie. Instead, it is the period drama's audacious commingling of style and substance that continues to amaze and unsettle viewers.

When it first hit theaters in 1967, *Bonnie and Clyde* was condemned by some outraged reviewers as a grotesquely comical treatment of dead-serious subject matter. (A *Newsweek* critic originally roasted the movie in a brief, brutally dismissive review — only to later announce an unprecedented change of heart in a cover-story rave.) Worse, according to the most disapproving pundits, the filmmakers appeared to glorify the murderous antics of their title characters. *New York Times* critic Bosley Crowther went so far as to condemn *Bonnie and Clyde* as "a cheap piece of bald-faced slapstick comedy that treats the hideous deprecations of that sleazy, moronic pair as though they were as full of fun and frolic as the jazz-age cut-ups in *Thoroughly Modern Millie.*"

But *Bonnie and Clyde* was never that simple, and seems even more complex today. There's a long tradition of Hollywood dramas about lovers on the run who turn to crime — and, in the process, turn each other on — only to wind up being force-fed their just deserts. But director Penn and screenwriters Robert Benton and David Newton were among the first post-modernist filmmakers to view such outlaws as neither cunningly sinister nor tragically misguided, but rather as absurdly self-deluded.

The Bonnie and Clyde of Penn's film are not quite evil, and not entirely dim-witted. They turn to crime primarily because there's nothing else to do to dispel the soul-dimming boredom of small-town life in Depression-era Texas. (Also, it's a good way for Clyde to compensate for his impotence.) Once they decide to become criminals — impulsively, as they do everything else — they want to be superstars in their field. Early on, when Clyde meets a farmer whose home has been foreclosed by a bank, he introduces Bonnie and himself with a bold claim: "We rob banks." In point of fact, neither has done anything quite so serious up to that point. But after Clyde boasts so heartily in front of Bonnie, it's only a matter of time before he must make good on his promise.

Bonnie and Clyde is a comedy of sorts, but the humor is midnight dark and the punchlines are real killers. Joined by Clyde's bumptious brother (Gene Hackman) and whiny sister-in-law (Estelle Parson), and a dim-bulb driver (Michael J. Pollard) who inadvertently causes the movie's first serious bloodshed, Bonnie and Clyde conduct a crime spree throughout the Southwest, always mindful of their own newspaper coverage and sometimes willing to supply what might be described as publicity stills. Long after they get in way over their heads, they don't recognize that they're drowning.

Bonnie has a glimmer or two of what's in store for them — note the tragic ending for her self-aggrandizing poem — but Clyde remains ludicrously unaware and unapologetic. Near the end, when Bonnie wistfully asks what he'd do if, by magic, they could somehow start over, Clyde blithely responds that he would take pains to never rob a bank in a state they would call home.

Penn firmly places his characters in the context of their time, and gives a strong sense of the fear, loathing, and star-worship they inspired among their contemporaries. And yet *Bonnie and Clyde* remains remarkably timeless in its double-edged view of ordinary folks who achieve extraordinary notoriety — who romanticize themselves as outlaws, even revolutionaries, but remain as banal and smaller-than-life as a stereotypical dysfunctional family.

Many later movies have attempted to use *Bonnie and Clyde* as a template. But the original, unlike most imitators, never makes the fatal mistake of reducing everything to cartoonish excess or ironic posturing. Bonnie and Clyde may be foolhardy killers, but they also are recognizably human. We are not asked to excuse or forgive them. But we cannot help caring as they suffer, bleed, and die without fully comprehending who they are and what they've done.

SPECS:

Bonnie and Clyde — Stars: Warren Beatty, Faye Dunaway, Michael J. Pollard, Gene Hackman, and Estelle Parsons. Directed by Arthur Penn. Screenplay: David Newman, Robert Benton. Running time: 112 minutes. Year of release: 1967. DVD distributor: Warner Home Video.

SUBJECTS FOR FURTHER RESEARCH:

Boxcar Bertha (1972) — *Bonnie and Clyde* spawned scores of copycat dramas about Depression-era outlaws (including *Killers Three*, a 1968 B-flick starring — no kidding — Dick Clark as a bespectacled psycho). *Boxcar Bertha*, a 1972 Roger Corman quickie starring Barbara Hershey as a white-trash *femme fatale*, is the most notable of the wanna-bes, if only because it's the first commercial film directed by Martin Scorsese.

Badlands (1973) — Terrence Malick's spare, semi-absurdist drama takes a chillingly deadpan approach to violent crimes of a Kit (Martin Sheen) and Holly (Sissy Spacek), none-too-bright fugitives who either can't or won't comprehend the enormity of their actions. The movie was inspired by the 1958 killing spree of Charles Starkweather and Carol Fugate, with names changed to protect the guilty.

Natural Born Killers (1994) — Echoing Bonnie Parker's poetic self-promotion, Oliver Stone's hallucinatory social satire imagines vicious killers (Woody Harrelson, Juliette Lewis) who transform themselves into multimedia superstars in a voyeuristic age of blood-and-guts television, sensationalistic tabloids, and true-crime best-sellers.

LESSON FOR FILMMAKERS:

A few critics can make or break films. Even fewer films can make or break critics. Pauline Kael ignited her ascent as the doyenne of American film critics with her insightfully celebratory review of *Bonnie and Clyde* in the *New Yorker*. For Bosley Crowther, however, his *no comprende* pan of the same movie signaled the beginning of the end of his tenure at the *New York Times*.

GOODFELLAS

Take your pick: *GoodFellas* is (a) an epic gangster melodrama of white-hot passion and blood-red mayhem; (b) a darkly hilarious comedy of bad manners about lethal impulses and unbridled ambition; (c) an absurdist satire of middle-class morality gone perverse, voracious consumerism as a way of life, and the ties that bind only until they're hacked off or blasted away; or (d) all of the above.

The correct answer, of course, is (d), though you might amend it to read: "All of the above, and much more." Ever since it blasted its way into the pop-culture pantheon in 1990, *GoodFellas* remains — arguably, even more than Francis Ford Coppola's *Godfather* trilogy — the touchstone for all subsequent mob-scene movies, and a prime influence for everything from *Analyze This* and *Mickey Blue Eyes* to *Donnie Brasco* and TV's *The Sopranos*.

This teeming saga of life and death among mid-level Mafiosi is consistently electrifying, charged by director Martin Scorsese with alternating currents of wonderment and repulsion. Like Henry Hill, the movie's POV protagonist, viewers may be amused at first by the swaggering vitality of the villains on view. But then Scorsese rubs our noses in what these people really are all about, and even Henry is aghast.

Working from a screenplay he co-wrote with Nicolas Pileggi — author of *Wiseguy*, the nonfiction book on which the movie is based — Scorsese dramatizes three decades in the life of Henry (played by Christopher Serrone as a teen-ager, Ray Liotta as an adult), an Irish-Sicilian Brooklyn kid who greets us with a simple, heartfelt statement: "As far back as I could remember, I always wanted to be a gangster."

Henry begins as a gofer for neighborhood hoods, and impresses them enough to be "adopted" into their family — even though, because of his Irish background, he can never be accepted into the Mafia hierarchy. He begins, and remains, an observant outsider, making him all the more useful as the movie's narrator. Right from the start, Henry appreciates the value of having good friends in low places: When Henry's parents are informed of their son's frequent truancy, mobsters warn the neighborhood mailman not to deliver another letter from the school board.

Later, Henry ignores the round-the-block line of waiting customers and strides into the side door of the Copacabana nightclub with Karen (Lorraine Bracco), his future wife, on his arm. He doesn't have to wait, other people have to wait on him, because "being a gangster is like being president of the United States." It's a stunning sequence, a long continuous shot propelled by Scorsese's breakneck virtuosity and Michael Ballhaus' relentlessly gliding Steadicam. Here and elsewhere, *GoodFellas* is about nothing so much as the rush of feeling totally in control, among the chosen few.

Trouble is, that exuberance can turn toxic. On the final day of his freedom, Henry races through a sardonically twisted yuppie-Mafia nightmare of balancing home life and career. He frantically divides his time between preparing a lavish family meal, visiting his mistress, delivering stolen guns, avoiding a pursuing helicopter, readying a drug shipment — and repeatedly charging himself with cocaine. As always, Scorsese picks the perfect pop tunes to underscore the sequence. Ry Cooder's slide guitar intro for *Memo from Turner* dips low and ominously as a coke-addled Henry lurches deeper into paranoia. Then Harry Nilsson's *Jump Into the Fire* explodes in our ears, and the harshly yelped lyrics — "You can jump into the fire, but you'll never be free!" — have the impact of a slap across the face.

Henry has two Mafia "brothers," neither of them reliable. Tommy DeVito (Joe Pesci) is the more obvious sociopath, a volatile hothead who will shoot a waiter in the foot for fun, then shoot him through the heart when the wounded fellow makes a rude remark. But James Conway (Robert De Niro) is even more dangerous in his cold calculations, especially when he begins to exterminate his partners in crime.

The chronically underrated Liotta is riveting as Henry, the ambitious outsider who recognizes much too late the bloody underpinning of his romanticized Mafia fantasyland. De Niro is subtly imposing in what basically is a supporting role, while Pesci — who won a richly deserved Oscar for his performance — is at once hilarious and horrifying as Tommy, the free-wheeling loose cannon who's ultimately destroyed by a bloody ricochet of his own violence.

This is a man's world, but Lorraine Bracco — who takes a more analytical view of mob life in *The Sopranos* — asserts herself as dynamically as the character she portrays. When Karen tires of her husband's infidelities and threatens him with a gun, Bracco makes you believe that, hey, she might really pull the trigger.

SPECS:

GoodFellas — Stars: Robert De Niro, Ray Liotta, Joe Pesci, Lorraine Bracco, and Paul Sorvino. Directed by Martin Scorsese. Screenplay: Nicholas Pileggi and Martin Scorsese, based on Pileggi's book *Wiseguy*. Running time: 146 minutes. Year of release: 1990. DVD distributor: Warner Home Video.

SUBJECTS FOR FURTHER RESEARCH:

Mean Streets (1973) — Martin Scorsese's breathtakingly self-assured breakthrough drama about a small-time hood (Harvey Keitel) and his dangerously unstable buddy (Robert De Niro) contains many distinctive stylistic flourishes (especially the inspired use of a pop-music soundtrack) that would later serve Scorsese so well in *GoodFellas*.

Casino (1995) — *GoodFellas* was a tough act to follow, even for the people who made it. Still, this second Martin Scorsese–Nicholas Pileggi collaboration is a thrilling and vibrant piece of work on its own terms. In fact, this drama of mob action in Los Vegas can be viewed as a counterpoint to their earlier film — colder, harder, and far less empathetic in its view of overweening ambition among Mafiosi.

Boogie Nights (1997) — Paul Thomas Anderson's stunning drama of life and love in the '70s porn-industry demimonde repeatedly "quotes" *GoodFellas* to good effect. Note the opening nightclub sequence, the first party scene at Jack Horner's house, and the final scene at the same abode — all of which feature extended Steadicam tracking shots inspired by the *GoodFellas* Copacabana sequence.

LESSON FOR FILMMAKERS:

Avoid the obvious — until you're ready to embrace your background. To a casual observer, it might seem that Martin Scorsese — an Italian-American filmmaker raised on the mean streets of Manhattan's Little Italy — was predestined to direct a movie such as *GoodFellas*. And yet, largely because he felt it was such a predictable career move, he actively shunned the gangster-movie genre for the first two decades of his career. (*Mean Streets* doesn't really count as a "gangster movie," per se.) It wasn't until he read Nicholas Pileggi's account of mobster-turned-informer Henry Hill that Scorsese felt ready to deal with characters he knew all too well. "I grew up with a lot of these people," he says of Mafiosi like those on view in *GoodFellas*. "Before I knew what it was they did, I thought it was normal."

THE KILLER

ong before Hong Kong action master John Woo dove into the mainstream of North American pop-culture consciousness, his name was whispered with equal measures of awe and amazement by venturesome festivalgoers and video renters.

A Better Tomorrow (1986), his HK box-office breakthrough, jolted even jaded audiences with its exhilarating rush of full-throttle excitement. *A Bullet in the Head* (1990), his audacious commingling of *The Deer Hunter* and *The Good, The Bad and the Ugly* in a slam-bang vengeance melodrama, exponentially increased his loyal following. On the night *Hard-Boiled* (1992) premiered at the Toronto Film Festival, impatient fans could barely contain their pre-screening enthusiasm: They shouted "Woo! Woo! Woo!" like some sort of manic incantation until the lights dimmed and the show began.

But Woomania didn't reach epidemic proportions until *The Killer* (1989), arguably the greatest of his made-in-HK extravaganzas, began reaching international audiences beyond festivals and video stores in 1992. The first of Woo's films to receive even a cursory theatrical release in the United States, this *Killer* thriller introduced the uninitiated to a new breed of action flick: Operatically intense, deliriously passionate, thunderously kinetic — and well-nigh intoxicating in its one-damn-thing-after-another exuberance.

Many other filmmakers — including Quentin Tarantino, a devoted admirer who cribbed from *Better Tomorrow* for his own *Reservoir Dogs* — had already begun to emulate Woo's trademark tropes and rapid-fire stylistics by the time a clumsily English-dubbed version of *The Killer* appeared on the U.S. art-house circuit. (Even the heroine's cat sounds like it was dubbed, probably by the same person who dubbed the heroine.) But after *The Killer* invaded America — followed shortly thereafter by *Hard-Boiled*, Woo's final Hong Kong production, and *Hard Target* (1993), his first made-in-USA opus — the cult-fave filmmaker rapidly evolved into a brand-name product and, more important, a mentor for other moviemakers.

What many of his students forget, however, is that there's as much heart and soul as sound and fury in Woo's cinema. In *The Killer*, the entire plot is propelled by the title character's quest for spiritual redemption after he accidentally blinds a pretty singer (Sally Yeh) during the aftermath of a gangland rubout. The incomparably ultra-cool Chow Yun-Fat plays Jeff, the guilt-racked hit man, who agrees to one last job to pay for the young woman's eye operation. Unfortunately, the hit man is betrayed — first by his employers, then by his best friend (who must then redeem himself by accepting beatings, then bullets, as his just deserts). Jeff meets his fate during an epic gun battle in which he and the blind singer appear to be reenacting the infamous climax of King Vidor's *Duel in the Sun* (1946).

The body count is staggeringly high in *The Killer* — more people are gunned down in the first scene than in all the *Lethal Weapon* movies — but the rock-'em, sock-'em mayhem has an almost surreal quality, balletic and bodacious until it achieves a kind of lunatic beauty. Woo freely admits being inspired by the revisionist Westerns of Sam Peckinpah and Sergio Leone. But in his movies — which, like *The Killer*, often seem like urbanized updates of Wild West melodramas — the slo-mo gunplay usually escalates into something not unlike Armageddon (the one prophesized in the Bible, not the one directed by Michael Bay). Surprisingly, maybe mercifully, much of the rapid-fire carnage is as bloodless as the bad-guy gundowns in '40s B-movies. It's not the occasional vividness, it's the sheer volume of the violence that makes *The Killer* seem so overkilling.

Jeff never shoots one adversary when he can cut down ten or twelve instead. Occasionally — like, after he fires twenty-five or thirty shots from a single pistol — he runs out of bullets. As a matter of fact, something like that happens early on in *The Killer*, just as a bad guy (or, to be more precise, a worse guy) gets ready to fire back. But does this faze our ever-resourceful Jeff? Hell, no. He simply gives a card table a well-placed kick, catapults a slain gangster's gun into his hand, and starts shooting again. Cowabunga!

But don't misunderstand: Just because Jeff is a professional killer doesn't mean he's not a sensitive guy. When a little girl is wounded during a shootout with his treacherous cohorts, he risks capture by taking the child to a nearby hospital. (As he waves his gun, nobody, not even the admitting nurse, questions whether the girl has medical insurance.) And, of course, there's that obsession with healing the sightless girl.

(*Village Voice* critic J. Hoberman likely was first to note the allusion to *Magnificent Obsession*, Douglas Sirk's stylish 1954 weepie about a drunken playboy who becomes a dedicated surgeon in order to treat a woman he accidentally blinded. The big difference, Hoberman wrote, is that *The Killer* plays like "*Magnificent Obsession* remade by Sam Peckinpah.")

All this nobility impresses Detective Lee (Danny Lee), the maverick cop — hey, every country has them! — who's after Jeff. Asked to describe the killer for a police artist, Lee waxes poetic: "He looks determined without being ruthless . . . He acts like he has a dream . . . full of passion." Gleefully perverse in its genre-bending playfulness, *The Killer* pushes way, way out to the forefront what, in other, tamer thrillers, might merely be a subtext: The homoerotic attraction between the antagonists. Woo knows squat about subtext. If he wants the audience to, uh, suspect that Lee and Jeffrey are flirting, he has them wave their handguns in each other's faces. And, oh, yeah, they give each other cute nicknames: Mickey Mouse and Dumbo. No, I'm not making that up.

The Killer contains a lot of talk about fate, friendship, and honor, and you actually can hear much of it above the sound of gunfire. (You can also spot examples of the religious imagery – most notably, fluttering doves as incongruous symbols of peace — so common in Woo's *oeuvre*.) Even as they're mowing down entire platoons of bit players, however, Jeff and Lee sound so sincere, so irony-free, that you can't help taking them as seriously as Woo intends.

It helps, of course, that Woo knows how far even he can push existential musing between the gun battles. "I can do my job," the maverick cop complains at one point, "but nobody trusts me." "I have the same problem," the killer responds. And then, with that out of the way, the shooting resumes.

SPECS:

The Killer — Stars: Chow Yun-Fat, Danny Lee, Sally Yeh, and Kong Chu. Written and directed by John Woo. Running time: 110 minutes. Year of release: 1989. DVD distributor: The Criterion Collection.

SUBJECTS FOR FURTHER RESEARCH:

Le Samourai (1967) — John Woo credits Jean-Pierre Melville's existential thriller about an ice-cold hit man (Alain Delon at his best) as a primary influence on *The Killer*. Here, too, a hired killer precipitates his own downfall by making the fatal mistake of caring too much for an innocent bystander.

Hard-Boiled (1992) — After playing tarnished anti-heroes in *The Killer* and *A Better Tomorrow*, Chow Yun-Fat moved to the other side of the law in Woo's rock-the-house action-adventure, playing a Hong Kong police detective who makes Dirty Harry look like a civil libertarian.

The Matrix (1999) — Armed with overloaded guns in either hand, an impossibly poised dude and an equally lethal dudette wear way-cool sunglasses while blasting inconvenient objects (especially windows) and faceless bit players into slo-mo shards. Throughout the first chapter of their sci-fi trilogy, the Wachowski Brothers demonstrate how much they learned from John Woo movies in general, and *The Killer* in particular.

LESSON FOR FILMMAKERS:

Try not to be terribly disappointed if audiences insist in misinterpreting your work. John Woo says his *The Killer* "is my most romantic film to date, and many people just talk about the action and violence in it." Uh, yeah. Audiences often speak admiringly of a visual calling card first glimpsed in *The Killer*: The hero and the villain wind up standing face-to-face with their handguns pointed at each other's foreheads. To Woo, the image represents the duality of human nature. "The standoff is my trademark," he explained to a SplicedWire.com interviewer. "In my theory, I always feel no one is perfect in this world. There is no real good guy or bad guy in this world. You can see yourself in the bad people. The bad people can see themselves in the good people. So that's why I created the movement of the standoff scene. No matter if it's a good guy or bad guy, they're all equal."

≈10≈
ACTION!

FLASH GORDON

Lion Men and Tigron and bears — oh, my! To say nothing of shifty Shark Men, high-flying Hawk Men or — gasp! — The Mighty Masked Swordsman of Mongo.

Throughout thirteen chapters of spectacular spills and thrills, *Flash Gordon* offers an awesome abundance of fierce creatures and ferocious characters, spectacular scrapes and hairbreadth escapes. This classic 1936 serial is the quintessential cliffhanger, a multi-part Saturday matinee fantasy that remains irresistibly entertaining and relentlessly exciting in spite of — or perhaps *because* of — the hilarious hokiness of its overstated performances, borderline-cheesy sets, and archaic special effects. All is takes is a quick perusal of a few randomly chosen episodes for you to fully appreciate its enduing influence on later, more lavishly produced action-adventures — everything from *Star Wars* (1977) and *Raiders of the Lost Ark* (1981) to the *Lord of the Rings* trilogy (2001-03). But really, you owe it to yourself to feast on the entire extravaganza, preferably during a single evening of delirious indulgence.

Patterned after the serialized novels of Charles Dickens, Arthur Conan Doyle, and other literary notables, serials such as *Flash Gordon* originally were intended to be viewed on a week-to-week basis over a period of three or four months, with each chapter presented as a curtain-raiser for a discrete feature attraction. Most of these chapter-plays were Westerns, action-adventures, or sci-fi fantasies, and almost every episode ended with a moment of suspense, uncertainty, or seemingly unavoidable peril — the "cliffhanger" that gave the genre its nickname — leaving the audience eager for a resolution that, of course, would not come until the next chapter.

Film historians credit *The Perils of Pauline* (1914), a twenty-chapter adventure melodrama starring Pearl White, as the serial that made the genre internationally popular. But it was not until the advent of talking pictures — and, specifically, the release of *Flash Gordon*, one of the first and only serials produced on something more than a frayed-shoestring budget — that cliffhangers emerged as the reliably potent audience draws that they remained until the mid-1950s.

Faithfully adapted from the then-popular comic strip by Alex Raymond, *Flash Gordon* is a perpetual motion machine that careens from incident to incident, pitfall to pitfall, propelled by the buoyant charisma, irony-free sincerity, and all-American athleticism of Olympic swimming champ Buster Crabbe in the title role. (Crabbe repeated his career-defining performance in two sequel serials — *Flash Gordon's Trip to Mars* [1938] and *Flash Gordon Conquers the Universe* [1940] — and essayed another intergalactic hero in *Buck Rogers* [1939]). The first chapter — forebodingly titled "The Planet of Peril" — quickly establishes the immensity of the challenge facing our hero: As panicky crowds stampede through the streets of world capitals, sage scientists in a mountaintop observatory note the impending approach of the planet Mongo on a collision course toward Earth. But don't worry: The first time we see Flash Gordon, the studly blond son of the gloomiest scientist, beaming a megawatt smile while being shaken and stirred during a bumpy airline flight, we know we have a hero who's more than capable of personally pre-empting any possible interplanetary cataclysm.

Just how cool is this Flash fellow? When the plane begins an irreversible dive, Flash calmly retrieves a parachute that's conveniently stashed beneath his seat, and graciously offers to share it with pretty passenger Dale Arden (Jean Rogers). Fortuitously, this fun couple hits the ground near the domain of Dr. Zarkov (Frank Shannon), a brilliant eccentric who has built a super-duper spaceship in his very own backyard. Zarkov needs a co-pilot for his journey to Mongo, which he hopes to somehow halt before its close encounter with Earth. (Hey, if you can build your own spaceship, why *shouldn't* you think you could control an entire planet?) Flash immediately volunteers to go along for the ride. So does Dale, if only because, what the hell, outer space might be a safer place than a seemingly doomed Earth.

With exposition out of the way, director Frederick Stephani was free to boldly go where no filmmaker had gone before, to explore the outer limits of his audience's willing suspension of disbelief. He cleverly pinched pennies by recycling sets, props, and scores from more expensive movies — including music from *The Bride of Frankenstein* (1935), rocketships from *Just Imagine* (1930), Egyptian statuary from *The Mummy* (1932), Roman warrior breastplates and headgear from God only knows where — while more or less establishing the cliffhanger tradition of scrambling historical periods in costume and production designs, to manufacture a fantastical crazy-quilt of comic-book reality.

Zarkov and his companions make their way from Earth to Mongo with a remarkable display of no-sweat sangfroid. (Zarkov: "We're safe! We've just passed the Death Zone!" Flash: "Wow! That's something!") After their landing, however, it's one damn thing after another, as Flash and friends tussle variously with oversized lizards, burly minions, sword-wielding centurions (who, oddly enough, also are armed with high-tech ray guns, which they rarely use) and, worst of all, the dreaded Emperor Ming (Charles Middleton), a sneeringly haughty and impetuously cruel tyrant who wants to destroy or conquer Earth, depending on his mood, and turn Dale into his very own love slave.

While Zarkov pretends to perfect weapons of mass destruction for the easily duped Ming, Flash does most of the heavy lifting while fighting for Dale's honor and Earth's future (though not necessarily in that order). When he isn't busy trekking through tunnels or dropping through trapdoors, he manfully maneuvers through a series of daunting challenges: Dodging dragons, wrestling octopi, slugging security guards, grappling with an Orangopoid (a gorilla with a unicorn-like horn), strangling a Tigron (a tiger with attitude), and leading a slave rebellion.

Along the way, Flash is aided or abetted by Princess Aura (Priscilla Lawson), Ming's va-va-voom daughter, who covets a hunka-hunka burnin' Flash; Prince Barin (Richard Alexander), rightful heir to the Mongo throne and, not incidentally, bashful suitor of Princess Aura; Prince Thun (James Pierce), leader of the rebellious Lion Men; and King Vultan (John Lipson), the lusty Hawk Man who tries (and fails) to woo Dale Arden in his Sky City, a floating metropolis that obviously served as the model for similarly aloft real estate in *The Empire Strikes Back* (1980). As it turns out, Flash needs all the help he can get: He's a brave and resourceful hero, no doubt about it, but he has to be rescued by Dale, Aura, or Zarkov in a surprising number of episodes.

Speaking of surprises: For a movie presumably aimed primarily at children, *Flash Gordon* is not exactly shy when it comes to wink-wink hints of steamy sensuality. Time and again, director Stephani finds some new excuse to rip away Flash's shirt, all the better to expose Crabbe's well-oiled biceps. (Crabbe bared even more beefcake in the guilty-pleasure cult-fave *Tarzan the Fearless* [1933]). Ming — whose name, manner and Fu Manchu mustache suggest the worst sort of "Yellow Peril" stereotype — can barely refrain from soggy drools and wolf whistles whenever he sees Dale in skintight attire that bares her midriff and accentuates her heaving breasts. Not to be outdone in the heaving department, the bosomy Aura tends to hyperventilate whenever she casts her admiring gaze upon Flash (even when he's wearing a shirt). All of which may explain why so many little boys (and more than a few girls) who view *Flash Gordon* at an impressionable age want to make their own serial-style adventures when they grow up.

SPECS:

Flash Gordon — Stars: Buster Crabbe, Jean Rogers, Charles Middleton, Priscilla Lawson, Frank Shannon, Richard Alexander, Jack "Tiny" Lipson. Director: Frederick Stephani. Screenplay: Frederick Stephani, George Plympton, Basil Dickey, and Ella O'Neill, based on the comic strip by Alex Raymond. Running time: 245 minutes. Year of release: 1936. DVD distributor: Image Entertainment.

SUBJECTS FOR FURTHER RESEARCH:

Barbarella (1968) — Jane Fonda strips for action in Roger Vadim's notoriously racy and deliciously campy sci-fi spoof, loosely based on a European comic strip, about a forty-first-century adventuress in pursuit of a villain armed with a humongous death ray. Take note of Pygar (John Philip Law), the blind, beatific angel who resembles a slimmed-down, well-scrubbed Hawkman.

Raiders of the Lost Ark (1981) — A rip-snorting, slam-bang homage to Saturday matinee attractions of yesteryear, Steven Spielberg's thrilling action-adventure about a globe-trotting, whip-cracking archaeologist was aptly dubbed a "Cliffhanger Classic" in a Newsweek cover story during its opening week.

Sky Captain and the World of Tomorrow (2004) — In Kerry Conran's retro-revisionist homage to *Flash Gordon* and other '30s sci-fi cliffhangers, Jude Law, Gwyneth Paltrow, and Angelina Jolie are among the high-flying heroes who battle an evil genius bent on destroying the world.

LESSON FOR FILMMAKERS:

Imitation can be the most lucrative form of flattery. Eager for a change of pace after the '60s nostalgia of *American Graffiti* (1973), George Lucas considered doing a feature-length remake of the '30s *Flash Gordon* serials. Trouble is, he couldn't afford the rights to the original Alex Raymond comic strip, which already were owned by producer Dino De Laurentiis. And so — well, hey, can you say *homage*? Take another look at *Star Wars*, and note the many similarities to Frederick Stephani's serial: Screen wipes, set designs, title crawls, etc. "I started out with a modest little movie," Lucas says, "that was designed to be in the motif of a 1930s action-adventure serial that they used to show on Saturday matinees. So the whole style was kind of '30s and very cliffhanger-ish."

GUADALCANAL DIARY

The war-movie convention of the multi-ethnic platoon — the emblematic band of brothers that purposefully epitomizes the demographic diversity of America — has long been razzed and satirized by critics, academics, and stand-up comics. During World War II, however, the cliché was a deadly serious element of many Hollywood movies. But wait, there's more: The cliché was viewed in some quarters as a secret weapon in the fight for truth, justice, and the American way. No kidding.

Driven by equal measures of patriotism and profit motive, producers dutifully stressed any and all symbols of national unity in war stories such as Lewis Seiler's *Guadalcanal Diary*, one of the first and best of the flag-waving, crowd-pleasing WWII combat dramas designed to honor U.S. soldiers, boost home-front morale, enhance America's image abroad — and, of course, attract masses to movie theaters. Whatever the reason for their inclusion, those symbols were greatly valued and actively encouraged as potent propaganda tools by the Office of War Information's Bureau of Motion Pictures, the agency charged with advising and influencing the film industry's contributions to America's war effort.

To be sure, OWI lacked the authority of an official, government-sanctioned censorship board. But, then as now, "suggestions" by any Federal agency seldom go unheeded by image-conscious Hollywood moguls.

Guadalcanal Diary was not, strictly speaking, the first Hollywood-produced WWII combat film released in the aftermath of December 7, 1941.

It wasn't even the first to depict real-life U.S. military activity: *Wake Island* (1942), the tragic yet inspiring story of an American defeat, and *Bataan* (1943), a drama about the doomed defenders of the Philippines, beat Seiler's movie to theaters. But *Guadalcanal Diary* was the first film of its kind to celebrate an American *victory* against Japanese forces.

Based on Richard Tregaskis' best-selling nonfiction book about the Marine invasion of the Solomon Islands, this reasonably gritty and generally well-acted drama is remarkably persuasive for a movie supposedly set in the South Pacific, yet shot on location at Camp Pendleton, California. Its episodic depiction of day-to-day survival under enemy fire has repeatedly been used as a template for similar jungle-combat scenarios filmed during and after WWII. Likewise, its introduction of a fighting unit entirely comprised of stereotypical characters is the first significant deployment of a lineup that would reappear, with only minor variations, in countless other war films.

Right from the start, Seiler calls attention to the variety of ingredients in his all-American melting pot. During the opening minutes, as the Marines attend a Sunday religious service on the troop ship transporting them to Guadalcanal, an onboard Christian soldier compliments his buddy: "Say, Sammy, your voice is okay." His friend smiles and responds: "Why not? My father is a cantor in the synagogue." After the service, another fellow speaks longingly of sailing his yacht on Chesapeake Bay. A more humble-born Marine describes a more plebian pastime: Rooting for the Dodgers at Ebbets Field.

In short order, we're introduced to other instantly recognizable types: The supportive company chaplain (Preston Foster), the blunt-spoken, Brooklyn-born cabdriver (William Bendix), the grizzled veteran sergeant (Lloyd Nolan), the tough-talking but inwardly anxious raw recruit (Richard Jaeckel), the gravel-voiced comic relief (Lionel Stander), and so on. To provide some much-needed color — much-needed, that is, because the U.S. armed forces were racially segregated during WWII, an unpleasant reality that the image-conscious OWI preferred Hollywood not to mention — we have Anthony Quinn as a lusty Mexican solider who proves that, doggone it, every American boy can pull his weight and do his part.

Brothers in arms, indeed.

For audiences accustomed to more graphically violent and morally ambiguous renderings of men at war, *Guadalcanal Diary* may seem a quaint relic from a distant past when the Greatest Generation fought the good fight. (I don't have to tell you that one of the soldiers adopts a stray dog, do I?) But even cynics have to admit the movie has quite a few undeniably affecting moments.

For something designed in large part as spirit-boosting propaganda, Seiler's drama is surprisingly upfront about acknowledging the terrors experiencing by soldiers under fire. ("Anyone who says he ain't scared is a fool or a liar," the sergeant tells a weeping private.) William Bendix, representing the common man as citizen soldier, improvises a prayer during a long dark night of Japanese bombardments. He doesn't talk about glory or honor or any other abstraction. Rather, he describes — in plain and simple words that doubtless resonated with wartime audiences — the doubts and determination of an ordinary man in extraordinary circumstances: "I'm no hero, I'm just a guy. I'm out here because somebody had to come. I don't want no medals. I just want to get this thing over with and go back home. I'm just like everybody else..."

SPECS:

Guadalcanal Diary — Stars: Preston Foster, Lloyd Nolan, William Bendix, Richard Conte, Anthony Quinn, and Lionel Stander. Director: Lewis Seiler. Screenplay: Lamar Trotti and Jerry Cady, based on the book by Richard Tregaskis. Running time: 93 minutes. Year of release: 1943. DVD distributor: 20th Century Fox Home Entertainment.

SUBJECTS FOR FURTHER RESEARCH:

The Thin Red Line (1964) — Two years after co-directing *The Longest Day*, Andrew Marton filmed this crudely efficient WWII drama based on James Jones' novel about American soldiers fighting the enemy, and each other, while taking Guadalcanal from Japanese forces. Terence Malick's more lavishly produced 1998 remake is better known, but Marton's grungier low-budget version — starring Keir Dullea as a rebellious private and Jack Warden as his borderline-psychotic sergeant — is much less pretentious and plodding.

Too Late the Hero (1970) — Robert Aldrich's violent and revisionist WWII action-adventure plays like a stern critique of *Guadalcanal Diary* and other gung-ho movies of its kind. Japanese forces steadily decimate a British-American commando unit (including Michael Caine and Cliff Robertson) on a suicide mission deep in a Pacific island jungle. Released during the height of the Vietnam War, Aldrich's bracingly cynical drama was sold with an advertising tagline ("War: It's a Dying Business!") intended to position the film as anti-war statement.

Saving Private Ryan (1998) — Steven Spielberg's remarkably harrowing WWII drama begins and ends with graphically bloody battles that unstintingly render the horrors of combat. In between, however, the film tells a more traditionally inspiring war story, complete with a platoon comprised of various social and ethnic types. Tom Hanks' deeply moving speech about his character's personal reasons for completing his mission echoes William Bendix's improvised prayer in *Guadalcanal Diary*.

LESSON FOR FILMMAKERS:

Even producers of wartime propaganda must be mindful of political correctness. In an early version of the *Guadalcanal Diary* script, a priest tells the Marines they are fighting "a righteous war" while representing "a righteous nation," which he defines as "economically sound, politically sound, and spiritually unassailable." Unfortunately, those sentiments upset the bureaucrats at the Office of War Information's Bureau of Motion Pictures. As Clayton R. Koppes and Gregory D. Black report in their book *Hollywood Goes to War*, OWI claimed the rousingly pro-American speech "was not only 'bad theology' but also 'bad political philosophy' because China, Greece, and Yugoslavia, among others, would hardly qualify as righteous nations under this standard." To avoid possible offense to allies in the war against Axis powers, OWI suggested that the speech be cut. It was.

LAWRENCE OF ARABIA

Oxymoronic though it may sound, David Lean's *Lawrence of Arabia* is a textbook example of an intimate epic. To be more precise, it is a larger-than-life spectacle that never loses sight of the singular life at its center.

Almost everything you have ever read – or, better still, vividly remember — about its unparalleled visual majesty is true. Stunningly photographed by F. A. Young, *Lawrence of Arabia* fully immerses you in Super-Panavision panoramas of desert splendor, inviting you to not merely watch the film so much as experience it. At times, the rocky, wind-blasted wilderness resembles some angry red landscape of Mars. At other moments, the bleached-yellow sands are shifting seas, ever ready to ensnare with a hidden whirlpool. And in one of the film's most indelible images, the desert is a shimmering silver plane, above which floats an approaching rider who could very well be a mirage — until he demonstrates his corporeality by firing a fatal gunshot.

The battle scenes, though arguably not as stirring as those of John Ford or Akira Kurosawa, are nonetheless powerful, terrifying, and horrifyingly beautiful. Teeming masses have been choreographed into quarrelsome clashes, fearsome charges, exultant dances, and, perhaps most impressively, still and foreboding threats.

In short — admittedly, a phrase one usually doesn't associate with this must-see movie — *Lawrence of Arabia* is a work that fully realizes film's unique capacity for sweeping epic gestures. Generations after its initial theatrical release, it remains one of the yardsticks by which all movie epics are measured.

But there is more to Lean's masterwork than eye-popping pageantry. Freely adapted from T. E. Lawrence's autobiographical *The Seven Pillars of Wisdom*, *Lawrence of Arabia* is one of the most literate epics in the history of Anglo-American cinema. The screenplay by Michael Wilson (a blacklisted writer who didn't receive full credit until 1996) and Robert Bolt is at once a thrilling adventure story and a provocatively ambiguous psychological portrait.

After establishing the legendary status of their hero in a short prologue, Bolt and Wilson reach back in time to find the man behind the legend. Lawrence, played with an almost giddy anxiety by an incredibly young Peter O'Toole, is introduced as an obscure, somewhat effete officer posted to the British General Headquarters in 1917 Cairo during World War I.

Partly through luck, and partly through his own self-dramatizing drive, Lawrence is ordered to report on the feuding Bedouin tribes that are revolting, ineffectually, against the Ottoman Empire.

Lawrence enters the desert as an eager observer, fortuitously earns the respect of a revered Arab leader (Alec Guinness), and transforms himself into a warrior god through sheer force of masochistically obsessive will. As a leader, he unites and inspires the Bedouin tribes, driving them to victory against the Turks. As a man, however, Lawrence is horrified by the pleasure he takes in killing, and traumatized by a brutal flogging (and, though this is never made explicit, an equally brutal sexual assault) while held prisoner by Turkish soldiers.

Worse, Lawrence as a British soldier plays an unwilling role in the post-WWI takeover of Arab lands under the terms of the Sykes-Picot Agreement. Arab unity collapses after the common enemy, the Turkish army, is driven from Damascus. (Some things never change: The Middle East seems as torn by internecine warfare here as it is today.) *Lawrence of Arabia* may be the only epic ever made, that anyone has dared to make, in which the hero is last seen as defeated and disillusioned, as a humbled giant who wishes for nothing more than anonymity.

In the role originally offered to Marlon Brando and later to Albert Finney, Peter O'Toole, then twenty-nine and relatively unknown, gives a star-making performance of startling range, diversity, and sharply focused intensity. One moment as fey as a virgin bride, the next moment as mesmerizing as a charismatic visionary, he actually seems more at ease in his flowing Arab robes than in his spit-and-polish army uniform. It's almost as though going native liberates him.

O'Toole plays Lawrence as a man who invents himself, then finds his handiwork wanting. He runs the risk of going over the edge, and once or twice tumbles into what seems like excessive flamboyance even by Lawrencian standards. Much more often, however, O'Toole is wonderfully, painfully persuasive as a tragic hero with a touch of the poet, condemned to gallop across the blindingly bright desert until he reaches his own heart of darkness.

The supporting cast, for the most part, is excellent. Guinness as the wise Prince Feisel, Omar Sharif (never better) as the impulsive Sherif Ali, Anthony Quinn as the boisterous Auda Abu Tayi, Anthony Quayle as the skeptical Colonel Brighton, Arthur Kennedy as reporter Jackson Bentley (a slightly fictionalized stand-in for wartime correspondent Lowell Thomas), Jack Hawkins as the crudely conniving General Allenby, and Claude Rains as the much more elegantly duplicitous diplomat, Dryden.

The only false note is sounded by Jose Ferrer, who, while hamming it up as a Turkish officer, looks like he's getting ready for the lead role in *The Salvador Dali Story*. But never mind: The virtues of *Lawrence of Arabia* are large enough, grand enough, to overshadow any minor flaw.

SPECS:

Lawrence of Arabia — Stars: Peter O'Toole, Alec Guinness, Anthony Quinn, Jack Hawkins, Omar Sharif, Jose Ferrer, Anthony Quayle, Claude Rains, and Arthur Kennedy. Directed by David Lean. Screenplay: Robert Bolt and Michael Wilson, based on the writings of T. E. Lawrence. Running time: 228 minutes. Year of release: 1962. DVD distributor: Columbia/TriStar Home Video.

SUBJECTS FOR FURTHER RESEARCH:

Patton (1970) — Originally released in a year when America seemed irreconcilably divided over the ongoing Vietnam War, Franklin Schaffner's intelligent WWII epic (co-scripted by Francis Ford Coppola) takes an intriguingly even-handed approach to Gen. George A. Patton (brilliantly played by George C. Scot), a warrior-scholar almost as complex as T. E. Lawrence.

Veronica Guerin (2003) — The title character, an Irish investigative reporter (Cate Blanchett), is killed during the opening minutes, leading to an extended flashback. Any resemblance to David Lean's magnum opus is *not* coincidental. "I used *Lawrence of Arabia* as a template," producer Jerry Bruckheimer acknowledges. "Beginning your movie like that serves two purposes. It kind of softens the blow of what's going to eventually happen. But it also creates a lot more tension for your lead character throughout the drama."

The Last Samurai (2003) — Another tortured hero goes native and becomes a legend in Edward Zwick's massively scaled yet intimately detailed historical drama, an intelligent and exciting tale about a guilt-racked Civil War veteran and Indian fighter (Tom Cruise) who gets a shot at redemption while learning the way of the samurai in nineteenth-century Japan.

LESSON FOR FILMMAKERS:

Steven Spielberg describes his first viewing of *Lawrence of Arabia* at age fifteen as "the biggest seminal moment in my life... After that experience, I wanted to make films — not just as a hobby, but I wanted to go into the profession — and I began looking for ways to do that." It's easy to believe that David Lean's masterwork had such a profound impact on Spielberg. Very easy, as a matter of fact, if you consider how Spielberg lifted several of its most memorable images for his own *Close Encounters of the Third Kind* and *Raiders of the Lost Ark*. But he has always given credit where it's due: The deluxe DVD edition of *Lawrence* contains "A Conversation With Spielberg" in which he gratefully acknowledges the influence of his mentor.

4 8 Hrs.

NICK NOLTE

EDDIE MURPHY

48 HRS.

It wouldn't be entirely accurate to cite *48 HRS.* as the very first example of a genre best described as mixed-combo, slam-bang action-comedy. But Walter Hill's hugely entertaining 1982 opus clearly set the standard for dozens of subsequent buddy-cop capers — everything from *Running Scared* (1986) and *Lethal Weapon* (1987) to *Bulletproof* (1996) *and Rush Hour* (1998) — and remains the yardstick by which most audiences and almost all critics judge such high-concept concoctions.

Much of the credit must go to Hill, master of the rapid-fire montage and role model for the likes of John Woo and Quentin Tarantino. Prior to *48 HRS.*, Hill had grabbed attention with his frenetically kinetic style of storytelling in *The Warriors* (1979) and *Southern Comfort* (1981). But *48 HRS.* allowed him to rev up the speed and pump up the volume in ways that forever changed the rules of the game for the action-comedy genre. Alternating between laughter and splatter with dizzying abruptness, Hill audaciously mixed shockingly graphic violence and raucously foul-mouthed humor. Just as important, he infused conventionally dead-serious action sequences — a gunfight in a hotel hallway, a cat-and-mouse pursuit in a subway station — with the kind of quick-cut, rapid-fire urgency that would later be a hallmark of MTV videos and Hong Kong shoot-'em-ups.

Take a close look at *48 HRS.*, and you'll see that, even when a scene involves nothing more dramatic than exposition or transition, Hill doesn't let you pause for breath. Of particular note: A thrillingly sustained tracking shot that encompasses a series of encounters in a police squad room. It's a virtuoso flourish that crackles with excitement without calling undue attention to itself.

Still, if that's all *48 HRS.* had going for it, the movie would be of little more than academic interest. What gives this action-comedy that ineffable something extra — the borderline-magical quality that can transform a slick piece of commercial filmmaking into a true-blue Hollywood classic — is a happy accident of casting. At the time they were hired, Nick Nolte sorely needed something to jump-start his stardom after the back-to-back flops of *Heart Beat* (1980) and *Cannery Row* (1982), while Eddie Murphy needed a sure-fire vehicle to take him to the next step beyond TV's *Saturday Night Live*. Both men got precisely what they needed, thanks in large measure to the potent chemistry they generated as a classically mismatched pair of action heroes.

Nolte, sounding like a rusty drainpipe and looking like an unmade bed, plays Jack Cates, a San Francisco police detective on the trail of two fugitive killers. It's a personal vendetta for Cates, since one of the bad guys — a psycho named Ganz (James Remar) — swiped his gun and fatally shot one of Cates's cohorts. So the grizzled white cop seeks info from a slick black convict, a jive-talking jailbird named Reggie Hammond (Eddie Murphy). Cates has Hammond released on a 48-hour pass, hoping Hammond will lead him to the killers. Hammond doesn't mind betraying Ganz, because the psycho covets loot that Hammond has hidden. But the convict has little desire to work for a cop. Especially a white cop.

Although he doesn't appear until nearly twenty-five minutes after the opening credits, Murphy radiates more than enough youthful sass and self-confidence to hold his own opposite his more seasoned co-star. If Nolte nonetheless manages to dominate most of their shared scenes, it's because of his ability to authoritatively underplay, even when he's growling obscenities. It also helps that Nolte has an underrated gift for eloquent physicality. Cates is hulking and hunched-over for most of the movie. But during the final confrontation in a fog-shrouded alley, he calmly steps out of the darkness, ramrod straight and unmistakably lethal, to give Ganz the bad news: "You're not going to make it."

The byplay between Nolte and Murphy is aggressively profane and rich with inventive insults. (Four writers are credited with cobbling together the script, but long stretches of the movie sound improvised.) It comes as no surprise that the cop and the con eventually lower their guards and work together. What *is* surprising — almost shocking, even more than two decades after the movie's premiere — is the off-handedly blunt depiction of racially-charged animosity between the two lead characters. In fact, you would have to go back to *In the Heat of the Night* (1967) to find an earlier mainstream Hollywood movie in which an integrated odd couple swapped so many non-P.C. epithets.

Throughout the first hour or so, Cates repeatedly addresses Hammond as "Boy" or "Watermelon" — or worse — and doesn't hesitate to slap the convict around to loosen his tongue. (It requires a willing suspension of disbelief — and a bemused acceptance of Murphy's prerogatives as an above-the-title co-star — when the much smaller Hammond stuns the burly Cates by slapping back.) And during the movie's most famous scene — the scene that instantly established Murphy's superstardom — Hammond reveals a streak of exuberant savagery while posing as a cop and hassling the Caucasians in a country-and-western bar. "I don't like white people," he sneeringly informs the seething crowd. "You people are rednecks. That means I'm enjoying this…"

Much later — in a considerably funkier sort of hangout, where Cates is the one whose pigmentation makes him conspicuous — the cop and the con edge warily toward, if not a color-blind friendship, then at least a non-aggression pact. Even here, however, *48 HRS.* refuses to turn soft and sentimental. Cates half-heartedly apologizes for his race-bating remarks: "I was just doing my job, keeping you down…" Hammond is dubious: "Well, doing your job doesn't explain *everything*, Jack." And, to his credit, Cates fesses up: "Yeah, you're right." Not surprisingly, Hammond laughs out loud. So does Cates. The good news is that, by that point, they're able to laugh with, not at, each other.

SPECS:

48 HRS. — Stars: Nick Nolte, Eddie Murphy, Annette O'Toole, Frank McRae, James Remar, Sonny Landham, and David Patrick Kelly. Directed by Walter Hill. Screenplay: Running time: 96 minutes. Year of release: 1982. DVD distributor: Paramount Home Video.

SUBJECTS FOR FURTHER RESEARCH:

Lethal Weapon (1987) — One of the first and best of the *48 HRS.* clones, Richard Donner's frenetic buddy-cop action-comedy starring Mel Gibson (as a borderline-suicidal supercop) and Danny Glover (as his older, more sobersided partner) spawned a formidably resilient franchise. Unfortunately, Gibson's death-wishing daredevil seems increasingly less distinctive as he becomes more conventionally heroic with each succeeding sequel.

Rush Hour (1998) — With Jackie Chan as an acrobatic Hong Kong cop and Chris Tucker as his motor-mouth partner in crimefighting, it's no surprise that the balance between hard action and broad comedy tips decisively toward the funny stuff in Brett Ratner's popular mixed-combo opus.

The Rundown (2003) — Can you smell what The Rock is cooking? So could the millions who flocked to Peter Berg's odd-couple adventure-comedy, in which the wrestling champ turned action-flick heavyweight (a.k.a. Dwayne Douglas Johnson) joins *American Pie* star Seann William Scott for a rumble in the Amazon jungle. The stars engage in not-so-friendly banter that recalls the Nolte-Murphy duets in *48 HRS.*

LESSON FOR FILMMAKERS:

Casting against type can pay off beautifully — even when the person you're casting has grave misgivings. Director Walter Hill admits that perennial bad boy Nick Nolte "had a very large resistance to the idea of playing a policeman. It's just not part of his makeup. So he had a terrific problem facing the material." (Remember: *48 HRS.* was filmed long before Nolte wore a badge in *Q&A*, *Extreme Prejudice*, and *Mulholland Falls*.) Nolte says he was able to play Cates only by imagining the character as an outcast who stands beyond the constraints and comforts of polite society: "You know that scene at the end, where Cates shoots the guy who's grabbed Eddie? That whole scene is set up to say that this man is dealing with killers, and he can kill. And to Eddie's character, that's a shock. No matter how much fluff there is on the surface, a police officer is involved with that. That's one of the things that we innocents — which is what they call us — are not capable of doing: Committing ourselves to purgatory."

DIE HARD

You don't often hear action heroes pray out loud — "Oh, God! Please don't let me die!" — before they attempt some dangerous derring-do. But that's exactly what Bruce Willis does during an especially nerve-racking moment in *Die Hard*, John McTiernan's genre-defining thriller. And largely because we're privy to this vulnerability — that is, because we fully understand Willis is playing a flesh-and-blood mortal, not a blood-and-thunder superman — *Die Hard* stands head and shoulders, heart and soul, above its many, many imitators.

Like most of the copycats that prowled in its wake, this must-see movie is all about the right man in the wrong place at the right time. John McClane (Willis), a veteran New York cop, flies to L.A. on Christmas Eve in hope of reconciling with his estranged wife, Holly (Bonnie Bedelia), and their two children. Holly moved west several months earlier, for a career-building promotion in a multinational corporation. She, too, is hoping for a happy holiday. But it won't be a silent night.

Shortly after John and Holly have a not-so-warm reunion at her office Christmas party, all hell breaks loose in the high-rise building. While John unwinds in his wife's office, terrorists storm out of the elevator. And, mind you, we're not talking about your garden-variety bomb-throwers. No, these terrorists are dressed like *GQ* fashion plates, and they're more interested in capitalism than class struggle. In short, they want a crack at the loot inside the Nakatomi Corporation safe.

Led by the ice-cold Hans Gruber (the great Alan Rickman in his big-screen breakthrough), the terrorists have prepared for every eventuality:

They have secured the bottom floors, booby-trapped the roof, recruited a computer genius to access the safe's security systems. But, of course, they haven't counted on dealing with a testy New York cop armed only with his service pistol. John tries to arrest a terrorist, and winds up killing him. That's the opening gambit, and the cat-and-mouse game begins.

In synopsis, *Die Hard* might sound like *Rambo in the Towering Inferno*. And yet, despite some familiar elements, the movie came off as fleet and fresh in 1988, and remains far more compelling than all other films (including *Die Hard* sequels) of its kind. For one thing, McTiernan and his scriptwriters are very deft at spiking their thrills and chills with some sharply honed satire. (Sensationalistic TV newscasters — then as now, every filmmaker's favorite straw men — get some particularly nasty jabs.) And when the time comes to play hardball, Team McTiernan pulls off the sort of hairpin curves and bravura flourishes that always impress action aficionados.

The real key to the movie's continuing appeal, however, is Bruce Willis. Then best known as smirking naughty-boy David Addison of TV's *Moonlighting*, he firmly established his movie star credentials here while perfectly cast as a reluctant man of action with a vulnerable streak. Indeed, Willis' John McClane is *extremely* vulnerable — at one point, he has to run across broken glass in his bare feet — even when he's most ticked off. His cocksure tenacity can easily rattle the normally unflappable Hans, although, deep down, John just *knows* he's no match for all the well-armed bad guys. His guerrilla campaign against the terrorists becomes increasingly inspired only as his panicky desperation mounts.

As he prepares to leap from the high-rise roof, hoping a fortuitously placed fire hose will prevent his free fall to the streets below, John moans: "If I get out of this, I promise I will never even *think* about going up in a tall building again!" That's the beauty part of Willis' performance: He plays John McClane as a Joe Average who's desperate to survive and terrified that he won't.

When he's not shooting at people, or being shot at, Willis spends much of his time on screen alone, more or less delivering soliloquies — exploding into rage one moment, sinking into tearful despair the next, then revving himself up again to handle the dangerous business at hand. It's an impressively detailed and shrewdly nuanced performance by any standards, and downright amazing in the context of a genre movie. The writers can be credited with providing the sharp dialogue, and the producers should be commended for their savvy offbeat casting. (If someone "safe" would have played John McClane — say, Stallone or Schwarzenegger — would there ever be any doubt about the hero's ultimate victory?) But Willis is the one who takes the concept and runs with it, carrying the audience along for the wild ride.

SPECS:

Die Hard — Stars: Bruce Willis, Alan Rickman, Bonnie Bedelia, and Reginald Veljohnson. Director: John McTiernan. Screenplay: Jeb Stuart and Steven E. de Souza, based on the novel by Roderick Thorp. Running time: 132 minutes. Year of release: 1988. DVD distributor: Fox Home Entertainment.

SUBJECTS FOR FURTHER RESEARCH:

Speed (1994) — The first and arguably best in the "*Die Hard* on a (fill in the blank)" cycle. Here, it's *Die Hard* on a bus, with Keanu Reeves and Sandra Bullock trying to defuse a bomb rigged by a scenery-chomping Dennis Hopper.

Independence Day (1996) — Taking a cue from the casting of "a TV actor" as the reluctant hero of *Die Hard*, director Roland Emmerich hired talented second-tier actors (like up-and-comer Will Smith) rather than "bankable" superstars as the leads for his sci-fi action-adventure. "When you have a big movie with a big action star," Emmerich explained, "you know his or her character will triumph. In our movie, everybody's fate is up in the air. Audiences will be surprised as to who survives — and who doesn't."

Unbreakable (2000) — For his second collaboration with director M. Night Shyamalan (*The Sixth Sense*), Bruce Willis returns to his *Die Hard* roots by memorably humanizing another genre stereotype (in this case, a literally superheroic character).

LESSON FOR FILMMAKERS:

Sometimes, the star makes the movie. Other times, the movie makes the star. Richard Gere and Charles Bronson were among the better-known actors reportedly considered for the role of John McClane before Bruce Willis nabbed the *Die Hard* lead. Despite his spotty box-office record up to that point — *Blind Date* (1987) and *Sunset* (1988), his only two previous co-starring vehicles, had flopped — Willis was offered the then-staggering sum of $5 million by producers who were absolutely convinced he was right for the role. The gamble paid off, eventually, but 20th Century Fox tried to cover its bets: The first posters for *Die Hard* stressed the high-concept plot with artwork of a high-rise building. Willis' face was introduced into the print ad campaign relatively late, and not conspicuously emphasized until after the opening-weekend grosses rolled in.

≈11≈
FUNNY
BUSINESS

DUCK SOUP

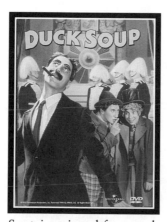

For connoisseurs of movie comedy, *Duck Soup* represents the purest distillation of Marxian anarchy. Indeed, all of the Marx Brothers — wisecracking Groucho, mutely zany Harpo, faux-Italianate Chico, and even straight-arrow Zeppo — are at their considerable best in this exhilaratingly rude 1933 farce. Unlike their earlier films for Paramount, which often creak and crawl while tangled up in stage roots, and their later Zeppo-free films for MGM, which sometimes seem overproduced and overextended, *Duck Soup* is stripped for speed and pared to essentials. No long-winded exposition, no insipid romantic subplots, no show-stopping musical turns by Harpo or Chico — just undiluted and uninhibited Marx madness.

Originally intended as a "topical" satire of geopolitical machinations — at a time when Adolf Hitler had just recently risen to power in Germany — *Duck Soup* remains as hilarious as ever in its cynical view of patriotic zeal, macho saber-rattling, and self-serving politicians.

Groucho stars as the fast-talking, double-dealing Rufus T. Firefly, a leering rapscallion who becomes ruler of Freedonia, a small European country on the verge of bankruptcy. For reasons that are never fully explained, perhaps because they defy rational explanation, the fabulously wealthy Mrs. Teasdale (the magnificently clueless Margaret Dumont) installs Firefly as president to "follow in the footsteps" of her late husband. But Firefly is more interested in lying down on the job, preferably with Mrs. Teasdale. While addressing his faithful Freedonians in song, he warns them to expect the worst: "The last guy nearly ruined this place, he didn't know what to do with it. If you think this country's bad off now, just wait 'till I get through with it."

But even a leader like Firefly needs some help while he's leading a country down the drain. Zeppo appears — sporadically — in the thankless role of Firefly's secretary. More important, Chico and Harpo are on hand as spies employed by the duplicitous leader of the nearby Sylvania. Occasionally, they take a paycheck from Firefly as well. And when that's not enough, they are self-employed as peanut-stand operators, leading to some madcap encounters with a slow-burning lemonade hawker (Edgar Kennedy).

Duck Soup contains many of the most famous one-liners and surreal exchanges associated with the Marx Brothers. ("Remember, we're fighting for this woman's honor — which is probably more than she's ever done!") And it features their very best sight gag, the much-imitated "mirror image" sequence that has a heavily-disguised Harpo mimicking Groucho's movements during a botched break-in.

As funny as all this is, however, what is most striking about *Duck Soup* today is the timeless quality of its raucously satirical rabble-rousing. When Firefly and his cohorts lead the populace in a spirited rendition of "The Country's Going to War," the elaborately hilarious production number seems only a slight exaggeration of what deadly serious world leaders do to ignite their own patriotic frenzies. Leave it to Groucho to have the last word on wartime heroics: "And remember — while you're out there risking life and limb through shot and shell, we'll be in here thinking what a sucker you are."

SPECS:

Duck Soup — Stars: Groucho Marx, Harpo Marx, Chico Marx, Zeppo Marx, Margaret Dumont, and Louis Calhern. Directed by Leo McCarey. Screenplay: Burt Kalmar, Harry Ruby, Arthur Sheekman, and Nat Perrin. Running time: 68 minutes. Year of release: 1933. DVD distributor: Universal.

SUBJECTS FOR FURTHER RESEARCH:

A Night at the Opera (1935) — Some die-hard Marxists insist this appreciably more lavish (and conspicuously more traditional) comedy is the best of the brothers' movies. It certainly contains many of their funniest routines, including the celebrated stateroom sequence and the "party of the first part" contract dispute.

Wag the Dog (1997) — Even darker and more audacious than *Duck Soup*, Barry Levinson's prescient political satire stars Robert De Niro as a Presidential advisor who tries to distract voters from a White House sex scandal by employing a Hollywood producer (Dustin Hoffman) to stage-manage a fake war.

Head of State (2003) — During his youth, comic actor Chris Rock says, "I remember people saying that Richard Pryor should play the President. That seemed like a good idea, in the spirit of *Duck Soup*." So good, in fact, that Rock eventually cast himself as a sassy Presidential candidate when he wrote and directed this freewheeling farce.

LESSON FOR FILMMAKERS:

Time is on your side, even if you "fail" in your own time. Despite the best efforts of Leo McCarey — arguably the only first-rate filmmaker to ever direct a Marx Brothers movie — and the gloriously unhinged exuberance of the brothers themselves, *Duck Soup* was a flop in 1933. Why? Joe Adamson, author of *Groucho, Harpo, Chico and Sometimes Zeppo*, theorizes that Depression-scarred audiences "were absolutely in no mood to watch an uncompromising, exasperating comedy that refused to truckle to their tastes and concerned itself with dictatorships and wars. Audiences found it easier to take the attitude normally afforded to the unconventional: They pronounced it Wrong. *Duck Soup* was not being daring and novel by ignoring customary plot development; it was simply cheating."

DR. STRANGELOVE

Still the funniest movie ever made about Mutually Assured Destruction – the tit-for-tat Cold War concept that assumed whoever shoots first, dies second — *Dr. Strangelove or: How I Learned to Stop Worrying and Love the Bomb* is unmistakably of its time and yet, for better *and* worse, undeniably timeless.

Stanley Kubrick's bold-as-brass 1964 farce vividly imagines a worst-case scenario — a demented Air Force general launches an unauthorized first strike against the Soviet Union, thereby ensuring the end of the world as we know it — and audaciously plays it as stone-faced black comedy. In doing so, Kubrick gleefully evokes and brashly satirizes the free-floating, wide-ranging paranoia of his age, a time when air-raid drills and fall-out shelters were not yet pop-culture punchlines, when military miscalculation and nuclear annihilation weren't supposed to be laughing maters.

Working from a screenplay he co-wrote with Peter George (whose novel inspired the script) and satirist Terry Southern (*Candy*), Kubrick grounds his outrageousness in a meticulously detailed reality — note how some scenes in the starkly black-and-white movie are shot in *faux* documentary style — while propelling his plot along three parallel tracks.

At a remote Air Force command base, Gen. Jack D. Ripper (Sterling Hayden), a psychotically self-righteous anti-Communist zealot, orders a squadron of B-52 bombers to pre-emptively nuke the Soviet Union. (The method behind this madness: The general blames his impotence on sneaky Soviets who have used water fluoridation to poison the "precious bodily fluids" of American men.) At Ripper's side, albeit reluctantly, is the increasingly anxious Capt. Lionel Mandrake (Peter Sellers), a visiting British exchange officer who gradually emerges as the movie's sole voice of reason.

Meanwhile, back in Washington, the seriocomically bland President Merkin Muffley (Peter Sellers again) hunkers down in the War Room with various political and military advisers, fretting about his limited options as the B-52s near their targets. The hawkish Gen. Buck Turgidson (a scenery-chewing George C. Scott) suggests that, what the hell, why not go ahead and finish what Gen. Ripper has begun? "I'm not saying we wouldn't get our hair mussed," Turgidson admits, "but I do say no more than ten to twenty million killed, tops, depending on the breaks."

But even Turgidson is intimidated by the Russian ambassador's revelation that the Soviet military recently constructed "The Doomsday Machine," a self-triggering retaliatory weapon. "When it is detonated," the ambassador (Peter Bull) fearfully explains, "it will produce enough lethal radioactive fallout so that within ten months, the surface of the Earth will be as dead as the moon." Dr. Strangelove (Peter Sellers yet again), the president's German-accented, wheelchair-bound military adviser, theorizes that government leaders and other important citizens may have to seek refuge below ground in mine shafts for, oh, about a century or so.

Unfortunately, not all of the B-52s can be recalled. Even more unfortunately, the only unrecalled bomber is commanded by Maj. T.J. "King" Kong (Slim Pickens), a good ol' boy from Texas who's been itching for a chance to go "toe-to-toe with the Rooskies!" Once he gets the good word from Ripper, Kong dons a ten-gallon hat and excitedly informs his crew that they're going to make history. He remains so determined to fulfill his manifest destiny that, when the bomb bay doors won't open as the B-52 nears its target, the Texan takes it upon himself to force the issue. It's one of the most indelibly memorable images in movie history: Kong jumps aboard one of the bombs like a rodeo cowboy mounting a bucking bronco, and rides the dad-blasted thing all the way down to ground zero.

Long before Kong causes the mother of all big bangs, *Dr. Strangelove* gravitates far beyond the level of the darkly comical, to thrive in the rarified realm of the bleakly hilarious. The beauty part is, the movie is all the more uproarious because Kubrick encourages his cast to maintain straight faces and grim attitudes as they stumble toward the Apocalypse.

Time and again, Kubrick invites his audience to consider the folly of relying on supposedly fail-safe systems and mechanisms — a theme he would later explore with HAL 9000 in *2001: A Space Odyssey* — and the disproportionate pettiness and puniness of those capable of unleashing something so monumental as nuclear Armageddon. Note the way a B-52 crewman dutifully erases errors and updates entries in his flight log moments before his inevitable vaporization. Or, better still, note how the hidebound Maj. Bat Guano (Keenan Wynn) reacts when Capt. Mandrake, using a pay-phone to transmit bomber-recall codes to the White House, tells the major to blast open a Coke machine for loose change. "Okay," Guano gruffly responds, "I'm gonna get your money for you. But if you don't get the President of the United States on that phone, you know what's gonna happen to you? You're gonna have to answer to the Coca-Cola Company."

Inevitably, the doomsday slapstick of *Dr. Strangelove* greatly offended some people, and frightened quite a few others, during its first-run engagements. *The Washington Post* critic fumed: "No communist could dream of a more effective anti-American film to spread abroad." Bosley Crowther, reviewing in the *New York Times*, damned the comedy as "malefic and sick," if not downright un-American, adding that he was deeply troubled "by the feeling, which runs all through the film, of discredit and even contempt for our whole defense establishment, up to and even including the hypothetical Commander in Chief."

Then as now, of course, it's amusing to appreciate how these and other outraged reactions suggest the full measure of Kubrick's ruthless accuracy: He had a killer instinct for knowing precisely where to aim his satirical thrusts so they would cause maximum discomfort. Indeed, he skewered his targets so effectively that, even now, it's difficult to hear some mealy-mouthed world leader try to place upbeat spin on horrific tragedy (or inconvenient scandal) without recalling President Muffley's desperate amiability while on the hot line with the Russian premier:

"Now, Dimitri, you know how we've always talked about the possibility of something going wrong with the bomb... The bomb, Dimitri, the hydrogen bomb... Well, now, what happened is, one of our base commanders, he had a sort of — well, he went a little funny in the head. You know, just a little funny. And, uh, he went and did a silly thing... Well, I'll tell you what he did... He ordered his planes... to attack your country..."

SPECS:

Dr. Strangelove or: How I Learned to Stop Worrying and Love the Bomb — Stars: Peter Sellers, George C. Scott, Sterling Hayden, Keenan Wynn, Slim Pickens, Peter Bull, and James Earl Jones. Director: Stanley Kubrick. Screenplay: Stanley Kubrick, Peter George, and Terry Southern, based on the novel *Red Alert* by Peter George. Running time: 93 minutes. Year of release: 1964. DVD distributor: Columbia/TriStar Home Entertainment.

SUBJECTS FOR FURTHER RESEARCH:

Fail Safe (1964) — Sidney Lumet's impressively intense thriller, released within months of *Dr. Strangelove*, takes a rather more serious approach to a similar doomsday scenario. When Air Force bombers are accidentally ordered to nuke Moscow, the U.S. President (Henry Fonda) tries to avoid World War III by sacrificing New York City.

Network (1976) — Sidney Lumet strikes again with a ferociously satirical fable (from an Oscar-winning screenplay by Paddy Chayefsky) about TV executives who will stop at nothing, not even murder, in their quest for higher ratings. As years pass, alas, the movie plays more like a behind-the-scenes documentary than an in-your-face comedy.

Canadian Bacon (1995) — Documentarian Michael Moore (*Bowling for Columbine*) tries his hand at feature filmmaking with an uneven political satire about a desperate U.S. President (Alan Alda) who plots to boost his re-election prospects by declaring war on Canada.

LESSON FOR FILMMAKERS:

For director Barry Sonnenfeld (*Men in Black*, *Get Shorty*), *Dr. Strangelove* is a masterpiece primarily because "it's a comedy in which no one in the movie is allowed to acknowledge that they're in a comedy... If any of these actors had tried to play *Dr. Strangelove* as a comedy, it would have been a disastrous movie." While screening Kubrick's film with Rick Lyman of the *New York Times*, Sonnenfeld acknowledged its profound influence on his own work: "I don't mean to imply that the movies that I make are anything near as good as *Dr. Strangelove*, but in all of them I'm always trying to make sure that the actors don't act like they know they're in a comedy."

ANNIE HALL

By 1977, Woody Allen already had five credits on his resume as a multi-hyphenate filmmaker. Six, actually, if you count his re-dubbing and retrofitting a Japanese spy movie to concoct 1966's madcap *What's Up, Tiger Lily?* His other early efforts — from *Take the Money and Run* (1969) to *Love and Death* (1975) — were cheeky scattershot spoofs and goofs, structured more or less as compendiums of blackout skits. Which doubtless explains why, in the opening moments of *Annie Hall*, Allen felt compelled to warn his audience that they were in for something radically different.

The movie begins with a medium shot of Allen, alone against a beige backdrop, breaking the fourth wall by addressing the audience like the stand-up comic he famously used to be. At first, you don't know how to react: Is this the real Woody Allen, inviting us into his manufactured world? Or is this Woody Allen in character, telling a couple of jokes by way of warming up to a more serious narrative?

As it turns out, this confusion between actor and role is the key to *Annie Hall*, a movie that relies heavily on the shrewdly sustained illusion of autobiographical intimacy. Even more than *Alfie* (1966), its most obvious precedent, Allen's first-person narrative lulls the audience into assuming the role of a conspiratorial confidant. It helps, of course, that even in 1977, when the movie first appeared in theaters, moviegoers knew enough about Allen's private life — including his off-screen relationship with co-star Diane Keaton — to assume this very funny fiction had to be based at least partially on fact. Allen plays skillfully on this assumption throughout *Annie Hall*, much as he would in many later movies, even as he slyly suggests — again, much as he repeatedly has in his filmmaking career — that any similarities to real life may be more apparent than real.

Allen tells two jokes in his opening monologue. The first is the oft-told tale about the woman who complains about the terrible food at a resort hotel. "Yes," her companion agrees. "And such small portions!" The second joke is the chestnut about the fellow who feels he would belong to no club that would have him as a member. The gags serve as metaphors for Alvy Singer, the comedy writer Allen portrays in the film. (Yes, the monologue is part of a character.) Although Alvy is wary of love, having survived two marriages, and pessimistic about life, he is sad that both love and life seem so evanescent. Worse, love will always be problematical for him because, unfortunately, he cannot understand what any woman would see in a self-deprecating kvetch such as himself.

The wit is visual as well as verbal throughout the rest of the movie. There are Alvy's hilarious memories of an anxious childhood spent in a home beneath an amusement park rollercoaster. There is Alvy's amusing encounter with a boorish intellectual in a movie theater lobby. There is a hilarious dinner scene in which the very Jewish Alvy breaks bread with a very WASP-ish family, and everyone assumes the worst about each other. There is a cleverly subtitled conversation between two people who struggle with small talk while they size up each other as romantic possibilities. There is a lot more.

And yet, for all that, an air of melancholy hangs lightly over even the funniest bits of comic business in *Annie Hall*, the story of a love affair that never quite works out right.

Amid the tangle of interlocking flashbacks, flashforwards, and fantasy sequences, Alvy, recently turned 40, finally finds someone he thinks will be the perfect woman for him: Annie Hall (Keaton), an awkward and easily flustered twenty-something singer who is even more ill-equipped than he to cope with stressful situations. During moments when she's too flustered to think of anything to say, she sighs: "Well, lah-di-dah! Lah-di-dah!" (For the benefit of those who tuned in late: Yes, *this* is where that line comes from.) Bless her heart, Annie sighs a lot.

At first hesitantly, then domineeringly, Alvy takes Annie under his wing, hoping to make her see the world from his disaffected-intellectual viewpoint. To his credit, Allen often makes his on-screen alter ego appear selfish, petty, and more than a little whiney. (He originally planned to call the film *Anhedonia*, a medical term for the inability to experience pleasure.) Alvy behaves like a petulant child whenever Annie evidences the least sign of independence. As she grows more self-assured, the romance starts to falter. They break up, then make up. Their final break, however, is a complete one, despite Alvy's frantic efforts to regain his last best chance for happiness — and, not incidentally, his role as dominant mentor.

Not surprisingly, Alvy winds up using the romance as material for a play, one in which he can control the destinies of the characters. Naturally, his scenario ends with a reconciliation. (As Alvy marvels — earlier in the movie, in a completely different context — "Boy! If only life were like this!") But Allen himself is more honest as an artist when it comes to tying up loose ends.

Annie Hall has loomed so large for so long in our collective pop-culture consciousness that its very familiarity can cloud your vision while you're attempting an appraisal of its original impact. Indeed, even those of us who bought tickets to see it during its first-run engagements can all-too-easily forget what a risk-taking, rule-breaking stunner it seemed in 1977.

It has been said that one measure of a classic is how difficult it is to imagine a time when it didn't exist. So you may have to just trust me on this: There really was a time, prior to *Annie Hall*, when American-made romantic comedies didn't focus so intently on the neuroses and insecurities of chronically self-analytical New Yorkers, when you had to seek out a foreign-language import to find a seriocomic love story so free-wheeling, self-reflexive, and essentially plotless. In fact, you would have to look at works by François Truffaut, Jean-Luc Godard, and other French New Wave masters — which, come to think of it, is probably what Allen did before starting work on his own masterwork — to find any films of the era in the same spirit and style as *Annie Hall*.

Diane Keaton fully deserved the Academy Award she received for her career-defining performance here as a woman who hesitantly makes the progression from dependant child to confident adult without losing her girlish vivacity. She also deserves a footnote in the history of American lifestyles for inspiring a fashion craze with her character's eccentric attire (vest, tie, and baggy pants) during the late '70s. As for *Annie Hall* itself: Its influence continues, unabated and undiminished. Whenever you hear someone describe a movie, play, or TV production as "like a Woody Allen movie," well, this is the Woody Allen movie they're most likely thinking about.

SPECS:

Annie Hall — Stars: Woody Allen, Diane Keaton, Tony Roberts, Carol Kane, Paul Simon, Shelley Duvall, Janet Margolin, Christopher Walken, and Colleen Dewhurst. Director: Woody Allen. Screenplay: Woody Allen and Marshall Brickman. Running time: 93 minutes. Year of release: 1977. DVD distributor: MGM Home Entertainment.

SUBJECTS FOR FURTHER RESEARCH:

L.A. Story (1991) — Call it *Annie Hall: The West Coast Edition* and you won't be far off the mark. Steve Martin does triple duty as star, screenwriter and occasional narrator in Mick Jackson's hugely entertaining mix of savvy social satire and bittersweet romantic comedy. Cast as an uptight TV weathercaster in love with a visiting British journalist (Victoria Tennant), Martin romanticizes Los Angeles with as much affectionate joshing as Woody Allen employs while polishing The Big Apple.

High Fidelity (2000) — After warming up by playing "the Woody Allen part" in Allen's *Bullets Over Broadway* (1994), John Cusack directly addresses the audience during flashbacks, fantasies and ongoing activity as a character trying to sort out his past and present romantic entanglements. (Sound familiar?) This sort of first-person approach is a tricky thing to pull off in cinema — for every *Alfie* or *Annie Hall*, there are dozens cringe-worthy embarrassments — but Cusack makes it work smashingly well in Steven Frears' whip-smart adaptation of Nick Hornby's novel.

Something's Gotta Give (2003) — Diane Keaton is supposed to be playing someone named Erica Berry, "the most successful woman playwright since Lillian Hellman," in Nancy Meyers' sharply observed comedy about over-50 romance. But it's not difficult to imagine she's really playing a long-lost twin sister of Annie Hall, older and wiser but no less easily flustered. (Taking a tip from Alvy Singer, she channels her romantic problems into a successful play.)

LESSON FOR FILMMAKERS:

Movies as diverse as *Tom Jones* and *Easy Rider* reportedly were "saved" in the cutting room. But *Annie Hall* may be the only film of its stature that was discovered during the editing process. Woody Allen originally envisioned his Oscar-wining film as a seriocomic murder mystery with a romantic subplot. And that's more or less how it was shot. But while he and editor Ralph Rosenblum were trimming down a rambling rough cut, Allen realized that all the best footage involved the Alvy-Annie relationship, so he restructured the movie as a romantic comedy. Waste not, want not: Allen kinda-sorta returned to his original concept fifteen years later, when he reunited with Diane Keaton and co-screenwriter Marshall Brickman for *Manhattan Murder Mystery* (1993).

NATIONAL LAMPOON'S ANIMAL HOUSE

Like some second-tier Marx Brothers comedies, and almost any movie starring Jerry Lewis, *National Lampoon's Animal House* seems much funnier — and more consistently madcap — when you replay it in your mind long after you actually see it. The classic bits and pieces of side-splitting, gut-busting hilarity are so deliciously rude and exuberantly anarchic in this 1978 production, you tend to forget the long stretches of conventional zaniness about unconventional cut-ups on a 1962 college campus.

To put it another way: When you hear the words *Animal House*, you immediately think of wild and crazy John Belushi, food fights, toga parties, and up-yours rebelliousness, don't you? But, tell the truth, it takes you considerably longer to recall any specifics of plot or character. And you don't remember the slow parts at all, right?

Set on the campus of Faber College, a not-so-august institution in small-town Middle America, *Animal House* is dedicated to the proposition that the purportedly innocent era of the early '60s — before Vietnam, student radicalism, and recreational drug use complicated everything — was a great time to party hearty.

Much to the displeasure of Dean Wormer (John Vernon), the rowdy frat rats of Delta House have become the stuff of legend with their constant carousing, practical joking, and authority-baiting antics. Determined to maintain decorum, Wormer enlists the aid of snotty crypto-fascists from a rival fraternity to punish — or, better still, expel — the unfettered party animals. But when the going gets tough, the Deltas simply party heartier.

In the role that, for better or worse, defined his on-screen persona, the late John Belushi blowtorches his way through *Animal House* as Delta dynamo Bluto Blutarsky, a walking sight gag with the most cunningly expressive eyebrows this side of Jack Nicholson. Despite his top billing, Belushi has relatively little time on screen, and hardly any dialogue. But that doesn't stop him from stealing the movie with his ingeniously crass version of silent-movie slapstick. To see Belushi robustly slurping Jell-O in a cafeteria line, or eagerly crushing beer cans on his forehead, or ogling undressed co-eds through a sorority house window, is to be reminded why his name remains synonymous with uninhibited, go-for-broke physical comedy.

Belushi is by no means the only performer of note in *Animal House*. As Boone, a droll Delta whose girlfriend (Karen Allen) has a fling with a pot-smoking professor (Donald Sutherland), Peter Riegert is the stand-out in an ensemble cast that also includes then-newcomers Tom Hulce, Bruce McGill, and (as the snide leader of the anti-Delta frat boys) Kevin Bacon. As the skirt-chasing Otter, Tim Matheson has some comically sexy interludes with the under-appreciated Verna Bloom (*Medium Cool*, *The Hired Hand*) as Dean Wormer's hard-drinking, tart-tongued wife.

But Belushi is the one who best personifies the overall air of beery anarchy and what-the-hell prankishness that has made *Animal House* so memorable and influential for more than a generation. At its frequent best, the movie is a gleefully lewd and boisterously crude testimonial to the empowering potency of swaggeringly bad behavior. Even when director John Landis and his spirited cast appear to be treading water while waiting for the next *really* funny gag, *Animal House* can be savored as a guilty-pleasure hangover from an age when hardly anyone making movies ever worried about the niceties of political correctness.

And whenever it pushes the envelope by springing something that, even now, is genuinely shocking in its nonchalant tastelessness — most memorably, an impudent exploitation of racial tensions when Delta white boys mingle with black regulars at a blues nightclub — *Animal House* still seems as fearlessly bold as all the gags about jammed zippers and semen-gelled hair in *There's Something About Mary*.

SPECS:

National Lampoon's Animal House — Stars: John Belushi, Tim Matheson, Peter Riegert, Tom Hulce, and Donald Sutherland. Directed by John Landis. Screenplay: Harold Ramis, Douglas Kenney, Chris Miller. Running time: 109 minutes. Year of release: 1978. DVD distributor: Universal.

SUBJECTS FOR FURTHER RESEARCH:

Meatballs (1979) — Bill Murray, John Belushi's *Saturday Night Live* co-star, established his own trademark movie style (i.e., subversive sang-froid with a smidgen of hostile looniness) in Ivan Reitman's *Animal House Lite* comedy about fun and games at summer camp. The movie spawned a few nominal sequels and an entire subgenre.

Porky's (1981) — Younger, cockier, and hornier than the Deltas, the rowdy '50s high-schoolers of Bob Clark's raunchy farce set the standard (in want of a better term) for teen-skewing, how-to-get-laid comedies throughout the '80s.

National Lampoon's Van Wilder (2002) — *National Lampoon* magazine is long defunct, but the brand name remains a marketing tool for purveyors of lowbrow, gross-out comedies. *Van Wilder* is a brazenly slapdash farce about college cut-ups, a neo-*Animal House* made by under-achievers with little regard for such niceties as original plotting and minimum-standard production values. And, yes, parts of it are laugh-out-loud funny. (Look for *Animal House* vet Tim Matheson as the hero's disapproving dad.)

LESSON FOR FILMMAKERS:

If you're specific in your direction, your actors are better equipped to improvise. Consider the moment in *Animal House*, during the celebrated toga party, when Bluto (John Belushi) impulsively destroys a folk singer's guitar — and then sheepishly apologizes. "That's not in the script," director John Landis said in a 2003 interview. "We just made that up. But that's key to Belushi's character — Bluto is sweet. That's the thing John was capable of doing... I told him he was like Harpo and the Cookie Monster (of *Sesame Street*), and both Harpo Marx and the Cookie Monster are about appetites. And what's unique about Cookie and Harpo is, they're both totally destructive and completely sweet."

≈12≈
FOREIGN
INFLUENCES

OPEN CITY

Ask six film scholars to define "neorealism" and you'll likely receive a half-dozen different responses. But don't worry: To paraphrase Judge Potter Stewart's oft-quoted explanation of pornography, you'll know it when you see it.

Generally speaking, the term refers to a distinctive type of cinematic storytelling that flourished in Italy throughout the decade following World War II. During this period, maverick moviemakers such as Vittorio de Sica (*Shoeshine*) and Luchino Visconti (*La Terra Trema*) made a virtue of their meager postwar resources by improvising a fresh and unvarnished style of social realism. Proudly distaining the lavish excesses of glitzy extravaganzas — often mocked as "white telephone dramas" — that typified Italian cinema of the 1930s, they shot their films on actual locations, often in a semi-documentary manner, usually with casts that included a large percentage of non-professional actors.

In this, the neorealists were fathers of the French New Wave — and, arguably, grandfathers of Dogma 95 (a back-to-basics movement whose advocates insist on handheld cameras, natural lighting, and other no-frills effects). Martin Scorsese, a passionate student and admirer of the postwar Italian auteurs, insists: "If you ever have any doubt about the power of movies to affect change in the world, to interact with life and fortify the soul, then study the example of neorealism."

Roberto Rossellini is widely acknowledged as the filmmaker who introduced neorealism to international audiences with *Open City*, his bold and bracing mix of brutally harsh naturalism, passionately contrived melo-drama, and what critic Andre Bazin aptly described as "reconstituted reportage." Shot within weeks of the Allied liberation, with scraps of film stock purchased from black marketers, *Open City* has the compelling immediacy of a newsreel — and, at the same time, the emotional frisson of a classic tragedy — as it offers a (literally and figuratively) black-and-white account of life and death during the repressive German occupation.

The plot, as simple and efficient as a blunt instrument, deals with doomed heroes of the resistance movement in the "open city" of Rome. Manfredi (Marcello Pagliero), a Partisan on the run from Nazi man-hunters, seeks help from Francesco (Francesco Grandjacquet), a comrade in arms, and Pina (Anna Magnani), Francesco's pregnant wife-to-be. Don Pietro (Aldo Fabrizi), a sympathetic priest, also figures into the story (co-written by a young Federico Fellini) as a loyal supporter of the Partisan cause.

Ultimately, Manfredi is betrayed when his former sweetheart, Marina (Maria Michi), a drug-addicted actress, spills the beans to a predatory lesbian allied with Major Bergmann, a diabolical Gestapo officer. But Manfredi withstands sadistic torture — his captors calmly light their cig-arettes with the blowtorch they apply to his chest — and dies without naming names. Don Pietro also is captured, and dies heroically before a Nazi firing squad. "It's not hard to die well," says the self-effacing padre. "What's hard is to live well."

But neither Manfredi's torture nor Don Pietro's execution is as shocking as the climax of an extraordinarily tragicomical sequence that illustrates Rossellini's mastery of shifting tones and upending expectations. Don Pietro nervously conceals Partisan weapons stashed in the apartment of a sickly old man. To keep the geezer quiet while *Fascisti* search the build-ing, the padre conks him with a frying pan. You're still laughing at the slapsticky comic relief when Pina — frantically pursuing a truck trans-porting Francesco, who's been rounded up during the apartment-complex search — is machine-gunned by a Nazi solider. She collapses into an obscenely leggy sprawl, her hemline rising above her garters. Don Pietro comforts her wailing son while reflexively attending to her corpse, pulling at her hem, as if to save the fallen woman the fur-ther humiliation of public exposure.

And then, giving one last twist to the sharp edge of dark irony, Rossellini shows how, just a few minutes later, Partisans ambush the truck carrying prisoners. Francesco is freed — too late.

Open City is not the subtlest of wartime dramas. Major Bergmann, played with effete arrogance by Harry Feist, appears to have walked in from an American-made B-movie of the period. Ingrid, the predatory lesbian played by Giovanna Galletti, does everything but wink lasciviously at the camera to convey her cunning. On the other side of the equation, the good guys are relentlessly stoic and heroic in their defiance, setting aside differences for the greater good of Italy.

And yet, even if the protagonists are types — at best, archetypes — Rossellini shrewdly allows them revealing shadings of character. *Open City* is especially intriguing, and in some ways strikingly prescient, as it notes fissures in the anti-fascist compact between Italian Catholics and Communists, two groups that would resume their fractious quarrels after a temporary wartime truce. Manfredi chides Francesco for agreeing to a church wedding, relenting only because he feels, what the hell, it's better to be married by a Partisan priest than a fascist court clerk. Later, Major Bergmann tries to turn Don Pietro against Manfredi by reminding the priest of the freedom fighter's atheism. But Don Pietro counter-argues that Manfredi, almost in spite of himself, is doing the Lord's work.

Because Rossellini succeeds so brilliantly at infusing the stock characters and the sometimes pulpish plot with such impassioned conviction, *Open City* transcends the specifics of time and place to remain a timeless work of art.

SPECS:

Open City — Stars: Anna Magnani, Aldo Fabrizi, Marcello Pagliero, and Maria Michi. Directed by Roberto Rossellini. Screenplay: Sergio Amedei, Federico Fellini. Running time: 105 minutes. Year of release: 1945. DVD distributor: Image Entertainment.

SUBJECTS FOR FURTHER RESEARCH:

The Bicycle Thief (1948) — Vittorio de Sica's harsh, heartrending neo-realist drama charts the mounting desperation of a long-unemployed man and his young son as they search for the stolen bicycle needed by the father for a menial job. The drama offers a vivid of portrait of hard-scrabble life — and fleeting moments of grace — in postwar Rome.

La Strada (1956) — Think of it as the bridge between hard-core neore-alism and sentimental melodrama. Federico Fellini's Oscar-winning road movie pairs a brutish circus strongman (Anthony Quinn) with a simple-minded waif (Giullietta Masina) for a tour through provincial Italy that turns into a tragicomical voyage of discovery.

The King is Alive (2000) — Kristian Levring, co-founder of the neo-neo-realist Dogma 95 movement, directed and co-wrote this fitfully fascinating drama about stranded bus passengers who pass the time while waiting for rescue by staging *King Lear* in a Namibian desert ghost town. Unlike most no-frills Dogma 95 productions, Levring's English-language feature features several familiar faces — including Bruce Davison, Jennifer Jason Leigh, and Janet McTeer (*Tumbleweeds*) — in its ensemble cast.

LESSON FOR FILMMAKERS:

Don't be afraid to make the most of the least. Granted, only distribution executives and easily-impressed journalists give a damn about how little your movie cost to make. (Rest assured, no one ever told a date: "Hey, let's go see 'Movie X.' I hear they filmed it for only $1.25.") But you really can produce something on a frayed-shoestring budget that's engrossing and uplifting if you're sufficiently talented, passionate – and patient. Also worth remembering: Despite the funny/scary things you see in SAG's cautionary trade-paper ads, it's possible to coax acceptable (and maybe even admirable) performances from non-professionals. Once again, however, patience is required.

RASHOMON

A bandit subdues a nobleman in a secluded woodland and forces himself on his captive's wife. The nobleman dies, the wife flees, the bandit is captured — and everything else in *Rashomon* remains open to conjecture. Decades before *The Usual Suspects* warned moviegoers not to accept subjective testimony as verifiable fact, Akira Kurosawa's breakthrough masterpiece suggested that no eyewitness can be entirely trusted, that truth itself may be forever elusive.

Four different accounts of the fateful, fatal incident — including one offered by the late nobleman through a court-ordered medium — are considered by three strangers in eleventh-century Japan. While stranded under the Rashomon gate during a raging thunderstorm, they wonder: Was the nobleman truly a man of honor? Was his wife an innocent victim or willing participant? Could the bandit (Toshiro Mifune at his most swaggeringly uninhibited) have twisted the truth for a selfless reason? The possibilities are perplexing. Each testimony is dramatized in flashback, and none seems more credible than the others. Indeed, Kurosawa strongly hints that all four stories are, to varying degrees, deceptions born of self-delusion. "Human beings," he wrote in *Something Like an Autobiography*, his acclaimed memoir, "are unable to be honest with themselves about themselves."

Rashomon has spawned many imitators, including *The Outrage*, a 1964 Americanized remake with Paul Newman miscast as a Mexican bandit. But Kurosawa's 1950 original continues to be the paradigm for this particular sort of beguilingly simple yet provocatively complex drama. Even now, the title is used to describe anything — from *Wonderland* to *Boomtown*, from Senate hearings to *Seinfeld* episodes — in which a story is told from multiple, and often contradictory, points of view.

SPECS:

Rashomon — Stars: Toshiro Mifune, Masayuki Mori, Machiko Kyo, and Takashi Shimura. Directed by Akira Kurosawa. Screenplay: Akira Kurosawa and Shinobu Hashimoto, based on stories by Ryunosuke Akutagawa. Running time: 88 minutes. Year of release: 1950. DVD distributor: Criterion Collection.

SUBJECTS FOR FURTHER RESEARCH:

Ikiru (1952) — Akira Kurosawa once again experimented with shifting perspectives and subjective interpretations in this deeply moving drama about a fusty bureaucrat (masterfully played by Takashi Shimura) who is devastated, then galvanized, when he learns he is dying of cancer.

The Bad Sleep Well (1960) — There's more than a hint of *Hamlet* in Kurosawa's profoundly fatalistic drama about a would-be avenger who is undermined by his own humanity during a private crusade against far less scrupulous opponents. Toshiro Mifune, wearing nerdy glasses that somehow make him look all the more foreboding, plays the vengeful son of a tradition-bound businessman who was driven to suicide by corrupt superiors.

Courage Under Fire (1996) — A troubled Army officer (Denzel Washington) seeks the elusive truth about the life and death of a Gulf War heroine (Meg Ryan) in this intelligently compelling *Rashomon*-style drama directed by Edward Zwick (*Glory*).

LESSON FOR FILMMAKERS:

Prophets aren't the only ones who are under-appreciated in their own countries. Akira Kurosawa is widely acknowledged as the director who single-handedly brought post-WWII Japanese cinema to the world's attention with *Rashomon*, which earned the grand prize at the Venice Film Festival and an Academy Award for Best Foreign Language Film. Even while it accumulated those accolades, however, the masterwork brought out the worst in some members of the Japanese film community, who dismissed the unprecedented honors as (to quote Kurosawa's memoir) "simply reflections of Westerners' curiosity and taste for Oriental exoticism." Later, as his fame and influence spread throughout the world, Kurosawa often found himself saddled with the dubious honor of being praised — and damned — as the "most Western" of Japanese filmmakers.

SEVEN SAMURAI

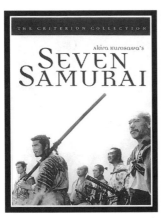

When Steven Spielberg hailed Akira Kurosawa as "the visual Shakespeare of our time," the American admirer likely was thinking of the Japanese master's *Seven Samurai*. Kurosawa's stunning 1954 epic is one of those absolutely indispensable films that practically everyone has heard about, regardless of whether they've actually seen it. Indeed, even if you haven't, you may *think* you've seen it, given its strong influence on so many other films and filmmakers. For five decades, directors ranging from John Sturges (who remade it as *The Magnificent Seven*) to John Sayles (who borrowed the basic plot while writing a 1980 sci-fi cheapie called *Battle Beyond the Stars*) have drawn from Kurosawa's tale of honor among warriors in sixteenth-century Japan.

By turns sage and savage, avuncular and authoritarian, the great Takashi Shimura (*Ikiru*) heads the ensemble cast as Kambei, an unemployed samurai who agrees to help peasants defend their village against periodic pillaging by marauding bandits. Even though the pay is meager — a few handfuls of rice — Kambei is able to recruit other hired swords who have little else to do after being cast adrift by the lords they once served. By appealing to their pride, sense of justice, and respect for tradition, he attracts such tough customers as Kyuzo (Seji Miyaguchi), a taciturn professional who never wastes a word or gesture, and Kikuchiyo (Toshiro Mifune), a bearish hothead who takes great pains to hide his less-than-noble ancestry.

Seven Samurai shows Kurosawa at the top of his form, demonstrating rigorous control of his medium with an inspired balance of formal precision and kinetic exuberance. His epic opens with rapid panning shots of bandits riding over hills, and climaxes with the thundering chaos of a rain-soaked, mud-and-blood battle. In between, there is scarcely a single shot that does not contain motion. Even when people in the frame are stationary, the camera itself glides, thrusts, and recoils like a restless animal. A half-century after its initial release, *Seven Samurai* still makes most other action movies seem positively pokey.

Appropriately enough, this classic by "the most Western of Japanese filmmakers" is, at heart, an old-fashioned Hollywood Western in even older-fashioned Japanese regalia. Kurosawa made no apologies for embracing the style and substance of Occidentals as diverse as John Ford and Vincent van Gogh. (He rendered the latter as a workaholic sage — played by Martin Scorsese, no less! — in his 1990 anthology film, *Akira Kurosawa's Dreams*.) A lifelong student of Shakespeare, he audaciously re-imagined *Macbeth* as *Throne of Blood* (1957), an epic drama of medieval warfare, and reconstituted *King Lear* as *Ran* (1985), his last incontestable masterpiece.

Even so, despite his borrowings from other cultures, Kurosawa remained forever mindful of his roots. And while he refused to err on the side of romanticized nostalgia in his re-creations of Japan's turbulent past, he viewed social changes, technological advancements, and other breaks from tradition as extremely mixed blessings. It is well worth remembering that in *Seven Samurai*, the sixteenth-century swordsman who best represents the ancient *bushido* code of honor is felled by a rifle shot.

SPECS:

Seven Samurai — Stars: Toshiro Mifune, Takashi Shimura, Daisuke Kato, Ko Kimura, Minoru Chikai, Seiji Miyaguchi, and Yoshio Inaba. Directed by Akira Kurosawa. Screenplay: Akira Kurosawa, Shinobu Hashimoto, and Hideo Ogumi. Running time: 203 minutes. Year of release: 1954. DVD distributor: Criterion Collection.

SUBJECTS FOR FURTHER RESEARCH:

Yojimbo (1961) — Akira Kurosawa's darkly comical samurai Western takes the hardboiled premise of Dashiell Hammett's novel *Red Harvest*

— a tarnished hero encourages two rival gangs to destroy each other — and outfits it with the trappings of traditional Japanese *jidai-geki* (period film). But there's nothing traditional about the cynical tone or the sardonic humor of this gleefully savage self-parody.

The Dirty Dozen (1967) — Robert Aldrich's much-imitated WWII action-adventure takes *Seven Samurai* to its logical extreme: A grizzled Army officer (Lee Marvin) assembles a group of "expert" killing machines (i.e., murderers, psychopaths, and other social outcasts) for a behind-enemy-lines commando mission.

A Bug's Life (1998) — *Toy Story* director John Lasseter scored another hit with this clever and comical animated adventure about a plucky ant (voiced by Dave Foley) who tries to defend his colony from marauding grasshoppers by recruiting warrior bugs. Unfortunately, instead of engaging samurai insects, he hires circus performers.

LESSON FOR FILMMAKERS:

Martin Scorsese wasn't exaggerating when he noted, "Kurosawa's influence on filmmakers throughout the entire world is so profound as to be almost incomparable." Almost equally significant, however, is Kurosawa's influence on film *actors*. Orlando Bloom admits that, prior to playing Legolas in Peter Jackson's *Lord of the Rings* trilogy, he studied the lead players in *Seven Samurai* "to find the same way of walking, the same posture that would give Legolas this aura of centeredness and focus."

THE 400 BLOWS

During his salad days as a notoriously contentious critic for *Cahiers du Cinema*, the celebrated French film magazine, François Truffaut proselytized for a "cinema of the first-person singular," encouraging the creation of movies "even more personal than an autobiographical novel, more like a confession or an intimate diary." When he was ready to make the transition from critic to creator as a founder of the maverick *nouvelle vague* ("new wave") movement, he took his own words to heart. And while he was at it, he made a timeless masterpiece.

The 400 Blows, Truffaut's profoundly affecting first feature, is a frankly autobiographical drama about growing up absurd in 1950s Paris. At once brutally specific and brilliantly emblematic, the film focuses on Antoine Doinel (Jean-Pierre Leaud), a 14-year-old boy whose acute sensitivity makes him tragically vulnerable to the hard knocks of an emotionally deprived childhood. Don't look for anything so comforting as rosy-hued nostalgia here. "Adolescence," Truffaut pointedly noted in a 1959 essay, "leaves pleasant memories only for adults who can't remember." Truffaut, who was 26 when he filmed *400 Blows*, couldn't forget.

Antoine is a lad of average intelligence, neither a dullard nor a genius, perhaps too imaginative for his own good. He is alert but confused, quiet but inquisitive, high-spirited with friends but instinctively reserved with grownups. He has ample reason to be wary around the adults in his world. At school, Antoine is methodically bullied by teachers who have zero tolerance for disruptions of their dull pedantry. At home, however, things are worse. "Antoine Doinel," Truffaut explained, "is the opposite of a mistreated child. He simply is not 'treated' at all."

Antoine's beautiful but careless mother (Claire Maurier) seems especially unsympathetic to his needs – largely, the movie suggests, because Antoine is the product of an unwanted pregnancy. She is affectionate, even "motherly," but only when she fears her son will spill the beans about having spied her in the arms of her lover. Her husband, Antoine's jovial but aloof stepfather (Albert Remy), married her long after Antoine's birth, out of the kindness of his heart, in order to give the child a name — as he never tires of reminding his wife.

Gradually, inevitably, Antoine channels his unhappiness into rebellion. (The film's French title comes from the idiom *faire les quatre cents coups*, which translates roughly as "to raise hell.") Misbehaving leads to playing hooky: Antoine never appears happier than he does during an AWOL visit to an amusement park, where he takes a ride on a centrifuge called The Rotor. The contraption begins to spin, and he is pinned to the wall, helpless yet happy, while the floor descends beneath his feet. (Look carefully, and you'll spot a young François Truffaut among the other folks pinned alongside him.) Trouble is, truancy requires inventing alibis. It speaks volumes about Antoine's sense of himself as an unloved son that, when pressured by his least favorite teacher (Guy Decomble, the grizzled police inspector of Jean-Pierre Melville's *Bob le Flambeur*) to explain one of his many absences, the boy blurts out that his mother has died. Wishful thinking? True to her nature, the very-much-alive Madame Doinel views Antoine's lie as a personal insult: "Why couldn't he have said *you* died?" she snaps at her husband.

One thing leads to another, the runaway child tries his hand at petty thievery and, of course, he's caught. The achingly sad story of Antoine Doinel ends with the boy's impulsive attempt to escape from a reformatory. This leads to one of the most famous and influential closing shots in movie history, a startling freeze-frame of Antoine alone on a wintry beach, unable to run any further — and anxious to see what new travail lurks over the horizon. The shot has been repeated countless times since 1959, in everything from *The Mod Squad* to MTV to Boaz Yakin's harrowing *Fresh* (1994), but the impact of the original remains defiantly undiminished in its shattering impact. Even if you know that Antoine survived — and thrived, actually — in three sequels and a short directed by Truffaut and starring Leaud, you can't help feeling you've witnessed the extinguishing of a soul.

Much of *The 400 Blows* has the raw, jumpy immediacy of a cinema verite documentary, particularly whenever Truffaut follows Antoine through the streets of Paris. In this, the film is very much a paradigm of *nouvelle vague* style: Like the Italian Neorealists of the post-World War II era, the French New Wave filmmakers made a virtue of their limited resources by going beyond the soundstage to capture life on the run, with handheld cameras and frequent improvisation. But what sets the late, great François Truffaut apart from most other filmmakers of his generation — from most other filmmakers, period — is the deeply humanistic understanding he extends to all his characters, even the more unpleasant ones, and the unadulterated joy he conveys in the very act of making films. A kind of joy, his first feature makes clear, that Truffaut seldom experienced during the melancholy days of his youth.

SPECS:

The 400 Blows — Stars: Jean-Pierre Leaud, Claire Maurier, Albert Remy, Patrick Auffray, and Guy Decomble. Written and directed by François Truffaut. Running time: 94 minutes. Year of release: 1959. DVD distributor: The Criterion Collection.

SUBJECTS FOR FURTHER RESEARCH:

Stolen Kisses (1968) — Just as François Truffaut survived his own hard-scrabble youth, Antoine Doinel, his cinematic alter ego, managed to live hopefully ever after in a short (*Antoine and Colette*) and three feature-length sequels. *Stolen Kisses*, the most affecting of the three, finds Antoine (Jean-Pierre Leaud) learning bittersweet lessons about love while pursuing a receptive yet elusive beauty (Claude Jade)

Fresh (1994) — Boaz Yakin's directorial debut is a gripping inner-city fable about a twelve-year-old African-American youngster (Sean Nelson) who uses his hard-won street smarts and crafty chess-master strategy to transcend his seemingly dead-end life as courier for a drug dealer. The stunning final scene indicates that, even when you're able to save your own life, you still can lose everything else that matters.

Joe the King (1999) — Actor-turned-filmmaker Frank Whaley freely acknowledges the influence of *The 400 Blows* on his own debut feature about the downward spiral of a troubled adolescent. Noah Fleiss stars in the rigorously understated yet hauntingly poignant drama about a problem child whose biggest problems are his dysfunctional parents (Val Kilmer, Karen Young).

LESSON FOR FILMMAKERS:

Norman Jewison admits he "didn't necessarily want to like" *The 400 Blows* when François Truffaut unveiled his first feature in 1959, "because I knew he had been a critic for *Cahiers du Cinema*, and there were a lot of things that I disagreed with him on. And when he said he was going to make a film, I said, 'Here you are, you asshole. Now you'll find out that it's not so goddamn easy.' And he was brilliant, totally brilliant." So brilliant, in fact, that he served as inspiration for directors as diverse as Steven Spielberg, Robert Benton, Lasse Hallström — and Oliver Stone. "I suppose what he taught me is, make your film personal," Stone says of Truffaut. "Do it about a boy, do it about your life, like *The 400 Blows*, *Stolen Kisses*, the Antoine Doinel pictures. Those films were very real. And he allowed us to be very real and personal. He encouraged us, as young filmmakers, to do that in our work. And that's very important."

DAY FOR NIGHT

Every so often, a motion picture will stake out a territory and lay eternal claim to it. Such is the case with *Day for Night*, a warm-hearted yet clear-eyed comedy-drama that persuasively argues, with ample evidence, that a movie set is the most magical place on earth.

The late, great François Truffaut's Oscar-winning masterwork was not, strictly speaking, the first movie ever made about the joy of making movies. But it remains, decades after its Paris premiere, the yardstick by which almost every film on the subject inevitably is measured. Its very title, which refers to a process through which night scenes can be shot in daylight, continues to serve as critic-speak shorthand in reviews of everything from Tom DiCillo's *Living in Oblivion* (1995) to Oliver Assayas' *Irma Vep* (1996) to Roman Coppola's *CQ* (2001).

Truffaut cast himself in the central role of Ferrand, the affable, over-worked auteur who's trying to complete a sudsy romantic melodrama, *Meet Pamela*, within seven weeks at the Victorine Studios in Nice. The production is beset by mishaps and misadventures, some amusingly minor (a recalcitrant cat refuses to perform in a sight gag), some shatteringly tragic (a star dies in an auto mishap before completing a key scene). At one point, an egotistically impulsive male lead threatens to abandon the film because his current sweetheart has spurned him. Desperate times call for desperate measures by a selfless team player: The American-born leading lady, still vulnerable after a recent nervous breakdown, nevertheless volunteers to keep her feckless co-star interested in the production by feigning romantic interest in him.

Throughout the barely controlled chaos, Ferrand maintains his sang-froid, though just barely, by keeping himself focused on the end that justifies any means. Making a movie, he says, is like taking a stagecoach ride in the Wild West: "At first, you hope for a nice trip. Then you just hope you reach your destination."

Unlike *Meet Pamela*, *Day for Night* brings out the best in everyone involved. The stellar ensemble cast includes Jacqueline Bisset as the beautiful but emotionally fragile Hollywood star, Valentina Cortese as a fading leading lady who's too flustered — and, quite often, too drunk — to remember her lines, Nathalie Baye as a frisky production assistant, and Jean-Pierre Leaud (a.k.a. Antoine Doinel, Truffaut on-screen alter ego in *The 400 Blows* and subsequent sequels) as the callow, self-absorbed actor who repeatedly poses a question that Truffaut himself often pondered: "Are women magic?"

SPECS:

Day for Night — Stars: François Truffaut, Jacqueline Bisset, Jean-Pierre Aumont, Valentina Cortese, Jean-Pierre Leaud, and Nathalie Baye. Directed by François Truffaut. Screenplay: François Truffaut, Jean Louis Richard, Suzanne Schiffman. Running time: 116 minutes. Year of release: 1973. DVD distributor: Warner Home Video.

SUBJECTS FOR FURTHER RESEARCH:

Sweet Liberty (1986) — Alan Alda does triple duty as director, writer, and star of this modestly amusing movie-within-a-movie comedy about a small-town history professor who writes a best-selling novel about the American Revolution. His triumph proves to be a mixed blessing, how-ever, when his community is overrun by a film company intent on turning his serious fiction into a raucous teen-skewing farce.

Through the Olive Trees (1994) — Iranian director Abbas Kiarostami blurs the lines between fact and fiction, drama and documentary, with a sometimes ponderous, sometimes fascinating film about a filmmaker intent on recruiting local actors in a region recently ravaged by an earth-quake. After casting a local woman and the unemployed bricklayer who adores her as romantic leads, the director is by turns amused and annoyed as he sees life imitating art imitating life.

American Movie (1999) — Just when it appeared *The Blair Witch Project* might encourage millions of impressionable wanna-bes to attempt their own no-budget extravaganzas, Chris Smith provided an invaluable service by focusing on the making of a far less successful horror flick. Smith's amusing and unsettling documentary about a wanna-be with far more enthusiasm than talent forces audiences to consider the other 99.9 percent of indie productions by neophyte auteurs. It is not a pretty picture.

LESSON FOR FILMMAKERS:

If you want to fully express your love for films and filmmakers — well, make your own film. And, just as important, acknowledge the influence of other people's films. As François Truffaut noted in a 1973 interview: "There are directors who boast of never going to the movies, but myself, I go all the time. And I am forever marked by the films I discovered before becoming a filmmaker, when I could take them in more fully. If, for example, in the course of *Day for Night* I pay special homage to *Citizen Kane*, it is because that film, released in Paris in July 1946, changed both the cinema and my own life. Through the young actor played by Jean-Pierre Leaud, I am always coming back to the question that has tormented me for thirty years now: Is cinema more important than life?"

≈13≈
BEYOND THE
MAINSTREAM

RETURN OF THE SECAUCUS 7

First he figured out which actors he could afford. Then he invented roles for them to play. Then he made up his mind what a movie with those characters could be about. Finally, with all the difficult decisions out of the way, John Sayles sat down and actually wrote — in two weeks! — the screenplay for *Return of the Secaucus 7*, the 1980 feature that established him as a founding father of American independent cinema.

This cart-before-the-horse method is never taught by esoteric theorists in the finest film schools. But Sayles learned his lessons from a more pragmatic mentor: Roger Corman, the schlock-movie mogul who also helped launch the careers of Jack Nicholson, Francis Ford Coppola, Martin Scorsese, and Peter Bogdanovich, among many others. Corman was impressed by Sayles' early efforts as a novelist and short-story author, and hired the then-twentysomething writer to churn out scripts for such low-budget quickies as *Piranha* (1978), *The Lady in Red* (1979), and *Battle Beyond the Stars* (1980). Sayles proved to be an attentive student as he observed how Corman's directors cut corners and pinched pennies while racing through production. When the time came to plan his debut effort as a feature filmmaker, Sayles put what he learned to good use, even as he contemplated using former student radicals — not gangsters or killer fish or belligerent extraterrestrials — as his *dramatis personae*.

The funny thing is, Sayles didn't intend for *Return of the Secaucus 7* to be anything more than a "calling card movie," one that would be viewed primarily by decision-makers who might hire him (or at least finance him)

287

for more ambitious projects. That it eventually was seen and enjoyed — and emulated — by so many people is the happily-ever-after ending for a Cinderella story that continues to inspire novice filmmakers.

Using a cast comprised of actors he had worked with at a summer-stock theater in New Hampshire, Sayles shot *Return of the Secaucus 7* in 25 days, on a frayed-shoestring budget of $60,000. The completed film was conspicuously lacking in lavish production values, Hollywood-style star power, and stirring scenes of action. All it had to offer was the spectacle of people talking and behaving pretty much like similar people do in real life, with all that mundane activity filtered through the humanist sensibility of a first-rate, natural-born film artist. This was more than enough for the movie to earn critical acclaim while attracting a respectably large audience. (The latter achievement was all the more impressive in an era before an indie movie could get a high-profile launch at the Sundance Film Festival.) Just as important, it also was enough to influence many other indie and mainstream moviemakers, from Lawrence Kasdan (*The Big Chill*) to Kenneth Branagh (*Peter's Friends*) to Denys Arcand (*The Decline of the American Empire*).

The "Secaucus 7" of the title are former activists who enjoy a weekend reunion some eight years after they were arrested and briefly jailed (in Secaucus, N.J.) while on their way to a political demonstration in Washington, D.C. As might be expected, the years have mellowed their anger and cooled their passions. Still, the friends remain idealistic, even hopeful. (Remember: The movie was completed *before* Ronald Reagan beat Jimmy Carter in the 1980 U.S. Presidential race.) As the story begins, however, each has a deeply personal problem to fret about. A couple wonders if it's too late to start thinking about having children. One of their friends contemplates leaving her long-time live-in lover. Another woman, a congressional aide, worries that she's being co-opted by The System. And so it goes.

Over the weekend, the old friends talk about past adventures and future plans, play games, skinny-dip, eat and drink — and, during painfully self-aware moments, consider what life may be like on the other side of the generation gap. For the most part, the mood is one of casual nostalgia and tolerant bemusement. Friends recognize warts on themselves and each other, but remain friends nonetheless.

All of which may sound like *Return of the Secaucus 7* would be as interesting as paging through a stranger's high-school yearbook. But don't worry: Sayles' dialogue is so flavorful, and his fresh-faced young players — including Gordon Clapp (of TV's *NYPD Blue*), David Strathairn, and, briefly, Sayles himself — are so ingratiating, you become deeply involved with these vividly drawn characters. Indeed, no matter how old you are, you may notice friends and acquaintances among the folks on screen. You may even notice yourself.

SPECS:

Return of the Secaucus 7 — Cast: Bruce MacDonald, Maggie Renzi, Adam LeFevre, Maggie Cousineau, Gordon Clapp, Jean Passanante, Karen Trott, Mark Arnott, David Strathairn, John Sayles, Marisa Smith, Amy Schewel, and Carolyn Brooks. Written and directed by John Sayles. Running time: 104 minutes. Year of release: 1980. DVD distributor: MGM Home Entertainment.

SUBJECTS FOR FURTHER RESEARCH:

The Big Chill (1983) — Lawrence Kasdan's extremely popular and much-imitated comedy-drama about a reunion of college classmates actually appeared three years after *Return of the Secaucus 7*. Even so, Kasdan's film is more frequently credited for kicking off the subgenre that both films inadvertently inspired. For better or worse, *The Big Chill* — even more than George Lucas' *American Graffiti* (1973) — also must be credited for sparking the tradition of movie soundtracks brimming with '60s golden oldies.

sex, lies & videotape (1989) — Arguably even more of a landmark film than *Return of the Secaucus 7*, Steven Soderbergh's sly drama about adultery and emotional voyeurism forever changed the way indie cinema was perceived and received in the United States. The movie's surprising critical and commercial success established Miramax as a major player in indie distribution, and the Sundance Film Festival as the premier launching pad for indie productions.

The Barbarian Invasions (2003) — Denys Arcand's ruefully wise and flawlessly acted comedy-drama invites us to spend quality time with some Montreal baby-boomers, aging ex-firebrands who vacillate between resignation and celebration as they measure their lives while one approaches death. The film is a sequel to Arcand's excellent *Decline of the American Empire* (1986), which owed more than a bit to *Return of the Secaucus 7* and *The Big Chill*.

LESSON FOR FILMMAKERS:

No stars? No budget? No problem: All you have to do is make a virtue of your limitations. While preparing *Return of the Secaucus 7*, John Sayles told me in a 1981 interview, "I realized that I wasn't going to have a lot of camera movement, because that takes a lot of time and money, and I wasn't going to have a lot of either. So I said, 'What reason will I have to cut and keep this thing moving a little bit, even though it's gonna be a very conversational movie?' And I thought of something like Robert Altman did in *Nashville* — that is, have a lot of subplots so you always have a reason for cutting. So I got the idea of doing an ensemble piece about a group of people, so that once people talked for two minutes, you could always cut to another group of people doing something else in a different location."

STRANGER THAN PARADISE

n the pantheon of American indie moviemakers, Jim Jarmusch is the patron saint of wonder-struck wayfarers. For interviews and photo ops, he cultivates the persona of a sub-zero New York hipster, complete with a Downtown wardrobe of black, gray, and more black. Yet his best films are infused with a warmer sensibility, indicating a generosity of spirit and a nonjudgmental empathy.

In movies such as *Down By Law* (1986), *Mystery Train* (1989), and *Night on Earth* (1991), Jarmusch gazes at everyday life on the fringes through the eyes of outsiders, and finds the view utterly exotic. Whether they're stuck in a tacky Florida hotel during the dead of winter, or wandering past ramshackle buildings on a Memphis street at twilight, his characters — often foreign-born, almost always displaced — find what they see at once familiar and fantastic. More often than not, however, they're too easily distracted by minutiae to linger on any phenomenon they encounter.

Stranger Than Paradise, Jarmusch's 1984 breakthrough film, is a no-frills, deadpan comedy shot in grainy widescreen black-and-white, and shot through with inventive looniness. Mind you, we're not talking about a rolling-in-the-aisles laugh riot, or a farce filled with snappy one-liners you can repeat to your friends. Here, as in most of his subsequent films, the humor springs from Jarmusch's askew point of view, the blithe assurance of his oddball characters, and the offbeat edges that his actors bring to their line readings. Jarmusch may encourage us to chuckle at self-regarding schemers and dreamers, but he inspires affectionate bemusement, not condescending mockery.

There's little point in quoting dialogue to illustrate the movie's humor, since most of the funniest lines mean nothing out of context. You have to experience *Stranger* for yourself to understand why its most devoted fans will smile knowingly, or even laugh out loud, if one says to the other, in a thick Eastern European accent, "I'm the winner!" (Or, more accurately: "I'm dah vinnah!")

Just as important, you have to experience it to fully appreciate how this must-see movie, a triumph of punk-minimalist chic, influenced hundreds of indie wanna-bes who have dared to dream on microscopic budgets throughout the past two decades. Indeed, some film historians often cite *Stranger Than Paradise* as the spark that ignited the New Indie Cinema of the 1980s and beyond, and view Jarmusch as the maverick role model who encouraged such diverse talents as Hal Hartley, Steven Soderbergh, and Quentin Tarantino.

Structured as a three-act misadventure, *Stranger* was filmed on the cheap over a few years in New York, Cleveland, and Florida. In the opening segment — titled "The New World," and originally exhibited as a self-contained short — we're introduced to Willie (John Lurie), a thick-lipped, broad-nosed Hungarian layabout who has lived for ten years in New York, and now feels he is completely assimilated. Willie, who often suggests a lobotomized Ed Norton, has no visible means of support, squanders money at racetracks and card games, and lives in a seedy East Village apartment that no self-respecting cockroach would enter. Even so, he believes he's living the good life in the land of opportunity. And he resents being reminded of his roots by the arrival of Eva (Eszter Balint), his sixteen-year-old cousin, who's passing through on her way to joining an aunt in Cleveland.

Willie feels more comfortable in the company of Eddie (Richard Edson), his best friend, another cheerfully satisfied ne'er-do-well. (The two men even look a bit like each other!) But the longer Eva stays, the more Willie feels something stirring in his heart for her. Not surprisingly, however, he refrains from acting on his inchoate feelings.

In the second segment, "One Year Later," Willie and Eddie impulsively travel to the snowy climes of Cleveland, where they gaze at frozen Lake Erie, see a kung-fu movie — and visit Eva. They also meet Aunt Lotte (Cecillia Stark), a Bela Lugosi soundalike who's always "dah vinnah" when the game is gin rummy.

Finally, in "Paradise," Eva joins Willie and Eddie for a journey to Miami. En route, they stop at a low-rent motel, discover the perils of betting at Florida dog-race tracks, and prove fate really can make life seem stranger than... well, you know.

Visually, *Stranger Than Paradise* is a sly cross-cultural joke. It doesn't matter whether we're in Cleveland or Miami, or whether we're viewing an interior or exterior shot: Everything on screen has the gray, wintry look of Eastern European cinema circa 1966. Each scene is a single, continuous take, climaxing in a blackout. Jarmusch uses the individual shots like pieces of a mosaic, cleverly arranging them to present a comically bleak vision of aimless, narrow-minded drifting through the lower depths.

As Willie and Eddie, Lurie and Edson are suitably laid back, almost to the point of catatonia, as their characters remain smugly superior to everyone they meet, and refuse to be fazed by anything that happens. But Balint is more than a match for either of them, especially when Willie makes the mistake of complaining about her repetitive playing of her favorite record. "It's Screamin' Jay Hawkins, and he's a wild man!" she responds. "So bug off!"

Zonked-out and absurd, yet subversively sentimental, *Stranger Than Paradise* slouches to the beat of a different drummer.

SPECS:

Stranger Than Paradise — Stars: John Lurie, Eszter Balint, Richard Edson, and Cecillia Stark. Written and directed by Jim Jarmusch. Year of release: 1984. Running time: 89 minutes. DVD distributor: MGM Home Entertainment.

SUBJECTS FOR FURTHER RESEARCH:

Smithereens (1982) — A precursor of Jim Jarmusch's knowing wallow in East Village bohemia, Susan Seidelman's somewhat harsher drama focuses on a self-deluding punkette who seeks fame and fortune in the rock world, despite her pronounced lack of social skills and discernable talent.

The Unbelievable Truth (1989) — Although clearly influenced by Jim Jarmusch (among others) in his approach to deadpan absurdism, Hal Hartley's low-budget debut feature is infused with a unique comic sensibility. The promise suggested by this droll farce was fulfilled in such later Hartley efforts as *Trust* (1990), *Simple Men* (1992), and *Amateur* (1994).

Coffee and Cigarettes (2003) — Still indie after all these years, Jim Jarmusch offers the equivalent of a short-story anthology: A collection of black-and-white mini-dramas, filmed over a seventeen-year period, involving animated conversations between close friends, passing strangers, and/or competitive power players. Taken together, the episodes chart currents of indie cinema from rough-edged minimalism to star-studded slickness. The good news: Jarmusch retains his trademark idiosyncrasy even with bigger stars and glossier production values.

LESSON FOR FILMMAKERS:

Spike Lee says he was inspired by a fellow NYU film school alumnus when he filmed his own low-budget breakthrough feature, *She's Gotta Have It* (1986). "The process really began," Lee said in a 2003 interview, "after a former classmate of mine, Jim Jarmusch, finished his first film, *Stranger Than Paradise*, a year out of NYU. Here was someone I knew, someone who went to the same school I did, who now had an international hit. I owe a great deal to Jim Jarmusch. He showed me and everyone else that we could do this."

BLUE VELVET

lue skies, sunny days. Kodachrome snapshots of small-town contentment. Red roses bloom along a white picket fence. A fireman passes by on his truck, waving heartily. A crosswalk guard helps children on their way to school. A homeowner waters his lawn as his faithful dog keeps watch.

And then the weirdness creeps in.

The homeowner collapses in agony as he's felled by a stroke. Jeffrey (Kyle MacLachlan), his cheerfully callow son, returns home from college to run the family hardware store. But Jeffrey is sidetracked when he discovers a severed human ear in a sunlit meadow. "Yes," a sobersided detective agrees, "that's a human ear, all right."

Sandy (Laura Dern), the detective's pretty, perky daughter, tells Jeffrey about a mysterious nightclub singer who might know something about the mutilation. Jeffrey takes one look at the *femme fatale*, and his curiosity — among other things — is aroused. So he plots to sneak into the woman's apartment, and hide in her closet. Why? "There are opportunities in life," Jeffrey explains to Sandy, "for gaining knowledge and experience."

And how. In *Blue Velvet*, arguably the definitive David Lynch mindtrip and certainly one of the most influential films of the 1980s, Jeffrey learns more about the evil within and around him than most folks ever want to know. And he pays dearly for his enlightenment.

Deep in the heart of Lumberton, a town seemingly wholesome enough to be home for a '50s sitcom, Jeffrey finds a pestilence is spreading. The chief cause for the infection: Frank Booth (Dennis Hopper), a manic-depressive drug dealer fond of sniffing nitrous oxide, dominating helpless women — and grooving on the golden oldies of Roy Orbison.

(You haven't lived until you've seen co-star Dean Stockwell, cast as an effete underworld type in league with Frank, lip-synching Orbison's *In Dreams*.) Jeffrey wants to help Dorothy (Isabella Rossellini), the sultry singer under Frank's grimy thumb. But before he can do her, or himself, any good, he has to come to grips with his own mounting appetite for psychosexual power plays.

Lynch concocted something indescribably wild and weird in *Blue Velvet*, a heady brew of blithe naïveté, scuzzy decadence, adolescent fantasy, and sadomasochistic humiliation. It's one of the most bizarre coming-of-age stories ever captured on film, as Jeffrey discovers just what lurks in dark corners on the sidestreets not so far away from his comfy-cozy neighborhood in Reagan-era America. ("I am seeing something," he tells Sandy, "that was always hidden.") But those dark corners inevitably spill their shadows into paradise: Dorothy, nude and badly beaten, staggers into Jeffery's orderly world at an extremely awkward moment, just when Jeffrey is arguing with a football hero over who should be dating the angel-faced Sandy.

It's easy to read Jeffrey as a surrogate for Lynch, a soft-spoken aesthete who spent his formative years in a Middle American hamlet much like Lumberton. (MacLachlan even dresses in what was widely recognized during the '80s as Lynch's trademark style: No tie, dark slacks, white shirt primly buttoned at the collar and cuffs.) But that's not the only indication that this is a deeply personal work. *Blue Velvet* begins and ends with massive close-ups of ears — one severed, the other not — suggesting the entire film is a journey through one man's mind, a fever dream of innocence lost and losing.

At various points in this 1986 masterwork, you can sense the spirit of *film noir*, those fatalistic thrillers of the '40s and '50s in which tarnished heroes discover their own darker impulses. At other points, however, *Blue Velvet* seems a straight-faced put-on, with MacLachlan and most of his co-stars delivering their dialogue with a deadpan sincerity that borders on the absurd. The film is a black comedy, of sorts. But the laughter never completely dispels the mood of chilly dread.

MacLachlan makes a most engaging hero, even when — or make that *especially* when — he reveals a decidedly kinky streak. Dern and Rossellini are perfectly cast as the embodiments of opposing forces vying for Jeffrey's soul. And in a career-defining role, Hopper vividly plays Frank Booth as a ferocious, foul-mouthed monster, as undisciplined and potentially lethal as a car careening down a mountain road without brakes.

Production designer Patricia Norris and cinematographer Frederick Elmes often give the film the brightly inviting look of a picture postcard. But appearances can be deceiving: *Blue Velvet* is a slick, stylish nightmare of perversion percolating beneath the surface of small-town placidity. Try to imagine what would happen if Beaver Cleaver went to hell, and found he enjoyed himself there, and you'll have some idea what to expect.

SPECS:

Blue Velvet — Stars: Kyle MacLachlan, Isabella Rossellini, Dennis Hopper, Laura Dern, and Dean Stockwell. Written and directed by David Lynch. Running time: 121 minutes. Year of release: 1986. DVD distributor: MGM Home Entertainment.

SUBJECTS FOR FURTHER RESEARCH:

Un Chien Andalou / An Andalusian Dog (1929) — It's the surreal thing. Filmmaker Luis Buñuel and artist Salvador Dali famously teamed for seventeen minutes of aggressively irrational imagery, much of it (including a scene in which a man severs a woman's eye) clearly foreshadowing the cinema of David Lynch.

Wild at Heart (1990) — David Lynch earned top honors at the Cannes Film festival for this exhilaratingly twisted and surreally violent road movie starring an Elvis-channeling Nicolas Cage and a hot-to-trot Laura Dern as lovers on the run.

Twin Falls, Idaho (1999) — Sibling filmmakers Mark and Michael Polish cast themselves as conjoined twin brothers in this oddly poignant drama that often looks — and sometimes even *sounds* — like one of David Lynch's wide-awake nightmares.

LESSON FOR FILMMAKERS:

Nearly two decades after his first viewing of *Blue Velvet*, German film-maker Tom Tykwer (*Run Lola Run*) remains fascinated by the film's "dream-like" qualities. "The identity of cinema is so related to dreams," Tykwer told the London Telegraph. "I think the reason why we love to see films is because we're put into a state of half-sleep — it's dark, and you get visions that seemingly make sense, but are actually completely illogical. And *Blue Velvet* is dream-like storytelling. When you remember it, you don't remember the plot: You remember an atmosphere, a feel." Just as important, "You cannot position this film in time. It feels some-how like the 1950s — there are these old cars — but then the phones and other things are obviously from the 1980s. I do this in most of my films; I love getting lost in time. *Run Lola Run* is very much a film of the 1990s, but it seems as if Lola is running in a dream, a nightmarish cir-cle. I hope if you see it in twenty years, it will still be approachable, because of this."

RESERVOIR DOGS

With a full-throttle self-assurance just short of brazen arrogance, writer-director Quentin Tarantino blazed into our pop-culture consciousness in 1992 with *Reservoir Dogs*, a neo-noir crime drama that, at the time, seemed louder, bloodier, and more indefatigably foul-mouthed than anything unleashed in theaters since Sam Peckinpah went to that great screening room in the sky.

But when you view this must-see movie with a coolly reappraising eye, you can better discern the craft and cunning beneath the sound and fury. And that makes it all the easier to appreciate how *Reservoir Dogs* — unlike most of the guns-and-poses knock-offs that have appeared in its wake — reinvented and reinvigorated the rules of the game.

Taking his inspiration from hardboiled pulp fiction (which, of course, also informed his second film), classic B-movies, and Top 40 radio ear-candy, Tarantino gives us a claustrophobically intense drama about a meticulously planned heist that goes horribly wrong. The premise is simple: Six cold-blooded professionals, each identified only by a color-coded alias, join forces under a despotic mastermind (Lawrence Tierney) to loot a diamond wholesaler. But the robbery is a bloody botch, two of the robbers are killed and a third, Mr. Orange (Tim Roth), is seriously wounded.

Reservoir Dogs opens with a profanely funny prologue in a diner where the criminals swap half-joking threats ("You shoot me in a dream, you better wake up and apologize!") and debate the meaning of Madonna's lyrics. We meet these tough customers before we understand just how tough they are, and for all we know, they're just another group of dis-content real-estate dealers from *Glengarry Glen Ross*. But that's only the first of Tarantino's nasty tricks.

Just after the opening credits, the movie jumps to the robbery's after-math, as Mr. White (Harvey Keitel) puts pedal to the metal while Mr. Orange lies, screaming and bleeding, in the back seat. Mr. White offers encouragement: "It takes days to die from that kind of wound! Time is on your side!" But Mr. Orange takes little solace from this pep talk.

Mr. White and Mr. Orange arrive in a deserted warehouse where, along with Mr. Pink (Steve Buscemi) and Mr. Blonde (Michael Madsen), they stew in their own rancid juices while waiting for the mastermind to arrive. And while they wait, they wonder which one of them is the undercover operative who tipped off the cops about their robbery.

Reservoir Dogs is aggressively, insistently cinematic, but Tarantino auda-ciously structures it like a work of literature. He even provides chapter headings — "Mr. White," "Mr. Orange," et cetera — for character-revealing flashbacks that provide counterpoint to the ongoing drama in the warehouse. This kind of trickiness might have tripped up a lesser director, or at least dissipated the suspense. (Several Tarantino wanna-bes have indeed tripped — and fallen on their faces — with similarly self-con-scious artifice.) But Tarantino knows exactly what he wants, and how to get it, and what he can do to enhance our anxious appreciation of it.

Occasionally, Tarantino appears to let everything — the gutter language, the macho posturing, the wild-eyed panic, *everything* — get deliriously out of hand. But that loss of control is more apparent than real. Like some high-wire performer who has every crowd-startling stumble metic-ulously planned, he never loses his balance. Not even when, at one point, it looks like he loses his nerve.

Mr. Blonde, a psychopath with a fiendishly goofy grin, thinks it might be a good idea to torture information out of a hostage police officer. Just when he begins to apply a straight razor to his captive's ear, Tarantino turns the camera away, as if to say, "Jeez! Even I don't want to see this!" But the nightmare won't go away: Mr. Blonde walks right back into the frame, a grisly trophy clutched in his hand. And that's when you can almost hear Tarantino say: "Gotcha!"

SPECS:

Reservoir Dogs — Stars: Harvey Keitel, Tim Roth, Chris Penn, Steve Buscemi, Lawrence Tierney, and Michael Madsen. Written and directed by Quentin Tarantino. Running time: 100 minutes. Year of release: 1992. DVD distributor: Artisan Home Entertainment.

SUBJECTS FOR FURTHER RESEARCH:

City on Fire (1987) — While filming *Reservoir Dogs*, Quentin Tarantino "borrowed" several characters and plot elements from Ringo Lam's Hong Kong heist melodrama about an undercover cop (Chow Yun-Fat) who's in the wrong place at the right time while infiltrating a gang of jewel thieves.

Pulp Fiction (1994) — Quentin Tarantino's fulfills the promise of *Reservoir Dogs* with an outrageously entertaining and ferociously funny triple-decker crime story. And if you can't take the violence, close your eyes and just listen: The virtually incessant, luridly colloquial dialogue is flamboyantly stylized and ingeniously foul-mouthed.

Go (1999) — Doug Liman borrowed a little from *Reservoir Dogs*, and a lot from *Pulp Fiction*, while structuring this thrilling, enthralling, and time-twisting comedy-drama about intersecting lives and crimes during a 24-hour period in L.A.

LESSON FOR FILMMAKERS:

If you're going to work on a high-wire, it might help to have a net, even if you never use it. Quentin Tarantino shot two versions of the infamous *Reservoir Dogs* ear-slicing scene. In the first version, the camera remains focused on Mr. Orange's psychotic mayhem. "But then, when I put the movie together," Tarantino told me in a 1992 interview, "it was the other one that had the power. It's the one where you *don't* see it that was the most powerful. It's almost like, when you see it, the graphicness of it lets you off the hook. Because you can almost dismiss graphicness, or wonder, 'Oh, I wonder how they did that?' But the other shot, the one where (the camera) went away — that is the one that knocks people out. That's the one that gets under their skin. And that is what I wanted to do to the audience more than anything else: I wanted to disturb them."

THAT'S A WRAP!

As this book goes to press, no fewer than thirty remakes and more than twice that many sequels are in various stages of development at Hollywood studios and indie production companies. And, mind you, that doesn't include unofficial (or unauthorized) remakes, or movies simply "inspired," to lesser or larger degrees, by other movies. It's hard to imagine that the makers of *Win a Date With Tad Hamilton!* never viewed *Bye Bye Birdie* (1963), or that the folks responsible for *Chasing Liberty*, another 2004 release, are ignorant of *Roman Holiday* (1953). Don't think of it as plagiarism, however. Think of it as affectionate homage. Or, better still, film literacy.

Every year, there are more movies inspired, influenced, or emulated by the must-see movies covered in this book. Of course, there are other movies to see, just as there are other books to write. For now, though, consider this: You are living in an age when nearly every great movie ever made is easily accessible through online shopping, cable-TV viewing, or a quick trip to your friendly neighborhood video store. And that's a good thing. Because there really is so much more to learn.

ACKNOWLEDGMENTS

The author acknowledges the copyright owners of the following home video releases from which images have been used in this book for purposes of commentary, criticism and scholarship under the Fair Use Doctrine. No endorsement or sponsorship of this book by the copyright owners is claimed or implied. Images have been reproduced as a guide to readers who may wish to buy or rent films analyzed by author.

All the President's Men – ©1997, Warner Home Video
Annie Hall – ©2000, MGM Home Video
The Birth of a Nation – ©1998, Image Entertainment
Blade Runner – ©1996, Warner Home Video
Cabaret – ©1998, Warner Home Video
Casablanca – ©2003, Turner Entertainment Co. and Warner Home Video
Citizen Kane – ©2001, Turner Entertainment Co. and Warner Home Video
City Lights – ©1999, Image Entertainment
Day for Night – ©2003, Warner Home Video
Detour – ©2000, Image Entertainment
Die Hard – ©2001, 20th Century Fox Home Entertainment
Do the Right Thing – ©1998, Universal Home Video
Double Indemnity – ©1991, Universal Home Video
Dr. Strangelove or: How I Learned to Stop Worrying and Love the Bomb – ©2001, Columbia/Tri Star Home Video
Duck Soup – ©1997, Universal Home Video
A Fistful of Dollars – ©1999, MGM Home Video
The 400 Blows – ©1998, The Criterion Collection
48 HRS. – ©1998, Paramount Home Video
Frankenstein – ©1999, Universal Home Video

The General – ©1999, Kino Video

Guadalcanal Diary – ©2001, 20th Century Fox Home Entertainment

His Girl Friday – ©2000, Columbia/Tri Star Home Video

High Noon – ©1999, Republic Entertainment Inc.

The Maltese Falcon – ©2000, Turner Entertainment Co. and Warner Home Video *Metropolis* – ©2002, Kino Video

National Lampoon's Animal House – ©1998, Universal Home Video

North by Northwest – ©2000, Turner Entertainment Co. and Warner Home Video *Nosferatu* – ©1997, Image Entertainment

Notorious – ©2001, The Criterion Collection

Open City – ©1997, Image Entertainment

Pillow Talk – © 1999, Universal Home Video

Psycho – ©1998, Universal Home Video

The Public Enemy – ©2000, Turner Entertainment Co. and Warner Home Video

Reservoir Dogs – ©2002, Artisan Home Entertainment

Return of the Secaucus 7 – ©2003, MGM Home Entertainment

Rio Bravo – ©2001, Warner Home Video

Rocky – ©1997, MGM Home Video

The Searchers – ©1997, Warner Home Video

Seven Samurai – ©1998, The Criterion Collection

Shane – ©2000, Paramount Home Video

Singin' in the Rain – ©2002, Turner Entertainment Co. and Warner Home Video

Smokey and the Bandit – ©1998, Universal Home Video

Snow White and the Seven Dwarfs – ©2001, Walt Disney Home Video

Stagecoach – ©1997, Warner Home Video

Taxi Driver – ©1999, Columbia/Tri Star Home Video

Vertigo – ©1999, Universal Home Video

About the
Author

JOE LEYDON is an award-winning film critic for *Variety, Dallas A.M. Journal-Express* and the *Examiner* newspapers of Houston. He also is host of the *MovingPictureShow.com* website, entertainment editor for *Cowboys & Indians* magazine, columnist for *Stereophile Guide to Home Theater* and adjunct professor at University of Houston and Houston Community College. Leydon was born and raised in New Orleans, where he acquired a taste for fine food and hearty partying at an early age. He graduated from Loyola University, where he developed an equally passionate regard for François Truffaut, Charlie Chaplin, and Michael Caine. From 1982 until 1995, he was film critic for the *Houston Post*. More recently, he has reviewed films for the *San Francisco Examiner, MSNBC.com,* NBC affiliate KPRC-TV, *Fort Worth Star-Telegram* and *Inside Houston* magazine. He has written features for the *New York Daily News*, the *Los Angeles Times, Newsday,* the *Boston Globe, IndieWire.com* and *Film Comment* magazine. He can be reached at JoeLeydon@yahoo.com.

MICHAEL WIESE PRODUCTIONS
www.mwp.com

We are delighted that you have found, and are enjoying, our books.

Since 1981, we've been all about providing filmmakers with the very best information on the craft of filmmaking: from screenwriting to funding, from directing to camera, acting, editing, distribution, and new media.

It is our goal to inspire and empower a generation (or two) of filmmakers and videomakers like yourself. But we want to go beyond providing you with just the basics. We want to shake you and inspire you to reach for your dreams and go beyond what's been done before. Most films that come out each year waste our time and enslave our imaginations. We want to give you the confidence to create from your authentic center, to bring something from your own experience that will truly inspire others and bring humanity to its full potential — avoiding those urges to manufacture derivative work in order to be accepted.

Movies, television, the Internet, and new media all have incredible power to transform. As you prepare your next project, know that it is in your hands to choose to create something magnificent and enduring for generations to come.

This is not an impossible goal, because you've got a little help. Our authors are some of the most creative mentors in the business, willing to share their hard-earned insights with you. Their books will point you in the right direction but, ultimately, it's up to you to seek that authentic something on which to spend your precious time.

We applaud your efforts and are here to support you. Let us hear from you.

Sincerely,

Michael Wiese
Filmmaker, Publisher

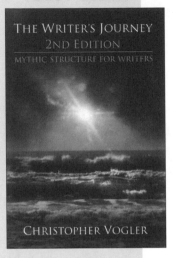

MYTH AND THE MOVIES
Discovering the Mythic Structure of 50 Unforgettable Films

Stuart Voytilla
Foreword by Christopher Vogler, author of *The Writer's Journey*

An illuminating companion piece to *The Writer's Journey*, *Myth and the Movies* applies the mythic structure Vogler developed to 50 well-loved U.S. and foreign films. This comprehensive book offers a greater understanding of why some films continue to touch and connect with audiences generation after generation.

Movies discussed include *Die Hard*, *Singin' in the Rain*, *Boyz N the Hood*, *Pulp Fiction*, *The Searchers*, *La Strada*, and *The Silence of the Lambs*.

Stuart Voytilla is a writer, script consultant, and teacher of acting and screenwriting and the co-author of *Writing the Comedy Film*.

$26.95, 300 pages
Order # 39RLS | ISBN: 0-941188-66-3

THE WRITER'S PARTNER
1001 Breakthrough Ideas to Stimulate Your Imagination

Martin Roth

This book is the complete source, as reliable and indispensable as its title implies. Whether you're looking for inspiration for new plotlines and characters or need help fleshing out your characters and settings with depth, detail, color, and texture, Martin Roth will turn your script into a strong, memorable work. This comprehensive classic covers every major genre, from action to suspense to comedy to romance to horror. With *The Writer's Partner*, you'll feel like you're in a roomful of talented writers helping you to perfect your screenplay!

Martin Roth is the writer of *The Crime Writer's Reference Book*.

$19.95, 349 pages
Order # 3RLS | ISBN: 0-941188-32-9

THE PERFECT PITCH
How to Sell Yourself and Your Movie Idea to Hollywood

Ken Rotcop *as told to James Shea*

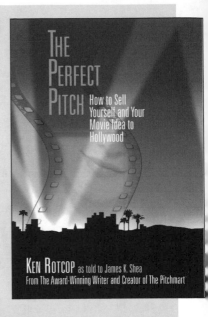

A good pitch can mean the difference between seeing your name on a lucrative studio contract or a form rejection letter. It's a well-known industry fact that film executives typically devote about two minutes of their attention to directors and screenwriters who bring them their ideas hoping for a deal. Can you capture their attention and pique their interest in the time it takes to order a latte at Starbucks? Your future as a successful screenwriter or director may depend on it.

Author Ken Rotcop writes from a unique perspective — he's made hundreds of pitches himself as a screenwriter and producer and heard many more as creative director of four studios. Using personal examples of successes and failures, Rotcop shows you how to walk the tightrope of a pitch meeting without falling off. Which attention-grabbing strategies can make a studio head put down his daily horoscope and listen to you? Once you've got his attention, how can you "reel him in" and get him excited about your idea? What if you forget what you were going to say? What if you make a faux pas? Does "no" always mean "no" in the language of movie deals?

Rotcop discusses these situations and others, as well as how to best present yourself and your idea, how and when to do "on-the-spot" pitching, and how to recognize and capitalize on future opportunities.

"Forget about snappy dialogue, characterization and plot. It's the pitch that gets a script read and a movie deal done. If it were not for Ken Rotcop, most new writers would be out of the loop."
— John Lippman, *Wall St Journal*

Ken Rotcop produces Pitchmart™, Hollywood's biggest screenplay pitch event.

$16.95, 156 pages
Order # 14RLS | ISBN: 0-941188-31-0

FILM DIRECTING: SHOT BY SHOT
Visualizing from
Concept to Screen

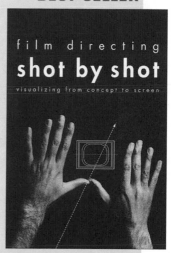

Steven D. Katz

Over 160,000 Sold! International best-seller!

Film Directing: Shot by Shot — with its famous blue cover — is the best-known book on directing and a favorite of professional directors as an on-set quick reference guide.

This international bestseller is a complete catalog of visual techniques and their stylistic implications, enabling working filmmakers to expand their knowledge.

Contains in-depth information on shot composition, staging sequences, visualization tools, framing and composition techniques, camera movement, blocking tracking shots, script analysis, and much more.

Includes over 750 storyboards and illustrations, with never-before-published storyboards from Steven Spielberg's *Empire of the Sun*, Orson Welles' *Citizen Kane*, and Alfred Hitchcock's *The Birds*.

"(To become a director) you have to teach yourself what makes movies good and what makes them bad. John Singleton has been my mentor... he's the one who told me what movies to watch and to read *Shot by Shot*."
— Ice Cube, *New York Times*

"A generous number of photos and superb illustrations accompany each concept, many of the graphics being from Katz' own pen... *Film Directing: Shot by Shot* is a feast for the eyes."
— *Videomaker Magazine*

Steven D. Katz is also the author of *Film Directing: Cinematic Motion*.

$27.95 | 366 pages | Order # 7RLS | ISBN: 0-941188-10-8

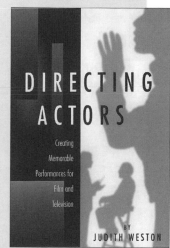

THE FILM DIRECTOR'S INTUITION:
Script Analysis and Rehearsal Techniques

Judith Weston

The craft of directing is well known to include shot composition and understanding of the technology. But directors need to know how to prepare so that their ideas achieve a level of intuitive truth. This means deep script analysis, until the characters' inner lives and private joys and problems are human and idiosyncratic, and as real to the director as his own. And it means reading the actors' impulses and feelings — including those that the actors themselves may not know they have.

A filmmaker's most precious assets — not just for directing actors, but for all the storytelling decisions — are his instincts, imagination, and intuition. Judith Weston gives away the secrets that can keep an imagination alive and free a director's intuition, so everyone on the set can function at full creativity.

Includes chapters on:
> Sources of Imagination
> Goals of Script Analysis
> Tools of the Storyteller
> The Lost Art of Rehearsal
> Director's Authority
> Sample script analysis of scenes from *sex, lies, and videotape*, *Clerks*, and *Tender Mercies*

"Judith's method is wonderful because it is practical. She has given me numerous tools to solve problems on the set and to earn the trust of actors. Her classes and her book are invaluable resources to any director."
> — Lawrence Trilling, Director
> *Alias*, *Ed*, *Felicity*

Judith Weston has taught Acting for Directors for over a decade throughout the US and Europe, and is the author of the best-selling book, *Directing Actors*.

$26.95 | 350 pages | Order # 111RLS | ISBN: 0-941188-78-7

ORDER FORM

MICHAEL WIESE PRODUCTIONS
11288 VENTURA BLVD., # 621
STUDIO CITY, CA 91604
E-MAIL: MWPSALES@MWP.COM
WEB SITE: WWW.MWP.COM

WRITE OR FAX FOR A FREE CATALOG

PLEASE SEND ME THE FOLLOWING BOOKS:

TITLE	ORDER NUMBER (#RLS _____)	AMOUNT
_____	_____	_____
_____	_____	_____
_____	_____	_____
_____	_____	_____
_____	_____	_____
	SHIPPING	_____
	CALIFORNIA TAX (8.00%)	_____
	TOTAL ENCLOSED	_____

PLEASE MAKE CHECK OR MONEY ORDER PAYABLE TO:

MICHAEL WIESE PRODUCTIONS

(CHECK ONE) ____ MASTERCARD ____ VISA ____ AMEX

CREDIT CARD NUMBER _____

EXPIRATION DATE _____

CARDHOLDER'S NAME _____

CARDHOLDER'S SIGNATURE _____

SHIP TO:

NAME _____

ADDRESS _____

CITY _____ STATE _____ ZIP _____

COUNTRY _____ TELEPHONE _____